Shakespeare and Trump

TEMPLE UNIVERSITY PRESS
Philadelphia • *Rome* • *Tokyo*

SHAKESPEARE
and TRUMP

Jeffrey R. Wilson

TEMPLE UNIVERSITY PRESS
Philadelphia, Pennsylvania 19122
tupress.temple.edu

Design by Kate Nichols

Library of Congress Cataloging-in-Publication Data

Names: Wilson, Jeffrey R. (Jeffrey Robert), 1982– author.
Title: Shakespeare and Trump / Jeffrey R. Wilson.
Description: Philadelphia : Temple University Press, 2020. | Includes
   bibliographical references and index. | Summary: "Shakespeare and Trump
   examines associations between Shakespeare's work and recent US politics,
   especially the presidency and character of President Donald Trump."—
   Provided by publisher.
Identifiers: LCCN 2019024286 (print) | LCCN 2019024287 (ebook) |
   ISBN 9781439919422 (paperback : alk. paper) | ISBN 9781439919439 (pdf)
Subjects: LCSH: Shakespeare, William, 1564–1616—Political and social
   views. | Shakespeare, William, 1564–1616—Adaptations. | Shakespeare,
   William, 1564–1616—Influence. | Politics in literature. | Power (Social
   sciences) in literature. | Politics and literature—United States. |
   Trump, Donald, 1946—Ethics. | Power (Social sciences)
Classification: LCC PR3017 .W55 2020 (print) | LCC PR3017 (ebook) |
   DDC 822.3/3—dc23
LC record available at https://lccn.loc.gov/2019024286
LC ebook record available at https://lccn.loc.gov/2019024287

♾ The paper used in this publication meets the requirements of the American
National Standard for Information Sciences—Permanence of Paper for Printed
Library Materials, ANSI Z39.48-1992

Printed in the United States of America

9 8 7 6 5 4 3 2 1

For my parents,

Tom and Jan Wilson

Contents

Preface and
Acknowledgments

A FOUR-HUNDRED-YEAR-OLD English playwright obsessed with monarchy should not be relevant to twenty-first-century American politics, but Shakespeare keeps showing up in our cultural response to President Donald Trump. This book asks why. It is not about Shakespeare—not really. It is about us: how we use Shakespeare today, how we make sense of Trump, and why these undertakings intersect. The goal is not to politicize the plays; it is to illuminate our politics through a Shakespearean intervention, enhancing interpretation by identifying core issues and hidden forces, going beyond the talking heads on cable news and even beyond political science. The aim is to exploit the analytical resources of literary criticism, history, and philosophy to reveal the abstract form of our moment, its plot, and its characters. For Shakespeare helps us to see *The Very Pleasant Comedy and Most Lamentable Tragedy of Donald Trump,* and to recognize its origins, structure, and possible outcomes. It is a story of self-serving and hypocritical career politicians preserving their power by perpetuating social and economic inequality; of the stunning moral compromises a resentful populace is willing to make for the comic relief provided by a charismatic clown; of an amoral Machiavellian, hungry for power, manipulating the people's anger, fear, and hatred of the government; and of the social catastrophe that can unfold when power is centralized in one man who becomes unstable. These Shakespearean resonances lead us onto difficult terrain. They demand that we consider Trump in world-historical terms, the level on which Shakespearean tragedy operates, but one that traditional political commentators are ill prepared to handle. How does one live through a time of tragedy? Are we in the realm of evil? Where will the restoration of social order come from? Or will we see the downfall of dynasties and the end of an empire?

This book came about through the prompting and generosity of several friends. In the heat of the 2016 presidential campaign, Jill Bradbury invited me to speak on "Shakespeare across the Disciplines" at Gallaudet University. Shortly after the election, Neema Parvini hosted me on his podcast, *Shakespeare and Contemporary Theory,* to talk Trump. The next summer, Lily Guttenplan recommended the project to Paul Lappin for the Moses Greeley Parker Lecture Series at the Pollard Library in Lowell, Massachusetts. Sara Cohen and Aaron Javsicas shepherded the manuscript through the publication process at Temple University Press, with key contributions from Ann-Marie Anderson, Jane Barry, Bruce Gore, Gary Kramer, and Joan Vidal. I am grateful for support from and conversations along the way with Kevin Birmingham, Isaac Butler, Andrew Cutrofello, Ambereen Dadabhoy, Olivia D'Ambrosio, Oskar Eustis, Rebecca Fall, Ewan Fernie, Timothy Francisco, Louise Geddes, Hugh Grady, Patrick Gray, Joshua Green, Stephen Greenblatt, Paul Hamilton, Julia Jones, Sean Keilen, Paul Kottman, Megan Kate Nelson, James Newlin, Scott Newstok, Stephen O'Neill, Asha Rangappa, Gabriel Rieger, Heather Schroder, Abigail Simon, Christian Smith, Daniel Spector, and Geoffrey Way. I am especially grateful to Peter C. Herman at San Diego State University for inspiring the kind of criticism pursued in this book. Julia Reinhard Lupton, Victoria Silver, and Robin Stewart at the University of California at Irvine remain major influences on my thinking. Hank Fradella, at California State University at Long Beach, was an early supporter of efforts to think society through Shakespeare. Karen Heath and Tom Jehn at Harvard University have been amazing role models for teaching and writing; Colleen Desrosiers Laude and Becky Skolnik helped me get to and from the classes and conferences where the ideas in this book took shape. My greatest thanks go to my family. My wife, Allison Dolan-Wilson, gives and gives endless love and support—an inspiration showing just how good a human can be. Our kids, Liam and Margaret, are my greatest source of joy. The Sunday night dinner crew—Dolans, Jareczes, Teixieras, and Tighes—

keeps life grounded. Chris Wilson and Anna Allen give me hope for Kansas. And because my parents, Tom and Jan Wilson, dedicated their life to teaching me how to lead mine, this book is dedicated to them, with thanks for their fight on the front lines of radical causes like *be nice to people, tell the truth,* and *art is important.*

All references to Shakespeare's plays are to *The Norton Shakespeare,* 3rd edition, edited by Stephen Greenblatt (New York: W. W. Norton, 2016). Spelling has been modernized throughout.

Introduction

I

WE TRIED to shield our four-year-old from American electoral politics. He overheard things, of course, people saying Donald Trump is not a good man. At four, you're taught to be nice and do the right thing. We didn't say anything the day after the election, but he heard about it at daycare. That night, he said to his mother as she was putting him to bed, "Mommy, Trump won the election." "Yes, sweetie, I know," she said. Then he broke down in tears. Rattled, she asked why he was crying. "I don't know."

Confusion was the most immediate response for many. Why had this happened? What was coming next? Why did it hit us so hard? I lost it a little myself the morning after, when I realized that my son and three-year-old daughter would first learn about the American president during the Trump years. I remember learning about the presidency with awe and inspiration. A child's naivety, sure, but I saw the president as an ideal, the best we can be. I don't want my children to hear the president talking about women the way Trump does. My son better never speak about women like that. No one better talk to my daughter that way.

What overwhelmed me was the symbolism. I thought then—still think now—that the lasting damage of Trump's election will not be the policies enacted, which can be checked and balanced or reversed over time, but the message sent to a generation of young girls and boys about how to achieve success. Whining, lying, cheating, and being an asshole are now demonstrable paths to success in America, a new generation socialized to behavior we had hoped to leave behind in the twentieth century.

I teach in a liberal bubble (Harvard University) within a liberal bubble (Cambridge) within a liberal bubble (New England). The day after the election, no one made eye contact on the subway. We stared at the floor in silence. No pleasantries with the teachers when I dropped my kids at daycare. *Was she a Trump voter?* They were asking the same about me. Could a preschool teacher support Trump? A college professor? Anything was possible. The rules had been rewritten. Nothing made sense.

"You know who wasn't surprised when Trump won?" asked many marginalized Americans. The day after, back in my conservative hometown in Kansas, there weren't any celebrations. If anything, they felt buyer's remorse: the symbolic votes cast to send a message to Washington brought a result that few thought possible. Those who bought Trump and his policies would now have to own them—the Oppenheimers of Trump.

The major players in the election—Trump, Clinton, Obama—spoke to the nation that day about unity, reconciliation, and putting the past behind us. They wanted to stave off unrest and violence from disaffected Americans who feared a Trump presidency. Those appeals were absurd: when a bully takes over the schoolyard, we don't tell our children that we owe him a chance to lead. And those desires for safety and security clashed with our equally valid desire for analysis and understanding. Why did things happen as they happened? How did we get here? What are we supposed to think now?

II

So first we felt it as human beings. Only later did we try to understand it as academics. *How do we explain this to our kids?* was the refrain at home. At work, *How do we talk about this in class?*

It became important for people in positions of authority (parents, teachers, ministers, governors, etc.) to affirm the value of honesty, kindness, respect for the dignity of all human beings, and the community's commitment to protect and support anyone feeling afraid, sad, or uncertain. I've always been pretty progressive in my politics but viewed such gestures as a little too precious for my tastes. Those values make up the unspoken moral fabric of America, I thought. That was no longer tenable. In the days after the election, a friend back in Kansas with a biracial daughter was called—to her face, in front of the kid, on two separate occasions—a slur so horrible I won't repeat it here. Our commitment to basic human decency needed to be made explicit, even if it felt hokey. *Don't feel guilty about opposing racism, sexism, and hypocrisy,* I had to say to myself. *Intolerance is the only thing to be intolerant of,* I heard the father of free speech, John Milton, saying.

My school sends out an email blast each morning about research being done around campus. The day after the election, experts coming from positions of disciplinary knowledge were asked to comment on the results: a professor of public health on the future of Obamacare, a professor of political science on the rise of populism at home and abroad. It was a testament to the value of academic expertise, and it was stabilizing to know what would happen next. Knowledge is power. So, on my way to campus, I asked, *What's the disciplinary perspective of my course?* I was teaching a first-year writing course about Shakespeare.

The course introduces students to scholarly interpretation and argument. On our first day, I tell them that academic writing—all academic work, really—is about one thing and one thing only: the search for truth. This pronouncement comes from my grad school teacher Stanley Fish's notion of "professional correctness."[1] Arguing against professors and institutions of higher education that view their mission as the cultivation of good character in students and a citizenry prepared to participate in democracy, Fish says to "aim low." Don't try to make your students better people; don't promote virtue; don't advocate for policies and politicians. Instead, do what you have been trained to do. As a Shakespearean, I have been trained to explain *King Lear,* but I should not draw an analogy between Lear's unhinged premodern machismo and the same in Donald Trump. Remain in an analytical posture, seeking knowledge and understanding; don't lapse into an ethical or political mode, seeking the betterment of society. The belief that academia is a venue for the discovery and dissemination of truth clashes with the idea that academics need to exert moral leadership, especially in perilous times.

You can imagine Fish's response when the Historians Against Trump penned an "Open Letter to the American People." "Today, we are faced with a moral test," they wrote. "As historians, we recognize both the ominous precedents for Donald J. Trump's candidacy and the exceptional challenge it poses to civil society. . . . We have a professional obligation as historians to share an understanding of the past upon which a better future may be built."[2] No, you don't, Fish wrote in a *New York Times* op-ed titled "Professors, Stop Opining about Trump": "Academic expertise is not a qualification for delivering political wisdom."[3]

But if academic work is, as Fish says, about the search for truth, wouldn't it be evading my academic responsibilities in a writing course—wouldn't it be professional malfeasance—not to address the problem of truth in the 2016 election? "Post-truth" ended up being the *Oxford Dictionary*'s word of the year.[4] Could I, with a straight face, tell my students that I was going to teach them how to search for truth and not acknowledge the attack on truth that was underway? So when we gathered on the day after the election, we talked about it—not as a political issue (Democrats versus Republicans), nor as an ethical issue (right versus wrong), but as an issue of truth, honor, and integrity in thought. Should health care be run by the federal government? That's not a matter of truth: reasonable people can disagree. Should abortion be illegal? Not a matter of truth. Should Trump have been elected president? Not a matter of truth.

But it was true that the United States had elected a man who flouts the truth. Trump disregarded facts, honesty, science, and knowledge derived from experts both academic and military. If you don't accept that as true, you also have an aversion to the truth. Outside our classroom was a place for anger and fear expressed in peaceful demonstrations, and reflection and reconciliation for the sake of national healing. Inside our classroom was a place for truth, for analysis, for understanding and debate about what is true and why. What was the significance of the fact that we elected a truth-less man as president? What is the status of truth in the age of Trump? Avoid doing politics, I asked students. Don't polemicize. At the same time, don't be fearful to speak the truth just because it makes some people look bad and others uncomfortable.

Having honed our skills of interpretation and argument all semester, we came to an understanding that quelled the confusion many were feeling. It was the justification for the humanities in action. Training in the humanities equips you with tried-and-tested strategies of analysis so that, when life serves up problems that are difficult to understand, you have the right tools ready at hand in your interpretive tool belt. Our conversation that day concluded that a time of felt economic recession had produced a nostalgia for 1950s American prosperity. Economic nostalgia had spilled over into a cultural nostalgia resistant to the increasing multiculturalism, ethnic diversity, and power and prominence of women in the nation. That is an analytical statement, not a political one—a thesis, or at least the first draft of one. We also, as is common in academic writing, identified questions for further thought. Why did economic anxiety, fear, anger, and resentment manifest in the kind of cultural rhetoric that the United States has disavowed in public for the past sixty years? Why does economic hardship speak the language of bigotry? Why didn't Trump's bigotry keep him from the White House? Those are political questions that require analytical answers. Don't do politics, yes. But don't let *don't do politics* prevent analysis.

III

That is one way we addressed the election in class. The other way, coming from the perspective of Shakespeare studies, was to look at the essay "An American Tragedy" published a day later by *New Yorker* editor David Remnick. "The election of Donald Trump to the Presidency," he wrote, "is nothing less than a tragedy for the American republic, a tragedy for the Constitution, and a triumph for the forces, at home and abroad, of nativism, authoritarianism, misogyny, and racism."[5] This was highly offensive to me, not as an American citizen—Remnick's narrative of the causes and consequences of Trump's election was educational— but as a literary critic. The word "tragedy" is bandied about in public to mean, vaguely, "something very bad." But tragedy is a highly formal literary device with a long history; its specialized meaning in literary studies points to a different understanding of the situation.

The first writer to theorize tragedy, Aristotle, describes it as a story about nobles—the wealthy, powerful, strong, brave, heroic, wise, and virtuous among us—who fall from prosperity to adversity, not because they are wicked, or victims of random misfortune, but because they make mistakes. The term in Greek is *hamartia*. The mistake causes the catastrophe, yet the gap between the smallness of the error and the severity of the catastrophe caused produces tragic pity and fear: pity for the person who did not deserve such a harsh outcome for such a small misstep, fear that a similar catastrophe could befall us for the routine mistakes we make daily.

Was there a *hamartia* in the 2016 presidential election? Did a great, heroic, noble, virtuous, well-intentioned person make a tragic mistake that brought about a catastrophe—one that was disproportionately large compared with the minuteness of the mistake? It is probably obvious that I am referring to Hillary Clinton's email scandal. While secretary of state, she used a private email account for official government business for the sake of convenience (to avoid having to carry multiple electronic devices). This was against State Department policy. Her decision to ignore that policy became scandalous when it was revealed that she had sent classified information on her nonsecure account and that her legal team had deleted 33,000 emails deemed non-work-related. When the scandal did not go away on its own, Clinton publicly apologized, though she obviously was not very remorseful and thought that the scandal was empty politics. Indeed it was, but the story dominated the final two weeks of the presidential campaign after Federal Bureau of Investigation director James Comey, who had declined to press charges against Clinton in July 2016, announced that the FBI was reviewing new emails discovered during an unrelated investigation into Anthony Weiner, the estranged husband of Clinton's aide Huma Abedin. In the words of Trevor Noah, host of the *Daily Show* on Comedy Central:

> The story is so Shakespearean. . . . Think about it: Hillary survives Bill's sex scandal, but now gets a scandal from her top aide's husband. And it was Bill who married them. Not to mention that Trump got his sex scandal from Billy Bush, whose uncle was defeated by Hillary's husband before Trump later defeated his cousin Jeb. There are only like fifteen characters in the entire story![6]

News outlets spent more time covering Clinton's email scandal than all her policy proposals combined. A story of modest importance consumed the election. To Elizabeth Drew at the *New York Review of Books*, "The damn spot that the server was on Clinton's presidential campaign turned out to be deadly."[7]

Whether we view it as an ethical lapse or a political miscalculation, Clinton slipped; she herself, repeatedly, called the private server a "mistake." Many factors contributed to the election of Donald Trump, but Clinton's email played a disproportionately large part in bringing America crashing down into a Trump presidency. In terms of retributive justice—*Does the punishment fit the crime?*—Clinton's mistake should not have cost her the election, but it did. If we are going to call the 2016 election a "tragedy," it is because a silly mistake brought about the downfall of a valiant politician who had given her life to public service. It was easy enough then—even easier now—to identify Clinton's shortcomings as a candidate. But the story of Hillary Clinton is tragic because she did almost everything right throughout her life, yet an utterly insignificant error not only kept her from becoming president but also—more importantly—initiated a massive catastrophe. As tragedy, Clinton's story generates pity and fear in us: pity because she deserved to be president, and fear because even if we do everything right, we too could be denied the success we would receive were the world logical and just.

IV

On the science side of campus, people feared the drying up of funding under Trump. On our side, the crisis in the humanities now had a clear and demonstrable consequence. The election revealed that the crisis is not about dwindling enrollments and decreased funding. It is about the waning, in mainstream American culture, of the knowledge and skills imparted by the humanities. The crisis is not *in* the humanities; it is bigger. It is in an educational system that devalues the humanities. Humanists are not, I think, interested in saying *I told you so,* but the election confirmed what we had been saying for decades: there is a dire need to foster the ability, among all our citizens, to interpret information amid the relentless data overload of the digital age.

Here's my take on the 2016 election: if you are a teacher, and you give the class an easy test, and half the class fails, there is something wrong with the way you are teaching the material. Humanists need to rethink how we have been teaching the material. More generally, there is something wrong with moral and civic education in America. Even if we fix the Trump problem, we will not have fixed the America problem. The United States needs to come to grips—we haven't even come close—with the fact that our celebrated nation, with deep roots in the Judeo-Christian religious tradition of love and kindness (especially for the most vulnerable among us) and the modern political tradition of liberal democracy (including the achievements of the women's rights and civil rights movements), elected a transparently immoral man with streaks of fascism.

With the increasing multiculturalism in the United States, and the continued decline of Christianity as the institution responsible for the cultivation of virtue, scholars will find themselves playing a more prominent role in the moral education of the country. The educational system is the only institution with the structural footprint to assume this role. I do not know if this is good or bad; many of us do not want this responsibility. Stanley Fish will kick and scream, but, like it or not, teachers are going to become secular ministers. This is not a call to action but a prediction. When it comes true, it will be our job to preach the gospel of truth, to practice the politics of truth. Preachers and politicians can't make truth great again: that is not what they have been trained to do. Academics are responsible for truth. That is what we have always claimed. It's time to support our argument with evidence.

V

Shakespeare offers a unique opportunity for the education of the American mind. He is widely taught in schools, creating a common language of sorts, and is especially cherished by those who want to conserve the traditions of America's European heritage. Conservatives love Shakespeare. Yet Shakespeare also forces us to reflect on the origins, uses, abuses, and outcomes of power. That is why many Shakespeareans are politically progressive.

That progressivism is palpable in my colleague Stephen Greenblatt's book *Tyrant: Shakespeare on Politics,* published in 2018. In the face of government censorship of politically incendiary material, he argues, "Shakespeare was the supreme master of displacement and strategic indirection."[8] He wrote plays related to current events, but did not make the connections explicit, leaving audiences to recognize the resonances. Shakespeare's "oblique angle" (184), Greenblatt says, made it "easier to tell the truth at a strategic distance from the present moment" (5). Greenblatt then imitates his idol, throwing shade at Trump without mentioning him by name in readings of Shakespearean tyrants like Richard III, Julius Caesar, Macbeth, and King Lear.

This was not a new strategy, as Greenblatt explained in a lecture at the Folger Shakespeare Library, invoking "the Janus face of new historicism," the movement in literary studies he founded in the 1980s.[9] New historicism has "a certain proud affinity with antiquarianism," he said, but what was new was its "heightened alertness to the pressures of the present." He pointed to his early book, *Renaissance Self-Fashioning* (1980), whose narrative of Renaissance colonialism evokes images of American troops setting fire to Vietnamese villages.[10] "It's not a question," he said at the Folger, "of being shy or coy. It was an attempt to use the preoccupations and passions of the present as a way to illuminate and to enter into and encounter the past." Turning to Trump, he concluded, "In certain circumstances, particularly in anxious or traumatic circumstances, it may be beneficial to look away from the present, and to distance oneself, if one can, from the disorientation of the daily news cycle— from the shock of one day's events after another—and to find some virtue in obliquity, in a look aside."

Greenblatt's "Janus faced" new historicism skirts Stanley Fish's "professional correctness," just as Shakespeare's "oblique angles" outmaneuvered Elizabethan censorship. But many Shakespeare scholars hated Greenblatt's *Tyrant*. After noting, with the taste of shit in their mouths, that he now writes for a popular audience, they derided the book as politics masquerading as literary criticism. It is a little ungenerous for scholars to lob bombs at a work with book jacket plugs from Philip Roth and John Lithgow. It smacks of the University Wits complaining about Shakespeare, *But he's not talking to us!* Scholars, like Renaissance playwrights and American progressives, rarely suffer from an excess of solidarity. But any critique of Greenblatt's book—including the one below— needs to be predicated on a celebration of his willingness to speak to the public rather than the profession. We have been calling for public humanities for years; let's support scholars heeding the call. Nitpickers need to recognize that Greenblatt leveraged his authority to allow Shakespearean drama to set the agenda for national conversations about politics. Surely that is a good thing. Analytical activism—academically informed yet publicly accessible, using the past to better understand life today—is the antidote to both political activism (nauseating polemics telling people what to do) and academic passivity (weak scholarly quietism doing nothing with knowledge).

"Oblique angles" elevate the conversation to an abstract level, denying the enemy entrance to the discussion by refusing to name him. That strategy reappeared at Shakespeare's Globe in London in July 2018 when Trump was in town. After a performance, the cast asked audiences to "speak and act against those like our visitor to the U.K. this weekend, He-Who-Shall-Not-Be-Named."[11] The audience erupted in laughter and applause, but this strategy of not-naming feels immature, and weirdly aligned with witchcraft superstitions (hence the Harry Potter reference). It does not empower Trump to name him. Refusing to name him is aligned with preaching to the choir, a move made when speaking with others who already agree, but a practice that does nothing to enlighten the audience most in need of education. Trolling the powers-that-be is not a crafty Shakespearean evasion of censorship; it is an evasion of a teacher's responsibility. Greenblatt's approach is not the one needed right now. If a slightly smug assurance that the Left is on the right side of history were all the country needed, Hillary Clinton would have won.

A week after reading Greenblatt's book, I heard a better alternative from Daniel Spector at a Shakespeare conference.[12] More actor than scholar, Spector runs the Shakespearean performance program at New York University, "training actors in the persuasive, other-centered ways of Shakespeare." Shakespearean characters are rarely thinking about themselves when speaking, he explained, so techniques for representing psychological realism, like method acting, are not especially helpful. Shakespearean drama is fundamentally a rhetorical negotiation: characters are both trying to persuade someone else and susceptible to change themselves. But Spector's students had been struggling with this approach. They were defaulting to fighting rather than arguing, a tendency that he connected to a shift in the way political opponents were imagined in the United States: from Obama in 2008 ("They get bitter, they cling to guns or religion . . . as a way to explain their frustrations") to Clinton in 2016 ("You could put half of Trump's supporters in what I call the basket of deplorables"). Obama's adversaries were persuadable. *Oh no they're not,* Clinton snapped. Spector extrapolated to Americans in general: our devotion to our own side in the 2016 election closed us off from the other side. This unrhetorical recalcitrance is fundamentally un-Shakespearean. Spector used it to explain his students' resistance to Shakespearean acting and to highlight the political potential of working with Shakespeare:

> Shakespeare may be just what my country needs right now to wrest us from this morass—not for any of its thematic content or cautionary tales or profiles in courage and weakness, but for its form: its setting of two opposing forces against, and at the same time, in collaboration with one another in a dialectical relationship that, regardless of the *outcome,* always maintains

the *possibility* for change, for transformation. [Emphasis in original]

Allow me to make explicit something that neither Stephen Greenblatt nor Hillary Clinton did: I am a progressive liberal, but I want to invite conservatives into a conversation. I am from middle America and hold strongly to the heartland values my parents instilled in me: hard work, toughness, calling it like I see it, sure—but also telling the truth and being kind to people. These are basic conservative values—the big-time conservativism upholding the moral ideals of America, not the bullshit conservativism dedicated to perpetuating the wealth and power of the wealthy and powerful. Conservative readers may not like all the ideas in this book. I'm eager to hear where you think I have misconstrued things. I am persuadable; I hope you will be too. You and I have much more in common than either does with the powers-that-be. I do not want to convince you as much as I want to try to understand your situation so that my ideas are fully accountable to it. I hope that being trained to interpret literary characters helps me see the world through your eyes. If my ideas are good enough, you might change your mind. You might change your vote. Or I might. Either way, it will not be because one has convinced the other. It will be because together we have gained clarity and allowed truth to guide politics and ethics.

VI

I didn't want to write this book. I'm not a very political person. Actually, I hate politics. But I love interpretation. That is why I love literature. The interpretation of literature is practice for the interpretation of life. That is why we read books: not to distract ourselves from what is going on around us, but to help us think about it. This book is not a political statement. It's an analytical statement. Politics is easy; analysis is hard. Everyone has an opinion, but a good interpretation is hard to find. And if *Hamlet* teaches us anything, it's that when you try to fix a world you don't understand, you and your whole family might die.

Knowledge is power. A better understanding of our political situation gives us power over both our current unease and our future direction, and Shakespeare can help: that is the basis of this book. It flows from the notion that we can do a literary criticism of life. The terms of literary studies—*plot, character, villainy, soliloquy, tragedy, myth, met-*

aphor, and so forth—identify not only features of fiction but also elements of society. What happens when someone trained as a Renaissance historicist applies those methods to current events? In literary studies, once you know the form of a text—sonnet, epic, satire, etc.—you have at your disposal a vast library of scholarship on that form, and on particular examples of it, to help you suss out its structure and logic: where it comes from, how it works, why it matters. If we can identify the formal features of the Trump phenomenon, we can mobilize the scholarly tradition to reveal its hidden causes, meanings, and possible futures. The imaginative power of literary expression can reveal what is going on behind the small slice of this moment in history we have access to.

Thus, *Shakespeare and Trump* pursues a criticism that revises the traditional relationship between Shakespeare and theory. Usually, scholars use literary and cultural theory to unpack Shakespeare, but understanding Shakespeare is not the be-all and end-all of life, at least not for me. Shakespeare studies are means to an end. By thinking society through Shakespeare, we can use Shakespeare to create new theory—working up from literary texts to generalizable ideas that explain life beyond the texts, such as *tragic populism* (Chapter 1), *cultural affirmative action* (Chapter 3), and *conscientious complicity* (Chapter 4). With that realignment comes a change in audience, Shakespeare scholars no longer writing only for other Shakespeare scholars. *Shakespeare for theory* is both *Shakespeare across the disciplines* and *Public Shakespeare.*

For instance, Greenblatt's thesis was "tyranny," a political term. Mine is "tragedy," a literary term shifting attention from a corrupt individual to a volatile social situation. Shakespeare's tragedies show that when power is centralized at the top, the state hangs on the fragile emotions of privileged men, and bad government amplifies routine individual moral failings—like deceit, revenge, and ambition—into social catastrophe, the suffering of helpless citizens, death, and the downfall of dynasties. Every empire falls. America will too. We might be watching it without knowing.

VII

The five numbered chapters that follow tell five stories. First, Trump's chief political strategist, Steve Bannon, wrote two far-fetched Shakespeare adaptations in the 1990s. Second, the 2016 election saw the rise of a new kind of literary criticism: the Shakespeare-inspired commentary on modern U.S. politics. Third, days after the election, students at the University of Pennsylvania protested against Trump by tearing down a monument to Shakespeare. Fourth, Trump's first 100 days in office can be read in light of the Netflix hit *House of Cards,* based on Shakespeare's *Richard III.* And fifth, in the summer of 2017, the onstage assassination of a Trump-esque Julius Caesar led corporate sponsors to pull their support for New York City's famed Shakespeare in the Park.

These stories reveal a surprising—even bizarre—relationship between William Shakespeare, provincial English playwright from the age of monarchy, and Donald Trump, billionaire president of the United States. Taking stock of these flashes of Shakespeare in recent U.S. politics, holding nostalgically to the notion that literature can help us understand life, I let Shakespeare elevate our conversation about Trump above daily headlines and comment sections to gauge how our moment fits into the larger themes of human history. Mired in the storm of the here and now, we have not yet thought imaginatively enough about how this all ends. Shakespeare both helps us comprehend the tragedy of our historical moment and teaches us where to find joy during times of turmoil. Shakespeare helps us see how our story might be told 400 years from now. That's why Shakespeare matters to me: because of the conversations his art enables across centuries, between his time and ours, through the steady flow of modernized performances, stretching back into the ancient world that was reborn during the Renaissance.

VIII

Why Shakespeare and Trump? Why have these two figures—so different in so many ways—consistently collided over the past few years? What, beyond bad hair, do they have in common? Why are Shakespeare scholars suddenly thinking about twenty-first-century politics? Why are political commentators turning to Shakespeare? What is the relationship between art and politics? And how does this discourse illuminate Shakespeare and Trump in ways more traditional analysis might miss?

It's not that Trump loves Shakespeare and regularly cites him, as Lincoln and Bill Clinton did. Instead, there is an alignment between what happens in Shakespeare's plays and what happens in Trump's politics. For one thing, both Shakespeare's plays and Trump's politics blend villainy and comedy *en route* to tragedy. For another, Shakespeare's plays are so political, and Trump's politics so theatrical, that their collision seems inevitable. Third, there is a tension between what Shakespeare and Trump symbolize. Shakespeare signifies art, creativity, thoughtfulness, understanding, the greatness of the human mind, joy, compassion, critique, skepticism, self-abnegation; Trump represents politics, instinct, raw power, Machiavellianism, self-assertion. Shakespeare's language is beautiful; Trump's is horrible. I want to resist saying that Shakespeare is good and Trump bad. Some will find it repugnant to put them on the same level, but, again, I am making an analytical statement about who we are, not a political statement about what we should do. We elected Trump; he represents us, politically and symbolically. As long as we continue to say *they* elected Trump—the Republicans, the Russians, the red states—we will continue to misunderstand our moment. We—Americans—elected him and need to figure out why.

Our question runs in both directions. From one angle, why *Shakespeare* and Trump? Why not Chaucer, Austen, or Faulkner and Trump? Perhaps it is simply that Shakespeare is the most popular Western writer; perhaps "Shakespeare and Trump" stands in for "literature and Trump." But we do not see massive discourses on Homer and Trump, Virgil and Trump, Dante and Trump, or Whitman and Trump. *The Lord of the Rings* and *Harry Potter* are both very popular, but there is relatively little discussion of Hobbits or Hogwarts and Trump. Something about Shakespeare speaks to Trump.

Shakespeare is a frequent point of reference for American presidents, in part, because—uniquely among authors in the Western canon—he wrote stories whose main character is a head of state. Dante and Milton emphasized encounters between the human and the divine; Chaucer and Dickens, between the upper class and the lower; Austen and Woolf, within the upper class; Twain and Steinbeck, among the working class; Dickinson and Whitman, within the self; Ellison and Morrison, among African Americans. With our democratic ideology, American writers are especially attracted to the Everyman: there are no great American novels about heads of state. Apart from classical epic (*Iliad, Odyssey, Aeneid*) and tragedy (*Oedipus Rex, Antigone,* the *Oresteia*), Shakespeare's plays are the only works in the center of the Western canon to focus at length on social conflict involving the highest in the land. So why not Homer and Trump, or Aeschylus and Trump?

From the other angle, why Shakespeare and *Trump?* There were blips of Shakespeare and Clinton, Shakespeare and Bush, and Shakespeare and Obama, but nothing like Trump. We haven't seen Shakespeare and Trudeau, Putin, or Merkel. The occasional Shakespeare-and-Brexit pieces are noteworthy because of parallels with Trump. But the tag "Shakespeare and Trump" is not just a stand-in for "Shakespeare and power" or "Shakespeare and politicians." Again, something about Trump calls for Shakespeare.

The best explanation I can offer is this. A figure from what scholars call the "early modern" age, Shakespeare stood between two epochs. He represented the politics of medieval times—brute force, kingship, dynasty, feudalism, servitude, the haves and have-nots perpetuated over time through family inheritance and structural social inequality—coming into contact with the politics of modernity, which increasingly emphasized liberty, equality, justice for all, and individual self-determination. All of Shakespeare's political rulers are medieval kings living in modern worlds. Donald Trump, with his privileged background, massive wealth, petulant personality, and penchant for making knee-jerk decisions based on his emotions of the day, has thrown us back into medieval politics. He is a medieval king living in a modern world. Shakespeare had a strategy for dealing with this situation. He called it *tragedy*: stark social inequality, self-important leaders of privilege, rampant corruption and hypocrisy in government, fear, anger, resentment, hostility, incivility, warring factions—and then some random event ignites this political powder keg, leading to widespread violence, pain, suffering, death, and the downfall of nations. Let's hope he was wrong.

1

Bannon's Shakespeare

STEVE BANNON: Goldman Sachs investment banker, Hollywood film producer, executive chair of the right-wing Breitbart News Network, Donald Trump's chief political strategist, economic nationalist, populist, . . . Shakespearean screenwriter? In the mid-1990s Bannon teamed with a writer named Julia Jones to pen two high-concept Shakespeare adaptations. One, titled *Andronicus,* is *Titus Andronicus* but in space: war between the Romans and the Goths becomes war between the "Andronicii," beings of light and goodness, and the "Shades." The other work adapts *Coriolanus* into a rap musical set in early 1990s South Central Los Angeles: Romans and Volsci become Bloods and Crips.

With some justification, press coverage of these scripts has been about ridicule. A piece in the *Paris Review,* "Titus in Space," mocked Bannon as a wannabe Hollywood producer whose pathetic artistry produced gems like this:

Aaron leans like a shadow into the doorway. He knocks.

BACK INSIDE

Attava approaches. Her dressing gown gapes open, revealing her breasts. She opens the door. Aaron enters, closing it behind him and leans against it, arms folded across his chest.

AARON I'm glad you called.

He grabs her. She leads him to the bed and pulls him down; laughing softly, she unwraps her gown.

ATTAVA Everything is always so . . . physical with you.

AARON Oh, yes. . . .

He climbs onto her and their forms dissolve, blend and blur in an erotic scene of ectoplasmic sex.[1]

Similarly, a tongue-in-cheek table read of Bannon's *Coriolanus* had actors sprinting to get through the dialogue without laughing (Figure 1.1). "Some of it came off as if he had never met a black person," one noted.[2] This deficit is especially obvious in lines mixing urban American and Elizabethan dialects: "More of this busta ass nigga talk would infect my brain. Peace now, let's parlay down."[3] But what if we take Bannon's Shakespeare adaptations seriously? What can they reveal that a more straightforward analysis of the man misses? And what can the Bannon of the Shakespeare adaptations reveal about the campaign, presidency, and ideology of Donald Trump?

———

Figure 1.1. Table reading of Bannon and Jones's *Coriolanus* for *NowThis Politics*, April 30, 2017.

These screenplays are not publicly available, but, interested in reading them from a Shakespearean perspective, my student Abigail Simon contacted Julia Jones, who generously shared them with us.[4] Upon reading them and interviewing Jones, I found Bannon's Shakespeare adaptations to give a view of his politics that was more nuanced than the one described in the popular press, but also more frightening.[5] The adaptations show Bannon to be a capable and sincere thinker, rather than the boogeyman he is often made out to be by the Left, and they reveal Bannon the man as more dangerous than Bannon the monster. Ultimately, I concluded that one does not see his later politics at work in these screenplays as much as one sees evidence of a mind that finds the politics of tragedy appealing. The early Bannon's mythic and tragic Shakespearean adaptations and the later Bannon's divisive politics of culture war are different manifestations of the same thing: a mind that sees war everywhere, that sees ethics as moot when brute forces clash, and that sees tragedy as the necessary evil we must suffer for order and stability to re-emerge.

I. Bannon the Author

How was the young Bannon drawn to literary expression in the first place? Born in 1953 in Norfolk, Virginia, to a working-class, Irish Catholic, and Democratic family, he was educated at Benedictine College Preparatory, a private, all-male Catholic military high school in Richmond, Virginia. One classmate remembers being taught that "Muslims could have taken over the world," but the Catholics defeated them in Spain 500 years ago.[6] In his earliest years, therefore, Bannon learned a mythologized Western history based in racial and religious conflict. The lesson would echo throughout his life. In the words of Joshua Green, who has chronicled Bannon's life and career, he was taken with the idea that Western civilization must be "constantly and vigilantly defended against shadowy, shape-shifting enemies."[7] These are the "Shades" that would show up thirty years later in Bannon's adaptation of *Titus Andronicus*.

After graduating from Virginia Tech in 1976, Bannon joined the Navy, where his belief in an epic clash of civilizations solidified. A voracious reader with time on his hands, he conducted, in his own words, "a systematic study of the world's religions," from Christian mysticism to Buddhist metaphysics.[8] According to Green, he landed on the philosophy of Traditionalism developed by the mid-twentieth-century French mystic René Guénon, who believed that secular modernity was erasing the universal spiritual truths of various ancient religions, both Western and Eastern. Most of recorded time has occurred, Guénon thought, in a phase of history known as the *Kali Yuga,* a Hindi term meaning "dark age," in which our "primordial spirituality becomes gradually more and more obscured."[9] We need not dwell here on Julius Evola, Guénon's devotee who developed the *Kali Yuga* into the racial politics of Mussolini's Italy and Hitler's Germany, because at this point an answer to our question is clear: Bannon was drawn to literary expression because he lives in a fantasy world. His crackpot religious, philosophical, and historical beliefs are the backdrop against which his political positions must be understood. That is why, while Bannon was in the Navy in the early 1980s, the Iran hostage crisis—Iranian students holding fifty-two Americans hostage for 444 days—sparked in him a sense that he was witnessing the latest stage of an ancient and ongoing battle between the West (Judeo-Christian good guys) and the Middle East (Muslim bad guys).

Bannon's proclivity to see himself as enmeshed in epic history was bound up with delusions of grandeur. He conceived every experience in his life as monumental. As an investment banker, he thought "the river of history runs deep through Goldman's M&A [Mergers & Acquisitions] department," according to one colleague.[10] In Hollywood, he was "constantly telling stories about great warriors of the past."[11] When he started a celebrity talent agency ("We're in the Vin Diesel business, or the Fred Durst business"), he declared, "It's the beginning of a revolution."[12]

Bannon's mythologizing of himself and world history clarifies why, once he became political, he constantly saw himself as engaged in epic conflicts between "us" and "them." By all accounts September 11, 2001, had a radicalizing effect on him, leading him to enlist in both "a global war against Islamic fascism" and "our current cultural and political war" in America.[13] He made the mythologically titled documentary *Reagan: In the Face of Evil* (2004), in which a figure from Hollywood rises up to destroy a Satanic conglomeration of Bolshevism, Fascism, Communism, and Nazism dubbed "the Beast."[14] "His belief in the beast was so real," Jones recalled.[15] Beyond Islamic terrorism, Bannon saw the clash of civilizations in immigration (addressed in his documentary *Border Wars: The Battle over Illegal Immigration* [2006]) and refugees (referring to "civilizational jihad personified by this migrant crisis").[16] Seeing war everywhere, always, Bannon sounded the alarm at a conference at the Vatican in 2014:

> I believe the world, and particularly the Judeo-Christian West, is in a crisis. . . . This will be looked at almost as a new Dark Age. . . . We're at the very beginning stages of a very brutal and bloody conflict . . . an outright war against jihadist Islamic fascism. And this war is, I think, metastasizing far quicker than governments can handle it.[17]

Years later, after being ousted from Trump's administration, Bannon declared "a season of war" against the Republican establishment with characteristically militaristic rhetoric: "I'm leaving the White House and going to war for Trump."[18]

This protean war was manifested, of all places, at the 2018 Golden Globe Awards when Dwayne "the Rock" Johnson showed deference to Oprah Winfrey. Bannon saw this as a turning point in Western history: "The anti-patriarchy movement is going to undo ten thousand years of recorded history. . . . Women are gonna take charge of society. And they couldn't juxtapose a better villain than Trump. He is the patriarch. This [the 2018 Golden Globe Awards] is a definitional moment in the culture. It'll never be the same going forward."[19] It was this grandiose disposition that drew Bannon to creative writing in the 1990s: imaginative fiction—as opposed to, say, history or philosophy or politics—was well suited to express his mythical historical vision of an ancient and ongoing cultural clash between the Western tradition and enemy outsiders.

II. Bannon the Filmmaker

Bannon finished his seven years in the Navy in a low-level position at the Pentagon. In 1983 he enrolled in the Harvard Business School with his eyes on the finance industry, earning his M.B.A. in 1985. He became an associate at the Wall Street investment company Goldman Sachs, venturing west in 1987 to Los Angeles to increase Goldman's presence in entertainment. He struck out on his own in 1990, forming the Hollywood investment company that became Bannon and Co. while raising money for *The Indian Runner,* a 1991 film written and directed by Sean Penn, Bannon became interested in producing. That year, he met Julia Jones.

Jones, who describes herself now as a "Bernie Sanders liberal," grew up not far from Bannon in Chapel Hill, North Carolina. "I was there when the drugstore sit-in happened in Greensboro," she told me:

> That actually started the whole Civil Rights Movement in the South. It preceded Rosa Parks. The whole town was surrounded by cretins, by horrible racists. When I used to walk home from school, the rednecks would line up on one side of the street, and the black people were all on the other side. I used to have to cross over to walk in front of the black people because the rednecks were so abusive. They were horrible. They were nasty, nasty, nasty people. Then, I was in school at UNC, and I saw Malcolm X speak in Hayti—it was a black section of Charlotte—over a gas station one night, no lights on or anything. We got in: they welcomed us because we were young; we were students. But nobody else there was white. And it was one of the most powerful things I've ever taken part in, been privileged to be a part of.

Jones transferred schools and earned her A.B. in English with honors at Harvard in 1970, studying Shakespeare with the actor, director, and scholar Daniel Seltzer and encountering an idea that came to consume her: "He challenged us, and threw out the question, 'Did Shakespeare really write the plays?' He put that idea in my mind—that someone else wrote the plays—and I glommed on to Christopher Marlowe, and did an exhaustive study on Marlowe." Jones remains a passionate detective in the Shakespeare authorship question, but the script she wrote petered out: "It was about how Marlowe faked his own death. I felt that once you established that he faked his death, then he became a viable candidate for the plays. I did a brilliant job of establishing that, but then after the faked death, I didn't really have anything to say. And so I sort of had to make up a relationship between him and Shakespeare, and it just kind of fell apart after that."

With no writing credits to her name, Jones's sixteen-year partnership with Bannon began with a chance meeting at a bar in Beverly Hills: "He had the uniform on. The white Polo shirt, the navy blue pants, the loafers without socks. Preppy. I went up to the bar to get a drink, and I heard him talking about 'Harvard this and Harvard that.' So—it's the most obnoxious pickup line in the world—I walked up to him and said, 'Hi Harvard, I'm Harvard too.' I think it endeared me to him forever because, if nothing else, he's a snob. He's not a racist. He's an elitist." Making small talk, Bannon asked Jones what she did for a living. "Then I sort of tried to get rid of him because he wasn't my type," Jones recalled. Sure that this would shut the conversation down, she told him she was working on a screenplay about Shakespeare and Christopher Marlowe. "And he flipped out—'I'm looking for a Shakespearean screenwriter!'"

Why Shakespeare? Why not Homer or Aeschylus or Euripides or Seneca or Dante or Dickens or Austen or Joyce or Ibsen or Shaw or Albee? What did Shakespeare's plays offer Steve Bannon? He was not merely attaching himself to a fad. His interest predated most of the 1990s Shakespeare adaptations: Richard Loncraine's *Richard III* (1995), Baz Lurhmann's *Romeo + Juliet* (1996), Kenneth Branagh's *Hamlet* (1996), and Gil Junger's *10 Things I Hate about You* (1999), for instance. Two arthouse adaptations, Peter Greenaway's *Prospero's Books* and Gus Van Sant's *My Own Private Idaho,* came out in 1991. The most successful Shakespeare films of the previous years, like Branagh's *Henry V* (1989) and Franco Zeffirelli's *Hamlet* (1990), played it straight with the text, an approach that did not interest Bannon.

Instead, he found in Shakespeare a way to express his apocalyptic sense of our moment. Bannon's current theory of history comes from William Strauss and Neil Howe's *The Fourth Turning: An American Prophecy* (1997), which claims to have identified the generational rhythms of history and uses this discovery to demonstrate that the United States is nearing a catastrophe: "Turnings come in cycles of four. Each cycle spans the length of a long human life, roughly eighty to one hundred years, a unit of time the ancients called the *saeculum*. Together, the four turnings of the *saeculum* comprise history's seasonal rhythm of growth, maturation, entropy, and destruction."[20] The "First Turning" is a "High" of prosperity and optimism (Strauss and Howe point to postwar America, 1946–1964). The Second Turning is an "Awakening" or transformation of cultural values (such as the sexual revolution and campus protests, 1964–1984); the Third Turning, an "Unraveling" (malaise, the MTV generation, 1984–2005); and the Fourth Turning, a "Crisis" involving political revolution (predicted to stretch from 2005 to 2025). Strauss and Howe identify other Fourth Turning moments in the American Revolution and the Constitution (1774–1794), the Civil War (about 1860–1868), and the Depression and the Second World War (1929–1945), all spaced about eighty years apart. Do the math, they argue, and expect a political revolution around 2025.

After reading Strauss and Howe, Bannon made a documentary about Fourth Turning theory titled *Generation Zero* (2010). Where they pursued their analysis of events with the detachment of historians, Bannon zealously embraced the size, intensity, and destructiveness of the war to come.[21] Just as Julius Evola had weaponized René Guénon's Traditionalism, Bannon wanted to make a militant program of action out of Strauss and Howe's theory of history.

Obviously, Bannon was not a Fourth Turning devotee when he was searching for a Shakespearean screenwriter in 1991. His affinity for Strauss and Howe's theory is a symptom of an attitude toward history that Bannon developed much earlier. Guénon's Traditionalism, after all, contradicts Strauss and Howe's *saeculum*: Guénon is all about the long and linear decline of tradition in the West; Strauss and Howe are about cycles and recurrence. The common denominator is tragedy. Both historical postures emphasize decay, corruption, destruction, and ultimately radical catastrophe, with the promise of a return to some ancient paradisial state lost in modern society. That is also Shakespearean tragedy: a mythical, sweeping view of world-historical narratives enchanted with a larger-than-life sense of the moral fabric of the cosmos. Every tragedy involves a catastrophic turn from one social and political order to another. And Shakespearean tragedy is cyclical, with patterns echoing, for example, from Roman to English history. Bannon's attraction makes sense because the genre of tragedy captures his sense of our political moment as one headed for crisis, revolution, and catastrophe.

III. Bannon the Historian

At their chance meeting in 1991, Bannon gave Jones his card and told her to call him. He had an idea for *Titus* in space. The following Tuesday she went to the Beverly Hills office of Bannon and Co. to pitch a story about *Titus* "on the moon with creatures from outer space" and "pyramids on a planet."[22] He loved it. The intergalactic war spoke to his thirst for cultural conflict, and they saw a market for the movie. "Basically, what we were doing was a cross between Shakespeare and *Star Wars*," Jones recalled.[23] Bannon paid her a small retainer to help turn his ideas into scripts. "It wasn't a lot," she said, "but enough to live on."[24] She got some space in the Bannon and Co. office, came and went as she wanted, and billed his accountant each month. "He had a picture of Reagan over his desk," she told me. "He was a cloth coat Republican." In those days their political differences did not matter: "Artistically, we agreed 99 percent on everything we did."[25] He talked, dictating plots and themes; she wrote, developing and polishing the prose. They worked on the *Andronicus* script for two years. "It was mostly his vision and he was in agreement, and enthusiastic, about what was written," she recalled.[26] "He was the conceptual force, and I did most of the work."

Bannon and Jones planned dozens of projects. Most fizzled out. *Those Who Knew* was supposed to be a television series about ancient philosophers and great thinkers. As Jones remembers it, Bannon felt an apocalyptic anxiety as they wrote the pitch for the show, which she showed me: "As we approach the coming millennium, we find ourselves in a world where our powers have become such that our choices determine the future of all life on Earth: which lands will be destroyed or spared, which species will live or die, the quality of the air, the oceans, where and how our fellow humans live—or if they live."[27] Most of the proposed subjects came from Bannon, pursuing his mystical interests: Helena Blavatsky ("'Mother of the New Age,' mystic, spiritualist and adventurer"), Geronimo ("Shaman and American Indian warrior"), William Blake ("English poet and mystic"), and Hildegarde von Bingen ("Composer and religious visionary"). Only by studying these mystics could we return to tradition and break the tragic cycle of modernity: "Each of us must go within and 'wake up' if we are to stop the ticking of the Imperial Clock and put an end to the unconscious cruelty of past centuries. Although many believe we need a new and better way, *Those Who Knew* will show that all we may really need is a return to the 'old ways'—the ancient ways—broadcast down through the centuries as universal truths" (5–6).

"He was really focused on changing the world," Jones told me. "His condo bedroom had just a mattress on the floor, and it was so full of books he couldn't sleep there. He'd sleep on the couch." He loved Plato, Marcus Aurelius, anything about Sparta or the Peloponnesian Wars. When asked why Bannon chose *Titus Andronicus* and *Coriolanus*, Jones noted, "They're both war plays and Roman plays. Steve was never interested in *Henry V* or in *Antony and Cleopatra* (too romantic, I suppose) so there's something about these two Roman plays that appealed to him."[28] Why not *Hamlet, Othello, King Lear,* and *Macbeth*? Why not the comedies or the histories? What did Bannon see in Shakespeare's Roman tragedies?

He clearly loved Roman history, but it was a version mediated by

Edward Gibbon's *The History of the Decline and Fall of the Roman Empire* (1776–1789), which Bannon cites as one of the six books that have most influenced him.[29] He sees the Romans as *virtuous* people in the etymological sense of the term, from the Latin *vir*, "man." In 2017 he said, "You can see that power of Roman virtue, these Roman virtues of manliness, and service to the state. And that's why everybody in the world wanted a part of that."[30] From his reading of Gibbon, Bannon came to believe that the Romans are "the people most like us. . . . They built this great empire and . . . it all slipped away over time."[31] In Gibbon's argument, it was the expansionist foreign policy of an imperial Rome, "who, in distant wars, acquired the vices of strangers and mercenaries," that led to the collapse of the culture; then "the Roman world was overwhelmed by a deluge of barbarians."[32] In applying the lessons of Gibbon's Rome to America, Bannon homed in on Gibbon's characterization of foreigners as corrosive to the culture of a great nation. The Roman Senate, he told his biographer, Keith Koffler,

> was bought and paid for by the elites. . . . The exact thing we face today! . . . What the Roman Empire faced is exactly what we face, that you lose the citizenship—and the power of citizenship—of the Roman Republic, you become an Empire, and that empire becomes a massive concentration of power and wealth, which is detached from the people. And then eventually, you're having people who don't want to serve in the legions, you have to go for foreign soldiers. Everybody is a mercenary. And therefore, no one really stood up or was prepared to die, really, in service to the country. And then what happened? Wave, after wave, after wave of migrations from the Goths, the Visigoths, the Huns. Coming into the empire and changing the culture and destroying the civic society they had in Rome. The empire could not withstand it.[33]

Using the past to interpret the present, Bannon allowed his understanding of Roman history to inform his attitude toward American politics, especially his isolationist foreign policy and restrictive immigration policy.

Whether he was fully aware of it or not, the Bannon who sought to use Roman history to lodge moral lessons for his contemporary audience found in Shakespeare someone who had done the same. This representational mode recalls Shakespeare's favorite source for his Roman plays,

Plutarch's *Lives of the Noble Greeks and Romans,* another of Bannon's six most influential books. Employing the rhetorical device of parallelism (the formal term is *synkrisis*), Plutarch juxtaposes two figures, one Greek and one Roman, elevating the discussion from the particulars of each life to abstract moral and political instruction. As Thomas North puts it in his translation of Plutarch's *Lives* (1579), used by Shakespeare, "It is a certain rule and instruction, which by examples past, teaches us to judge of things present, and to foresee things to come: so as we may know what to like of, and what to follow, what to mislike, and what to eschew."[34] The classical historian made explicit parallels between his subjects, whereas the English playwright let audiences discern for themselves any correspondences between past and present. Plutarch used Greek history to write Roman history; Shakespeare used Plutarch's Greco-Roman histories to write plays with parallels to Elizabethan politics; Bannon sought to use Shakespeare's anglicized Roman histories to write screenplays with parallels to modern American politics. This dynamic may have been bubbling beneath the surface, but I think Bannon was drawn to Shakespeare's Roman plays because their presentist political mode, coding the social problems of early-modern England in ancient historical narratives, aligned with his own habit of politicizing the past to critique the present.

IV. From Revenge Tragedy to
Space Opera in Bannon's *Andronicus*

When I sat down to read Bannon's Shakespeare adaptations, I expected a celebration of populism. Titus and Coriolanus are both offered leadership of Rome by the people, but both refuse: Titus because he is too old, Coriolanus because he is too proud. Tragedy ensues. I expected this tragedy to form the foundation of Bannon's adaptations, leading to the cautionary message that leaders must listen to the will of the people, or else. I read the screenplays with an open mind. Listening to the will of the people is one of the central tenets of liberal democracy. I found one text more artistically successful than the other: *Coriolanus,* sticking closer to Shakespeare's original story, provides a coherent conceit, and the language, mixing Elizabethan dialogue with urban African American speech, while often absurd, might just be pulled off by capable actors. *Andronicus* replaces Shakespeare's plot and language with shallow sci-fi foolishness that is a struggle to slog through. But the more important element I discovered in Bannon's adaptations of Shakespeare was an insidious racism clothed as culture clash. His *Coriolanus* suggests that African Americans will kill themselves off through black-on-black crime, while his *Andronicus* tells the story of a "noble race" eliminating its cultural enemies on the way to securing political power.

Shakespeare's *Titus* is a tragedy in the classical, Aristotelian sense of a story about a noble person, Titus, who is strong and good but makes a miscalculation that brings about catastrophic and disproportionate pain and suffering. More specifically, it is a revenge tragedy. Typically in revenge tragedy, someone in a position of power kills or rapes someone in the protagonist's family. As a civic authority, the perpetrator is supposed to be responsible for administering justice; with no justice forthcoming, the protagonist suspends civic law to bring about his or her own version of vigilante justice. He or she plots and schemes, fumes in soliloquies, delays, and sometimes goes mad because he or she is seeking to do the very thing that he or she is punishing someone else for doing—murder. Because both protagonist and antagonist are guilty, both die at the end of the play, usually with other family members. The more guilty parties, the greater the body count.

Showing the guilt of the tragic protagonist, Shakespeare's Titus starts the play by mercilessly killing the first-born son of Tamora, queen of the Goths, whom the Romans have just conquered, as a sacrifice to the gods. "Let's hew his limbs till they be clean consumed," Titus's son, Lucius, crows. "Oh, cruel irreligious piety!" Tamora wails (1.1.129–130). As revenge, she orchestrates the rape of Titus's daughter, Lavinia. The girl's hands are cut off and her tongue cut out so she cannot identify the rapists; Titus chops off his own hand; Tamora kills one of Titus's sons. Titus goes mad, kidnaps Tamora's remaining sons, kills them, grinds up their bodies and bakes them in a pie, serves it to Tamora, honor-kills Lavinia, kills Tamora, and is killed by the Roman emperor, Saturninus. The emperor is then killed by Titus's only remaining son, Lucius, who becomes the new emperor of Rome. It is difficult to sit through, but recognizing the villain Tamora as also a victim emphasizes the element of justice in her cause, helping us see *Titus* as more than a melodrama of good versus evil. That is what separates Shakespeare's play from Gibbon's *Decline and Fall of the Roman Empire*: the play upends the antithesis between civilized Roman and savage Goth because the enemy actually lies within Rome, in its toxic conception of manly virtue, epitomized by Titus.

Illustrating, in contrast, the nobility and perfection of Bannon's pro-
tagonists is the voiceover that opens his *Andronicus*:

> While out among the stars, men and women intermarried with
> the Divine Sparks of other worlds to produce a noble race, the
> Andronicii—half-human, half-spirit. . . . The new Beings drew
> strength from the pure air of the stars and bred a race, strong in
> body and pure of heart . . . a race of Star Warriors dedicated to
> defending Earth. (1–2)

Why the emphasis on race in these lines? The Andronicii are not a family but a "race," characterized as "pure" and "noble," on a mission to
save the galaxy. The light associated with the Andronicii contrasts with
the darkness of their enemies, Bannon's version of the Goths, "the
DEMON SHADES OF ALGOL, shadows that writhe and swoop over
the land like blackened ghosts" (3). Extending the color imagery, the
Shades serve "the Dark Lord" (9), who spawned Attava (Bannon's Tamora). Just as Tamora has a black-skinned paramour, Aaron the Moor, so
does Attava: "A dark, translucent figure of a man, AARON, a Lower
Human (half-Shade, half-human) hovers nearby in the shadows" (15).
Like Shakespeare's Aaron, who displays the hypersexuality stereotypically associated with Moors in Shakespeare's time, Bannon's has a mys-
terious allure: "At the rear, the Lower Human, half-shape, Aaron, limps
behind; sinister yet appealing, he has black hair, black eyes and a sexual
quality like the goat-god Pan" (19). White-and-black and light-and-dark
are classic literary symbols for good and evil, especially in myth and science fiction, yet that trope does not govern Shakespeare's tragedy, because his protagonist, Titus, has major flaws, and his antagonists, the
Goths, are sympathetic at times. Notably, Shakespeare's Goths are ultra-
white. Bannon seems to have taken the symbolic significance of Aaron,
vilified because of his skin color, and extrapolated this quality to his
stand-ins for the Goths, the Shades, making them ultra-black.

As the story plays out, the heroic Titus defeats the Shades in a battle
on Mars, enslaves them, and brings them to earth. Instead of sacrificing
Attava's first-born son, as Shakespeare's Titus had, Bannon's Andronicus kills Ghul, Attava's first-born, in self-defense. The revision turns
Titus from a tragic to a heroic protagonist, from a powerful-yet-flawed
nobleman to a morally pure space knight. He is presented as "good,"
the Shades as "evil" (20), in a stark contrast to Shakespeare's play. Fol-

lowing Shakespeare, however, King Saturnius, who rules Earth, becomes enamored of Attava, marries her, and welcomes the Shades into
Earth culture. Anyone familiar with Bannon's love of Gibbon knows
what happens next. Chaos, betrayal, sci-fi mumbo jumbo, and recently
terrestrialized severed limbs cover the planet. Andronicus and the
Shades kill each other off. Titus's son, Lucius (his name from the Latin
lux, "light"), emerges as the hero of the play. In terms of genre, *Andronicus* is not a tragedy in the vein of Shakespeare's play but a heroic
romance. A Roman tragedy depicting the downfall of a noble house
becomes a space opera in the tradition of *Star Wars* where good conquers evil. By pitting one group of beings symbolized by light against
another group characterized by darkness, Bannon's *Andronicus* makes
race the centerpiece of his story.

In later interviews Jones has been appropriately embarrassed about
the *Andronicus* script: "It's really dreadful, the dialogue and such."[35]
"Unfortunately, it wasn't a good script, but it was a great idea."[36] When
asked about the enormous budget needed for special effects, she laughed:
"I don't think we thought very realistically at all while we were writing
it. . . . We just assumed the studio would take care of all of that."[37] The
project went nowhere, but *Titus Andronicus* haunted Bannon. He saw
Julie Taymor's 1994 production of the play at the not-for-profit off-
Broadway Theatre for a New Audience, which framed the story as a
flashback experienced by a traumatized post–Vietnam War America.
Bannon was smitten. He optioned the movie rights to Taymor's *Titus,*
hoping to inject it with his space opera vision, and took it to Overseas
Filmgroup, where he was on the board. His radical take on the play led
to a falling out with Taymor, whose film version, while conceptually and
visually bold, sticks closely to Shakespeare's story and language. Although Taymor later insisted that Bannon "had nothing to do with the
actual producing or financing of [*Titus*]," he still received an executive
producer credit when the film was released in 1999.[38] But the film flopped
at the box office. According to Bannon, "If they'd done it my way, it
would have been a hit."[39]

V. Racial Cannibalism in Bannon's *Coriolanus*

Bannon hit the jackpot in 1993. While negotiating the sale of Rob Rei-
ner's company, Castle Rock, to Turner Broadcasting, he acquired a
profit share in the television show *Seinfeld,* then in its fourth season. It

made him filthy rich. But around the time *Seinfeld* starting paying off, Bannon's thoughts returned to Shakespeare. While visiting a friend in New York, he saw a performance featuring gumboot dancers from South Africa. "Steve just flipped out," Jones told me.

> These were guys that were worse than slaves in the mines in South Africa. They couldn't even talk to each other, so they developed this Morse code of stomping with the big rubber boots they wore. And that's the way they talked to each other back and forth. This show was a really extreme political statement about suppression in apartheid South Africa. Steve came back to LA really on fire. He just wanted to do this. He wanted to set *Coriolanus* in South Central, and these guys were going to emerge out of a manhole, and they were going to be like a Greek chorus throughout the movie. And he wrote the first page—which is really well-written—and I took it from there.

They added another element to their *Coriolanus,* which took shape in the late 1990s: "Make a rap film out of it set in South Central during the L.A. riots—that was Steve's idea," Jones recalled.[40] The dialogue combining Shakespearean verse with L.A. slang was written by Jones and the son of Bannon's longtime assistant, Wendy Colbert, who is African American, perhaps lending credibility to the project. "Steve [then] added stuff—all the 'dudes' are him," Jones recalled.[41] At times, he would chime in with an especially aggressive line.

In 2006 Bannon and Jones were still excited enough about their *Coriolanus* adaptation to organize a staged reading, produced by the African American actors Robert Guillaume and John Wesley, at the Nate Holden Performing Arts Center in Los Angeles. The invitation to the event, billed as a pitch for a $20 million feature film, started with the rap music hook and then pivoted to political themes:

> Shakespeare was a natural rapper. This becomes evident in the delivery of this updated blend of two seemingly disparate genres—street rap and Elizabethan drama. . . . Where does Shakespeare end and street rap begin? . . . *Coriolanus,* the adaptation, will shed light on the continuing subversive effects of racial abuse going back centuries—from the mines of Apartheid in South Africa, [to] slavery, prejudice and brutality, to gang

cultures and the growing disregard for the disadvantaged in society today. It will show how the culture of greed, elitism, discrimination and inhumanity repeats itself today in a self-defeating replay of atrocities.[42]

Depicting the mutual destruction of two warring Italian cities, Shakespeare's *Coriolanus* provides a deeply pessimistic—tragic—view of humans continually defeating themselves. There are two key sets of characters: the Romans and the Volsci. In the first act, the Romans decimate the Volscian forces at Corioli. In the second act, the Romans turn on their own general, Caius Martius, dubbed "Coriolanus" in honor of his earlier victory. Coriolanus defects to the Volsci and, in Act V, leads a vengeful attack on his former allies in Rome. When the Romans persuade him to cancel his attack, however, the Volsci turn on him and slaughter him. So, in Shakespeare's play, the Romans kill the Volsci and the Volsci kill the Romans; the Volscian general steps into the power vacuum at the end of the play, but audiences get the sense that this cyclical self-destruction is going to continue into infinity.

Shakespeare thematized this self-consumption in the metaphor of cannibalism. At the start of the play, a starving citizen complains that the upper-class patricians are hoarding grain: "If the wars eat us not up, they will" (1.1.77). When Martius (the future Coriolanus) shows up, plebeians rather than patricians are characterized as cannibals "feed[ing] on one another" (1.1.179). All of Rome becomes a cannibal when the tribunes demand Coriolanus's death and his friend Menenius laments that the city "like an unnatural dam / Should now eat up her own!" (3.1.284–85). Later, when Menenius invites Coriolanus's mother to dinner, she volleys back: "Anger's my meat. I sup upon myself / And so shall starve with feeding" (4.2.49–51). The play returns time and again to eaters eating themselves, a metaphor for the self-defeating tendencies of humankind.

That conceit is radically changed by the racial emphasis of Bannon's adaptation, which begins with a wacky vignette set deep in Africa:

Pitch black. An endless vein of gold. SILHOUETTES of MINERS as they attack the vein—jagged-faced, with picks, axes, and pneumatic drills. The noise is deafening, the smoke and dust, blinding. The only illumination is from the miner's helmet lights.

Temperature 140 Fahrenheit—intense humidity, moisture and dampness everywhere. This is a scene straight from Dante's

Inferno—center stage at the ninth circle of hell: "Abandon hope, all ye who enter here."

As we track along the vein, Miners begin turning towards us—faces of living machines, the modern slaves of the notorious South African gold mines. Stripped to the waist, massively built with bandanna's around their necks, sweating profusely.

Slowly, one by one, the miners begin to CHANT—one voice, then another, then another. A cacophony of voices chanting from the Serengeti for a lost homeland. (1)

The miners enter a cage elevator that delivers them—bizarrely—to South Central Los Angeles. Sirens and gunshots in the air, this is "ground zero of the 1992 L.A. riots" (2). Throughout the screenplay, the miners, "helmet lights on, naked to the waist" (4), are interlaced with crowds of impoverished African Americans, who, like Shakespeare's plebeians, are starving. The Bloods are the Romans, the Crips the Volsci. Bannon weaves American racial tensions into a plot that follows Shakespeare's closely. "You choose," Brutus, Bannon's version of a Roman tribune, tells the Bloods: "To act and die—or lie beneath the white folk's boot!" (3). When Sicinius, another tribune, calls Brutus his "dear brother," Brutus explodes:

Dear? We're cheap, not dear.

(to crowd, voice rising)

White folks are dear. Their kibbles 'n' bits would relieve us, but they call us "dear" and cast us nothing. Our suffering's their gain. Let's avenge with guns and knives. I speak from hunger. (4)

The scene flashes to a television—"The SOUND IS OFF but a well-coifed, smiling BLONDE ANCHORWOMAN is speaking" (5)—reporting on the riots and the police mobilization to quell them: "NEWS ANCHORS broadcast from other parts of the city surrounded by fire and carnage. . . . We see the police and National Guard moving in, tanks rolling through the streets of Beverly Hills to keep out the rioters. Cop cars closing off intersections; cops beating looters" (6–7). This frame of the white commentators on television was all Bannon's idea, Jones recalled.

The head enforcer for the Bloods is Marcius, Bannon's Caius Martius. He defeats the Crips, led by Aufidius, in a shoot-out at the Corio Electronics Store, earning the name Coriolanus. On television, "an Anchorwoman smiles in the foreground, perfect teeth, perfect hair," reporting that "the mayor is asking L.A.'s gangs to help end the violence" (28). Like Shakespeare's Coriolanus, however, Bannon's hates pandering to the public: "On a make-shift stage—mic's, cameras, film crews, MEDIA everywhere—Coriolanus stands out awkwardly among the upright citizenry, like a WWF wrestling hero: tight tee, muscles bulging" (35). Spurning media appearances and political rallies, Coriolanus complains, "I can not be other than I am" (37), elaborating: "I cannot get down in the white man's suit, or bare my wounds for pity's sake" (40). "I'm not a ghetto superstar" (41), he concludes. Brutus and Sicinius conspire with the media to persuade the Bloods to turn on Coriolanus. He spurns the gang, leaves the city, and joins Aufidius and the Crips. Reconciled, Coriolanus and Aufidius return to Los Angeles to wage war, but Coriolanus's mother persuades him to abate. Betrayed and outraged, Aufidius and the Crips slaughter Coriolanus. Then Bloods and Crips together lift his body. In a callback to the opening, the screenplay ends with "a cacophony of voices chanting for a fallen brother—or a lost homeland" (97). They bear him across a crumbling Los Angeles, through the mystical portal that connects the city to the Serengeti, and then "we are back in the mine": "We see the endless VEIN OF GOLD streaking the ninth circle of hell, and catch a fleeting glimpse of the gangsters, massively built, bandanna's around their heads, sweating profusely as they bear the body of Coriolanus underground. Then all goes pitch black" (97).

By shifting the story from a clash between two cities to a civil war within an American subculture, Bannon's *Coriolanus* reframes the Shakespearean image of a cannibalistic humankind so that it applies only to one race: African Americans. Bannon's Bloods and Crips war against each other like Shakespeare's Romans and Volsci, but Bannon added a third set of characters: White America, as represented by the police, the politicians, and the media. The Bloods kill the Crips and the Crips kill the Bloods, but instead of Shakespeare's endless cycle of human self-destruction, Bannon's screenplay suggests that White America is sitting on the sidelines and watching Black America destroy itself. The audience is left not with a sense of perpetual self-harm in human society but rather with the sense that Black America is killing itself off, opening a power vacuum for a White America that does not share those self-destructive tendencies.

"I never knew the 'racist Steve' that's being reported now," Jones said in 2016.[43] She was even more adamant when I spoke with her:

> I had a great deal of personal pain about the way the people I really cared about and admired were treated by the rednecks. It was painful. It was physically painful for me. So I'm very, very sensitive—incredibly sensitive—to racism, and I didn't pick it up from him. It's not as though, "Oh, no, I didn't notice." No, my antennae were out. Steve was genuinely outraged by the apartheid situation, the treatment of the miners. And he was genuinely outraged by the conditions in South Central.

Nor does Bannon consider himself a racist. "We're not a birther site," he said about *Breitbart,* rejecting the claim that Barack Obama was not born in the United States.[44] He called white supremacist Richard Spencer a "freak" and a "goober."[45] Most forcefully, in an interview he thought was off the record, Bannon contrasted his "economic nationalism" with "ethno-nationalism," turning his venom on the racist far Right: "It's losers. It's a fringe element. . . . These guys are a collection of clowns."[46] Yet this is the same Steve Bannon who once told Jones that only landowners should be able to vote. "That would exclude a lot of African-Americans," she replied. "Maybe that's not such a bad thing," he said.[47] And this is the same Steve Bannon who, in 2013, after the Conservative Political Action Conference banned several anti-Muslim speakers, organized a counter-event to give them a platform.[48] It is the Bannon who shrugged off racism in the far Right: "Over time it all gets kind of washed out. . . . That will all burn away over time."[49] In the 2016 campaign against Hillary Clinton, he took a purely utilitarian view of racism: "We polled the race stuff and it doesn't matter. It doesn't move anyone who isn't already in her camp."[50] Yet he hired Cambridge Analytica, a British political consulting firm, to suppress African American votes, according to a whistleblower who testified before Congress in 2018.[51] Bannon's blasé attitude toward race persisted after the election: "The Democrats, the longer they talk about identity politics, I got 'em. I want them to talk about racism every day. If the left is focused on race and identity, and we go with economic nationalism, we can crush the Democrats."[52] And in March 2018, an emboldened Bannon rallied the French National Front

Party: "Let them call you racists. Let them call you xenophobes. Let them call you nativists. Wear it as a badge of honor."[53]

If pressed, I would say that I do not consider Steve Bannon a racist in the traditional sense: someone who believes that one race is genetically superior to another. His racism is all the more troubling because he is not explicitly racist. Racism crept into his Shakespeare adaptations while he was articulating other ideas. Something similar happens in his politics. And the same thing happens in Donald Trump's politics. Unpacking how this works is the goal of the next three sections.

VI. Machiavellian Populism

In 2009, around the beginning of the Obama era, Bannon and Jones stopped working together. As late as August 2016, she still saw him as "absolutely brilliant," "incredibly generous," and "like family."[54] Two months later, however—during the height of the 2016 presidential campaign, which gave Americans a close look at Trump's politics and Bannon's role in them—Jones became furious with him. "I don't want to know him anymore," she told the *Daily Beast*. "I don't care if I lose the friendship anymore. I'm so disgusted at what Bannon has become."[55] "Over time," she said, "he went from great ideas to pure politics."[56]

The key moment in that shift came in 2012 when Bannon and Andrew Breitbart relaunched the defunct *Breitbart* website. A conservative media figure himself, Breitbart saw Bannon as "the Leni Riefenstahl of the Tea Party movement," a reference to the Nazi film propagandist.[57] But Breitbart died days before the launch, so Bannon stepped in as executive chairman, branding the site as a "platform for the alt-right."[58] As Joshua Green explains, "The alt-right is a rolling tumbleweed of wounded male id and aggression," adding that "the bulk of the energy and activism attributed to the alt-right is driven by nihilistic, meme-obsessed gamer types whose use of racist and anti-Semitic language and iconography seems driven mainly by a warped sense of irony and a desire to upset their targets."[59] Their mascot is Pepe the Frog, whose tagline "Feels good man," first affixed to an image of Pepe with his pants down and urinating, is a catch-all slogan for the psychological release a certain strain of angry young white male adolescents feel from spewing racist bile on the internet. That demographic turned out to be Donald Trump's base when he ran for president. On August 17, 2016, Bannon became chief executive of Trump's campaign. Days after Trump won the election, he appointed Bannon chief strategist and senior counselor, giving him a place on the National Security Council. After Trump's dark inauguration address (written in part by Bannon) spoke of "American carnage" stemming from globalist economics, and responded with the slogan "America first," Bannon declared his latest revolution: "Like [Andrew] Jackson's populism, we're going to build an entirely new political movement . . . conservatives, plus populists, in an economic nationalist movement."[60]

Bannon gave a hollow Trump a substantive worldview. Nebulously defined and variously dubbed "nationalism" or "populism" (there are important differences), Bannon's worldview includes a middle-American, blue-collar, white, working-class ethos; an appeal to the angry and dispossessed who believe the system is rigged; a dark and inflammatory style of politics; a vow to be the voice of the people; a distrust of government institutions (i.e., the establishment); a resentment toward wealthy, corporate America and cosmopolitan lifestyles, symbolized by Wall Street; a defiant opposition to secularism, globalism, and modernity; an America-first mentality; a pro-military patriotism; isolationist policies in relation to the economy, the military, and immigration; and a fixation on identity—specifically race and gender—as the platform for discussing these issues.

But populism jars with the fear of the people's voice in Shakespeare's plays. In *2 Henry VI,* the pretender to the throne, Jack Cade, whips up a populist uprising of easily manipulated rogues and murderers: "Was ever feather so lightly blown to and fro as this multitude?" (4.8.51). In *Julius Caesar,* the plebeians are easily swayed by the politicians; looking to kill Cinna the conspirator, they kill Cinna the poet: "It is no matter, his name's Cinna" (3.3.31). The people in the anti-immigrant mob in *Sir Thomas More* are "the simplest things that ever stood" (Add. IIc.22). In *Richard II,* "the wavering commons' . . . love / Lies in their purse" (2.2.128–129). In *2 Henry IV,* the populace is "the blunt monster with uncounted heads, / The still-discordant wav'ring multitude," spreading rumor throughout the land (In.18–19). In *Coriolanus,* "the many-headed multitude" is easily manipulated by the tribunes (2.3.12). Shakespeare hated the political fecklessness of the people. In our terms, he was a fierce antipopulist.

His Roman plays are especially suspicious of the multitude. *Titus* starts with politicians "striv[ing] by factions and by friends / Ambitiously for rule and empery" (1.1.18–19). Saturninus and Bassanius campaign for votes, but the people "have by common voice / In election for the Roman empery / Chosen Andronicus" (1.1.21–23). Saturninus thinks that Titus will "rob [him] of the people's hearts" (1.1.210), but Titus does the opposite: "I will restore to thee / The people's hearts, and wean them from themselves" (1.1.213–214). The people's will is changeable, easily manipulated. Titus tells them to support Saturninus, and they fall in line.

Bassanius fears that Saturninus will bring dishonor to the Roman throne, and that is exactly what happens. Saturninus makes a "sudden choice" on pure whim (1.1.321), taking Tamora for his wife, making her empress of Rome. She is then poised to exact her revenge, delivering a "civil wound" to the state of Rome in the process (5.3.86). Those in power can easily manipulate the people's will, and someone ill-prepared to run a government where power is centralized can make impulsive emotional decisions with catastrophic consequences for the state.

Coriolanus connects populism to tragedy even more explicitly, starting with Caius Martius's disdain for the people's inconstancy: "With every minute you do change a mind / And call him noble that was now your hate" (1.1.164–165). A feckless populace is molded by crafty tribunes who infiltrate "the stream o'th' people, / And this shall seem, as partly 'tis, their own, / Which we have goaded onward" (2.3.241–243). Unlike *Titus*, *Coriolanus* includes open contempt for the will of the people, "You common cry of curs, whose breath I hate" (3.3.118). Exactly like *Titus*, however, *Coriolanus* shows a fickle populace empowering a leader who is terrible at governing, with tragic results.

Bannon's adaptations hew closely to Shakespeare's critique of the multitude. In *Andronicus*, the people are a faceless, thoughtless, frenetic mob in an abject condition, desperate for a hero to save them. When Andronicus first comes to Earth, a rendering of his triumphant return to Rome in Shakespeare's play, a crowd gathers, chanting, "ANDRONICUS, ANDRONICUS, ANDRONICUS" (25). He kills Ghul, and the crowd reacts like spectators at a blood sport:

> The Crowd ROARS and cheers. . . . The crowd goes wild. Beside itself, it begins CHANTING Andronicus' name in a frenzy. . . . Saturnius raises his hand motioning for silence, but they call for Andronicus with a strange urgency, ignoring their king.
>
> CROWD Andronicus, Andronicus, Andronicus! . . .

SATURNIUS If my people had their way, you'd be their king.
(27–28)

This is Bannon's version of Titus's election, although there is no election.
The people are mere onlookers while a heroic drama plays out at the
level of intergalactic royalty. We do not hear from the people again until
the end of the screenplay, when Lucius emerges as the king longed for at
the start of the screenplay: "Andronicus, Andronicus, Andronicus!"
(102). Without agency, barely human, the people are desperate to be
ruled by some heroic superhuman. That is closer to authoritarianism
than populism.

The masses are no better in Bannon's *Coriolanus*, but this text, like
Shakespeare's, emphasizes the multitude's manipulation by political operatives. When Bannon's Brutus whips up hostility toward Caius Marcius, there is "Wild CHEERING in agreement," the crowd chanting,
"The truth! The truth!" (3). As "the Miners move into the crowd,"
mixed voices fume against Marcius (4). Brutus calls for rebellion; "the
crowd CHEERS!" (4). Brutus and Sicinius play a game of pool; "the
crowd follows and gathers to watch" (4), symbolizing their passivity in
relation to the active manipulation of Bannon's tribunes. "The Miners
stand in the front row of the crowd" (5); when Brutus calls for a riot,
"the denizens of the pool hall become a mob, suddenly mobilized, grabbing anything that can be a weapon, getting ready to move out" (6).
Agrippa pacifies the crowd as easily as the tribunes agitated them, but
Brutus volleys back, making the case for riot as "the crowd ROARS its
approval" (7). Agrippa shuts him down, calling Brutus "the lowest, bas-
est, poorest of this 'wise' rebellion" (9). Caius Marcius then dresses
down those fickle and unfaithful "dogs" (9), in a passage of Shakespearean antipopulism:

So fuck you! Trust you?! Ha! With each passing minute, you
change your common mind. You call him noble that was once
your enemy, then dis your king. You cry against the "other"—
crackers, Blood, Crip, popo, Pol, the rich—it don't matter, nig-
gas. Awe keeps you feeding on each another. (10)

The riot is stamped out as easily as it was stoked.

As the screenplay unfolds, the tribunes become the sort of populists who engineer the will of the people. They use Coriolanus's antipopulism to rally the mob against him, turning them into the mindless chanting mass of the *Andronicus* script: "Down with him, down with him, down with him" (50). Coriolanus is driven from the city, concluding that "the many-headed beast has had its say" (60), not realizing that political actors claiming the mantle of populism have manipulated the public they claim to represent and tamed the beast.

Similarly, while Bannon presents himself as a for-the-people populist, he holds—if we take his Shakespearean adaptations seriously—a totally dismissive view of the agency, intelligence, and virtue of the people. Rather than autonomous citizens with rights and liberties, Bannon sees the people as ignoramuses who can and should be politically manipulated for their own good. Bannon's populism is not the kind that abides by the will of the people; rather, it is a Machiavellian populism that tries to manufacture, rather than solicit, public support for its economically egalitarian policies. The (possibly fatal) problem for his Machiavellian populism is that the political means employed to garner support coalesce around a willingness to enfranchise bigotry and strip some groups of their inalienable human rights and dignity in order to secure the financial well-being of others. That is a bargain most Americans have rejected.

VII. Tragic Populism

Bannon's Machiavellianism is most apparent in his manipulation of online communities. He discovered these networks in 2005 when—in a bizarre career turn—he took a financing job in Hong Kong for Internet Gaming Entertainment. The job introduced him to gamer culture. Immature and petulant young working-class men were spending all day on internet message boards. "These guys, these rootless white males, had monster power," he found.[61] He hired one of them at *Breitbart*. This was Milo Yiannopoulos, whom Bannon saw as evil but useful: "Milo is an amoral nihilist. I knew right away, he's gonna be a fucking meteor."[62] Bannon described Yiannopoulos's audience: "They come in through Gamergate or whatever and then get turned onto politics and Trump."[63] Bannon may have seen Trump—who, as the epitome of corporate America, should be Bannon's enemy—in a similar way: evil but useful, or, in Bannon's words, "a blunt instrument for us."[64] To do what?

For one answer we can look at the relationship between the tragic outcome of populism in Shakespeare's drama and the destructive, burn-it-down temper of Bannon's mythological history and politics, symbolized by his obsession with the honey badger. In 2011 a YouTube video of a honey badger devouring various prey animals went viral within the online gamer crowd and beyond. Uttered in the stereotypically gay voice later affected by Yiannopoulos, its tagline "Honey badger don't give a shit" became Bannon's personal motto, while *Breitbart* made the honey badger its mascot.[65] "We're honey badgers," Bannon told critics. "We don't give a shit."[66] When Trump responded to the infamous *Access Hollywood* tape (where he brags about grabbing women "by the pussy") by attacking Hillary Clinton for her husband's infidelity, Bannon was awed: "You have to have a certain psychological construct to do that—he's got that. Classic honey badger. He crushed her."[67]

What happens when you put a honey badger in the White House? In 2013 Bannon declared: "I'm a Leninist. Lenin wanted to destroy the state, and that's my goal too. I want to bring everything crashing down, and destroy all of today's establishment."[68] Around that time, he described his politics as "virulently anti-establishment."[69] By November 2016, he had morphed into a comic-book supervillain: "Darkness is good. Dick Cheney. Darth Vader. Satan. That's power."[70] After Trump took office, Bannon pledged a "deconstruction of the administrative state."[71]

On the surface, Bannon supported Trump because Trump advocated economically and socially nationalist ideas. Viewed through the lens of Bannon's Shakespeare adaptations—where populism puts terrible leaders into positions of power, only to see them fail and take down whole governments—a possible ulterior motive appears. This possibility requires us to distinguish between two kinds of populism. One strain of populism seeks to enact government policies that enfranchise the working class and oppose the concentration of wealth in the top one percent of the population. This desire is shared by most Democrats, but it is not Bannon's populism. He wants to destroy the institutional mechanism perpetuating wealth inequality. Trump was the perfect candidate for Bannon, not because Trump's social policies were geared toward a white, working-class demographic, but because his economic policies were geared toward corporate America. If Bannon knew, via Shakespeare, that populism produces weak leaders prone to tragedy, it is possible—taking into consideration Bannon's preoccupation with world-historical war, delusions of grandeur, and honey badger strategies—that he wanted Trump to succeed only to fail. If you are Steve Bannon, and you want to destroy corporate America, one way to do so could be to support a candidate who is (1) sure to get, because of his economic policies, the full-throated backing of corporate America, and (2) sure to be, because of his social policies and personality, resisted into resignation, impeached, or decisively voted out of office, taking with him the corporate America and Republicans who hitched themselves to his wagon. Once Trump took over the Republican Party, his failure could be, in Bannon's eyes, more successful than success. Never mind that global financial markets might crash and national institutions fail—that is not only a price Bannon was willing to pay but his goal. The Shakespearean suggestion that populism ends in tragedy was not a liability for Bannon. It was populism's greatest asset.

VIII. A New View of Populism

We have worked our way through the forests and valleys of Bannon's thought to a summit where we can survey what populism is—not what it says it is, but what it actually is. For starters, populism pursues the same egalitarian economics that liberal progressives like Bernie Sanders pursue: anti-elitist, anti-establishmentarian, and hostile to corporate America's perpetuation of economic inequality. Both populists and progressives claim that the system is rigged against working Americans. Both see Washington and Wall Street in a corrupt partnership to empower wealthy, coastal elites at the expense of working men and women. Both encourage and exploit anger at the system. What makes Bannon's populism different is that it wants to destroy the corporate American system that socialism and progressive liberalism aim to reform. And that destructive impulse informs everything in Bannon's version of populism.

Like Bannon himself, populism exaggerates. Drawing upon apocalyptic Christian imagery, populism paints an image of a world at war. It adapts the Manichaean cosmology of good versus evil into a schematic view of history and culture as a battle between "us" and "them." It deals in conspiracy theories where shadowy figures are pulling the strings behind the apparent workings of government. These ideas appeal to the gut rather than the head, so populism seeks out capable propagandists like Bannon to intellectualize its predetermined politics. Populism turns to history and other scholarly traditions to bolster its claims, willfully ignoring any facts that contradict its political tenets and endorsing dubious, sometimes patently absurd interpretations, rendering history into detached-from-reality mythological ideas seen as hokey by actual historians.

Using entertainment media and journalism, populism adopts a win-at-all-costs attitude, prizing aggressive, merciless political maneuvers. It is willing to ignore, sanction, even encourage the unethical impulses of its target audience—including racism—if that energy can be harnessed for political support. It is not racist in the sense of believing that one race is inherently superior to another; its racism is strategic, using racist imagery and ideas to appeal to a subset of the population that is explicitly racist. It presents outsiders—marginalized citizens, other nations—as enemies, especially demonizing Muslims and Mexicans, shrugging off the fact that the nations it demonizes are always racially different from White America. It then presents patriotism—love of nation—as the key factor in economic prosperity, and immigration as a threat to patriotism.

Beyond racism, populism exhibits an instrumental immorality. It is Machiavellian in its strategic manipulation of public sentiment, willing to lie to move people to a politically advantageous position. It claims to be the voice of dispossessed and forgotten Americans, working hard and doing the right thing but uncompensated and unappreciated. But it views those people as unintelligent and fickle. Quite counterintuitively, populism sees public sentiment as something to be manufactured rather than heeded. It manipulates the public sentiment it claims to represent.

It does so by appealing to the anger of white, working-class, red-state Americans, actively pursuing impressionable young men of gamer culture who delight in breaking their parents' norms. Along with its apocalyptic view of history, populism exhibits delusions of grandeur, presenting itself as a savior. It frames social problems in pseudohistorical and mythological terms to promote strongman candidates. Populists know that an abject populace is desperate for a champion. They know that a frightened populace that believes cultural war is underway will cling to a bellicose warrior who promises to lead the charge against both the outside forces threatening the nation and the spineless politicians refusing to fight this war. They know that the fear and anger of the dispossessed can be transformed into energy and enthusiasm for a candidate in the guise of a heroic savior.

But populists of Bannon's stripe also know that the election of non-political cultural warriors can result in mismanagement, catastrophe, and collapse. They understand that warriors make terrible governors. They know that, in a democracy, bad political leaders will be held accountable by the people. They know that falling politicians can take venerable institutions down with them. For them, the downfall of the status quo is not just acceptable but the whole point. They want to tear the system down. They want tragedy.

IX. Bannon as Riot

Let's end with Errol Morris's 2018 documentary profile of Bannon, *American Dharma,* which climaxes in an allusion to Shakespeare.[72] It comes in a segment on Bannon's view of himself and his quirky notion of *dharma,* a mash-up of Eastern mystical concepts signifying "the combination of duty, fate, and destiny." Several analogues from literature and film are suggested—Milton's Satan, John Wayne, Gregory Peck— but Bannon and Morris dwell on Shakespeare's Falstaff as played by Orson Welles in *Chimes at Midnight* (1965).

Bannon looks like Welles's mountainous and scruffy Falstaff; Joshua Green calls Bannon "a Falstaff in flip-flops."[73] Loud, irreverent, and boastful, Falstaff is Prince Hal's tavern buddy, a mentor in mayhem, as the young prince neglects his royal responsibilities and wastes his time in the pubs. Falstaff is a nobleman but does not act like one; he is derided in *1 Henry IV* in terms that Bannon's detractors would happily apply to him: "That reverend Vice, that grey Iniquity, that father Ruffian, that Vanity in years" (2.4.412–413). "That villainous abominable misleader of youth, Falstaff, that old white-bearded Satan" (2.4.421–422). "Wherein crafty, but in villainy? Wherein villainous, but in all things? Wherein worthy, but in nothing?" (2.4.416–418). When Hal undergoes a "reformation" (1.2.188), matures, and becomes king in *2 Henry IV,* he banishes his former friend. There are tears in Welles's eyes; his Falstaff is devastated. But Bannon reads this moment differently when drawing a parallel between Falstaff's fate and his own banishment from the Trump administration. Morris recalls:

The interesting thing about Bannon's version of Falstaff is that it's a heroic Falstaff. It's Falstaff who does his duty, knowing that it may come to a dismal end, but nevertheless his obligation, his dharma, is to train, educate, and bring up Hal, the future king. In Bannon's view, Falstaff is delighted. And Bannon is delighted by what he was able to give Trump. He was the loyal courtier who educated the future president. He did his job and did it well. He fulfilled his dharma.[74]

Shakespeareans might jump to apply other interpretations of Falstaff to Bannon. "There are many men resembling him," John Dryden wrote in 1668: "Old, Fat, Merry, Cowardly, Drunken, Amorous, Vain, and Lying."[75] Elsewhere, Dryden describes Falstaff as "a lyar, and a coward, a Glutton, and a Buffon."[76] In the next century, Samuel Johnson wrote, "The moral to be drawn from this representation is that no man is more dangerous than he that, with a will to corrupt, hath the power to please; and that neither wit nor honesty ought to think themselves safe with such a companion."[77] And in the twentieth century, John Dover Wilson excavated the origin of Falstaff in the allegorical character Riot from a sixteenth-century morality play called *The Interlude of Youth*.[78] It starts with Youth banishing Charity and Humility from his presence. Youth is joined by his brother, Riot, a Bannon bursting into the room:

> *Huffa, huffa who calleth after me?*
> *I am Riot, full of jollity,*
> *My heart is light as the wind,*
> *And all of riot is my mind*
> *Wheresoever I go.*[79]

Riot recruits Pride and Lechery to join their group. "Youth is not stable," Charity laments, "But evermore changeable" (552). Youth and Riot put Charity in chains. It takes Humility to release Charity and banish Riot from Youth's company. Humility then chastises Youth: "For your sin look you mourn, / And evil creatures look you turn" (762–763).

In comparing himself to Falstaff, Bannon reveals himself as Riot, a misleader of youth, clever and witty yet totally destructive, with no substantive policy behind him. This identification also reveals the absurdity of Bannon's effort to cast himself and Trump as Falstaff and Hal. Falstaff does not make Hal king—he stands in the way. Hal's rejection of Falstaff is not a betrayal of the man who made him. Like Riot, Falstaff is the corrupter of youth, an elder and mentor who encourages youth to embrace immaturity but is rejected when adulthood arrives. Bannon's Falstaffian moment will come, if it does, when the alt-right gamer kids he has raised see him and say King Henry's words:

I know thee not, old man. Fall to thy prayers.
How ill white hairs become a fool and jester!
I have long dreamt of such a kind of man,
So surfeit-swelled, so old, and so profane;
But, being awaked, I do despise my dream. . . .
Reply not to me with a fool-born jest;
Presume not that I am the thing I was,
For heaven doth know, so shall the world perceive,
That I have turned away my former self.
So will I those that kept me company.
When thou dost hear I am as I have been,
Approach me, and thou shalt be as thou wast,
The tutor and the feeder of my riots.
Till then, I banish thee, on pain of death,
As I have done the rest of my misleaders,
Not to come near our person by ten mile.
(2 Henry IV, 5.5.45–63)

2

Public Shakespeare

The Bard in the 2016
American Presidential Elections

I N A MAY 2, 2015, op-ed column in the *New York Times,* Frank Bruni held up one of Hillary Clinton's chief campaign strategists, Joel Benenson, as an exemplar of the value of a good liberal arts education, specifically Shakespeare studies.[1] "I can personally attest to the value of Shakespeare in my current profession," said Benenson, who majored in Theatre at Queens College. The knowledge and skills gained from studying *Hamlet* and *Macbeth,* he explained, were just as useful as statistics and political science. Bruni and Benenson's celebration of liberal arts education is a subtype of what has recently become an identifiable genre: the Defense of the Humanities essay. Over the past ten years—partly in response to increased funding for the STEM fields (science, technology, engineering, and math), partly in response to plummeting enrollments in the liberal arts—scholars have felt pressure to justify the very existence of the humanities. It is often public intellectuals who pen these defenses, but during the 2016 American presidential campaign an identifiable and unprecedented group of "Public Shakespeareans" emerged to illustrate the value of Shakespeare studies—both the instrumental value of skills acquired interpreting Shakespeare and the substantive value of knowledge of what happens in his plays.

These Public Shakespeareans were not simply exercising their rights as U.S. citizens to voice their political opinions (as a plumber or accountant might). Nor were they "crossing over" from their academic work to the public sphere (as a political scientist might). Instead, they were demonstrating the political value of Shakespeare studies, which fosters skills of analytical and ethical reasoning while supplying a body of examples of politics gone wrong. It turned out that Shakespeare scholars were uniquely positioned to comment on the 2016 presidential campaign because it exhibited the tone, characters, and structure of a Shakespearean tragedy. There was (1) a traditionally noble protagonist whose fatal mistake led to a surprising and disproportionately large catastrophe, and (2) an unceremonious, ignoble antagonist who provided comic relief but who also exploited (3) an economically stratified society filled with suffering, fear, anger, and resentment. Shakespeareans had explanatory authority because the election prompted the question Shakespeare's tragedies train us to answer—*Why did this happen?*

I. Citational Opportunism and Public Shakespeare

It feels absurd to cite a centuries-old English playwright from an age of monarchy in discussions of a modern democratic election. Yet Shakespeare has been invoked in connection with American presidential politics since at least the nineteenth century—in theatrical adaptations, in argumentative essays, and in other media. *Macbeth* has been especially prominent. Barbara Garson's play *MacBird!* (1967) used a Shakespearean framework to depict John Kennedy's assassination and the transfer of power to Lyndon Johnson. In 1992 the journalist Daniel Wattenberg dubbed Hillary Clinton the "Lady Macbeth of Little Rock": "consuming ambition, inflexibility of purpose, domination of a pliable husband, and an unsettling lack of tender human feeling, along with the affluent feminist's contempt for traditional female roles."[2] That same year Alan Woods's *Macbush* wrote George H. W. Bush into Shakespeare's play, and in 2003 Michael Hettinger's identically titled play did the same for a hawkish George W. Bush.[3] In 2004 Harold Bloom followed suit with a parody in *Vanity Fair* titled "Macbush: The Tragicomical History of Dubya the Great, King of America and Subsequently Emperor of Oceania."[4] If those Macbethifications of Bush II came from a Democratic angle, the Republican response was to dub him an American Henry V, as Mackubin Thomas Owens did during the Iraq War: "As a youth [Prince Hal] is dissolute to say the least. . . . Upon his father's death, he becomes a war leader of the first rank. President Bush's youth was never as dissolute as Hal's, but like the future Henry V, he became an effective war leader after 9/11."[5]

The Henry V–George W. analogy led Scott Newstok and Harry Berger Jr. to coin the term "citational opportunism" to refer to tendentious political analogies to Shakespeare's characters.[6] They point out that the analogy reflects poorly on Bush if one does a close reading of Shakespeare's character, starting with the "Redeeming time" soliloquy in *1 Henry IV* that inspired the comparison: "Harry's is a contentious, meanminded, and cynical speech even as it solicits moral self-justification. . . . Nothing in the remainder of the tetralogy changes this impression" (148). Shakespeare's Henry V wages war against France, not for the betterment of the English nation—as a good king would—but because of his "dynastic guilt and bad conscience," making this "an analogy ripe for Henrification of a negative rather than positive variety" (149). Bush waged war against Iraq neither in a display of newfound heroism nor for the betterment of America, but because of his own "dynastic guilt and bad conscience": his father deployed U.S. forces in the Middle East during the Gulf War but left the brutal dictator, Saddam Hussein, in power. Thus, Newstok and Berger trumpet close reading as "an antidote to citational opportunism" (145).

Not all allusions to Shakespeare in the popular press are citational opportunism. Consider the 2004 op-ed in the *New York Times*, "Friends, Americans, Countrymen . . ." by Stephen Greenblatt, a scholar no one could accuse of being bad at close reading.[7] Here, Greenblatt chose to write about Shakespeare in a public newspaper, in an accessible way, unencumbered by the conventions of academic writing, and explicitly with reference to modern presidential politics. For Greenblatt, the recent presidential debate between George W. Bush and John Kerry (each candidate calibrating his response to the unpopular Iraq War) shows an affinity to the orations of Brutus and Antony in Shakespeare's *Julius Caesar*, where each character adopts a different persona and posture toward Caesar's death. After qualifying the analogy ("Shakespeare lived in a monarchy, not a republic"), Greenblatt proceeds with a reading—close but quick and clear—of the play, quoting evidence and analyzing it, as literary critics do. He cites Brutus's love-hate relationship with Caesar—"As Caesar loved me, I weep for him . . . but, as he was ambitious, I slew him" (3.2.23–25)—showing how "the honorable, principled Brutus . . . lays out a complex and seemingly contradictory argument." In contrast, Antony "addresses not the listeners' heads but their gut feelings." Then Greenblatt shifts from analyzing Shakespeare to analyzing modern politics by looking at it through the Shakespearean lens. Bush was Antony; Kerry, Brutus:

> One man, the incumbent, insisted again and again on the need at all costs to avoid mixed messages. Everything for him was reduced to an apparently simple war-making strategy and a single enemy. The other man, the challenger, had a more complex account of the task. He expressed commitment to winning the war, but doubted its wisdom; he honored the sacrifice of our troops, but lamented our relative isolation from the rest of the world.

This is not citational opportunism. Greenblatt can read Shakespearean texts closely, and do the same for non-Shakespearean "texts" like the 2004 presidential debate: this ability to analyze information is the instrumental value of literary studies touted by their defenders. At the same time, he also makes sense of a modern political situation based on its similarity to a scene he has studied over and over in one of Shakespeare's plays. This is the substantive value of Shakespeare studies and what separates a Public Shakespearean like Greenblatt from the citational opportunist.

Shakespearean citational opportunism was satirized on national television four years later when Greenblatt appeared on the *Colbert Report* in October 2008.[8] On this show, host Stephen Colbert mockingly adopted the persona of a blow-hard conservative political commentator modeled on Fox News's Bill O'Reilly. Backstage before the show, he would inform guests that he would remain in character, and "willfully ignorant of what we're going to talk about, so disabuse me of my ignorance."[9] In the segment leading up to his interview with Greenblatt, Colbert asked indignantly, "Did you know that *Beverly Hills Chihuahua* is loosely based on *Troilus and Cressida*?" His feigned idiocy usually took the form of over-the-top conservative ideology, but on Greenblatt's episode it surfaced as citational opportunism. Referring to the 2008 presidential candidates, Colbert blustered, "Obama and McCain's stories are right out of Shakespeare," noting that "*McCain* sounds a lot like *Macbeth*: a passionate man prized for his military heroism." Obama, in contrast, is an "egghead elitist who can't make up his mind. Clearly, Obama is

Hamlet." Greenblatt played along with Colbert's shtick but also lodged a Shakespeare-inflected critique of McCain by reminding Colbert that *Macbeth* is a tragedy:

GREENBLATT I think Shakespeare thought all his life about precisely military heroism, and whether it could translate into leadership.

COLBERT And, of course, it always did.

GREENBLATT And, of course, he thought it almost never did.

Greenblatt's Democratic sympathies—another prominent feature of Public Shakespeareans—became even more apparent when he compared McCain's running mate, Sarah Palin, to Bottom, "a horse's ass," and demurred when Colbert compared Puck to Obama: "I think that Obama does have a certain magic," Greenblatt said. "I think the magic is the magic of offering people some hope when they're miserable."

II. Citational Opportunism in the 2016 Election

In the 2016 election, Shakespeare's presence in political commentary occurred on a different order of magnitude. A textbook example of citational opportunism, appearing in August 2015, is a piece for the daily humor website *McSweeneys* by Emily Uecker, an amateur pop-culture commentator. "'Hell Is Empty and All the Devils Are Here': A Shakespearean Guide to the 2016 Republican Primary" attaches a quotation to each of the sixteen candidates vying for the Republican nomination.[10] Donald Trump gets a line from *The Comedy of Errors*: "Many a man hath more hair than wit" (2.2.83–84). At this point, the clownish businessman and celebrity was just a bad-hair joke, not a serious contender. Jeb Bush, whose nomination seemed inevitable, gets a line from *Antony and Cleopatra*: "Give me my robe. Put on my crown. I have immortal longings in me" (5.2.276–277). Mike Huckabee, the governor of Arkansas, whose religiosity came across as hateful and retrograde to many, is tagged: "The devil can cite scripture for his purpose" (*The Merchant of Venice*, 1.3.92).

Uecker followed up in October 2016 with "'The Crown Will Find an Heir': A Shakespearean Guide to the 2016 Democratic Primary."[11] This piece is noticeably less caustic: the Democratic pool was much smaller, the Democratic primary was less of a circus, and Uecker's political inclination was firmly Democratic. Hillary Clinton gets a line from *Henry VIII:* "There's order given for her coronation: / Marry, this is yet but young, and may be left / To some ears unrecounted" (3.2.46–48). Bernie Sanders—who funded his campaign (as he obsessively bragged) with $27 donations from middle-class Americans—gets a line from *Julius Caesar:* "For I can raise no money by vile means" (4.3.71). For Jim Webb, a fiery former senator from Virginia whose candidacy was over before it began, the tag is simply *"Exeunt, fighting."*

The form of Uecker's pieces—Shakespearean quotation quippily connected to modern politician—was followed in January 2016 by Katy Weniger, an English major at Rider College with clearly liberal sensibilities ("I'm particularly interested in the variety of contestants we have running for the Republican party nomination [read: I'm terrified]").[12] Her post, "The 2016 GOP Presidential Candidates: As Told by Shakespeare," appeared on the website *Odyssey,* which pledged its commitment to unconventional voices: "*Odyssey* democratizes content."[13] Shakespeare would have a blast "picking fun at these goons running for office," Weniger writes, offering from his works "a few choice phrases for each of the oh-so-qualified candidates." The hits are light and good humored, as if she has mined an online Shakespearean insult generator. The overweight Chris Christie is "highly fed and lowly taught" (*All's Well That Ends Well,* 2.2.3). Donald Trump is, among other descriptions, the "anointed sovereign of sighs and groans" (*Love's Labour's Lost,* 3.1.167). Significantly, he has a total of five Shakespearean quotations while the other candidates get one each.

In April 2016, Tom Blunt published "The Bard's Ballot: 2016 Candidates as Shakespeare Characters" on the website *Signature* (whose slogan is "Making well-read sense of the world").[14] Trump is Nick Bottom, "a mere tradesman-cum-showman who's conceited enough to consider himself a worthy consort for the Queen of the Fairies. Oh yeah, and he literally has the head of a donkey for most of the show." Sanders is Prospero, "a cantankerous wizard from a remote desert island . . . whose 'pie in the sky' leadership strategies are the product of literal magical thinking." Clinton is Prince Hal; Jeb Bush, Macbeth; Ted Cruz, Brutus; Marco Rubio, Mercutio; Carly Fiorina, Tamora; and Ben Carson, Polonius (Figure 2.1). The analogies are funny but shallow. I guffawed, but the points are easily forgotten.

A similar sense of disposability pervades "Shakespeare on Our 'Scurvy Politicians'" (from September 2016), where Michael Judge, culture

FIGURE 2.1. Illustration for Tom Blunt, "The Bard's Ballot: 2016 Candidates as Shakespeare Characters," *Signature Reads*, April 18, 2016.

and arts critic for the *Wall Street Journal,* suggests that "Shakespeare, speaking from the grave, tells us more about the players on our political stage than any Matt Lauer interview ever could."[15] Judge presents a Top 10 list of Shakespeare's lines about politicians and politics but, with a smug grin, writes, "I'll leave it to you to match today's politicians with the quotes that best suit them." Individual readers may disagree on the modern politician implicated in each line—for my part, I associate "I am a man more sinned against than sinning" (*King Lear,* 3.2.60) with Hillary Clinton; "Plain and not honest is too harsh a style" (*Richard III,* 4.4.360) with Trump; and "The commonwealth is sick of their own choice" (*2 Henry IV,* 1.3.87) with Trump's supporters—but that is part of the game. The dynamic of Judge's piece is the relationship between the self-satisfied author who struts out his knowledge of Shakespeare and the self-satisfied reader who recognizes both the plays remembered from college and the politicians those lines can be made to mock.

Reviewing these pieces together helps us formulate how Shakespearean citational opportunism works. First, it is usually about the line or the character, which is rarely considered in the context of the larger plot from which it has been plucked. No close reading is involved: citational opportunism employs Shakespearean quotations and allusions with little or no analysis, explanation, or qualification, as if the asserted analogy obviously, incontestably, speaks for itself. Readings are shallow (e.g., Bottom is an ass; Henry V changes from rogue to hero) and not situated in larger considerations of the plays. Citational opportunism suggests one-to-one correspondences between lines or characters and modern politicians that tend to crumble under the weight of closer attention to the specifics of either the Shakespearean text or the modern situation. The purpose of these analogies is almost always to satirize and mock (the Henry V–George W. analogy is an exception). The allusions suggest absurdity, elicit self-satisfied laughter, and affirm the intellect of both the writer (who makes the analogy) and the reader (who recognizes it) over and above that of the subject (the politician satirized).

III. The Rise of Required Shakespeare and the Rise of Digital Media

These examples of citational opportunism point to two recent phenomena contributing to Shakespeare's presence in the 2016 election: the rise of Shakespeare as "required reading" in American education and the rise of digital media as an outlet for political commentary. First, while Shakespeare's works have been prominent in American education for decades, his foundational role in the curriculum has been codified in the twenty-first century. In the Common Core State Standards Initiative released in 2010, which aims to prepare American high-school students for success by providing curricular guidance to parents, educators, and policymakers, Shakespeare is the only author mentioned by name as required reading. In grades 11–12, syllabi ought to "include at least one play by Shakespeare and one play by an American dramatist."[16] Coequal with the entire dramatic output of the United States, Shakespeare here assumes the status of a discipline. The propriety of reducing English drama to Shakespeare can and should be debated, but the effect has been the creation of a common knowledge of Shakespeare in the United States. First-year college students of mine report taking entire high-school classes about Shakespeare, something associated with upper-division undergraduate or even graduate education in generations past. The widespread dissemination of Shakespeare to the American public through the high-school curriculum allows writers like Ueckler, Weniger, Blunt, and Judge to (1) assume a knowledge of Shakespeare in a general readership; (2) rely upon his cultural capital for clicks; and (3) use his plays as a communicable language for humor and commentary.

If the educational curriculum has made Shakespeare central to American culture, the rise of digital media has provided a venue for unconventional political commentary. As far back as the age of Shakespeare, political commentary—from experts with disciplinary training—traditionally took place in print media. Writers worked for and with news outlets that shared similar methods, standards, and top-down hierarchies. News and commentary went from the experts to the people as hard copy in expensive-to-produce newspapers, magazines, journals, and books. The 1990s saw the rise of the internet. In the 2000s, Web 2.0—the second stage of the internet and related technologies, such as smart phones and social media—shifted much of the internet from static web pages to dynamic user-generated content and communication. Everyone has always had an opinion; now everyone can publish it. The availability of an array of inexpensive, user-friendly tools and the proliferation of online media outlets have led to a "post-industrial journalism" that is decentralized and participatory.[17] As news is being disseminated from diverse sources, often amateurs—a bystander's cellphone video rather than a reporter—it is being analyzed from unexpected perspectives. Traditional news outlets like the *New York Times,* CNN, and *The Economist* host blogs offering commentary on the hard news of the day; niche websites multiply by the minute. New platforms, formats, and voices of political commentary have emerged, often with porous boundaries between traditional analysis and other genres of expression. There is a related crisis in the book publishing industry. Thus, new ports of entry to the public sphere have opened up for citizens, amateurs, scholars, and public intellectuals alike. On the one hand, a student and amateur intellectual can publish her witty associations between Shakespearean lines and modern politicians to a wide audience. On the other, analogies to current events that scholars previously might have mentioned to students in classrooms or office hours, but left out of publications for the sake of decorum, are now appearing in public writing. The kinds of conversations about Shakespeare and modern politics once conducted over coffee with colleagues are now being formalized and sent out into the world through tweets, blog posts, essays, and online op-eds.

IV. The Rise of Donald Trump

But the combination of broad familiarity with Shakespeare and the explosion of digital communication does nothing to explain the ubiquitous criticism of Donald Trump in Shakespeare-inflected political commentary. His campaign exhibited something we can reasonably identify (using the language of literary studies) as political "villainy." Coming from the world of reality television, he crafted a political persona for himself reminiscent of the villain audiences love to hate—a figure primed for critique by Shakespeare scholars. Like many of Shakespeare's villains, the Trump of the 2016 election was highly irreverent, overtly theatrical, unapologetically ambitious, deceitful, manipulative, self-satisfied, narcissistic, and demagogic, operating with a hostile bravado, yet thoroughly entertaining. In calling him a "villain," I am not referring to policies on issues that reasonable people can disagree on: health care, immigration, taxes, trade, treaties. Trump's "villainy" resides in the tone, rhetoric, and strategies of the character adopted for the campaign.

His first foray into presidential politics was championing the "birther" movement, which sought to delegitimize Barack Obama's presidency by claiming that he was not born in the United States and thus by law could not be president. At best, the movement was willfully ignorant of evidence and reality. Even when Obama released his birth certificate, Trump refused to acknowledge the president's U.S. birth. The campaign came across as insidiously racist to most. It pushed an idea proponents knew to be false, exploiting the repressed racism of a subset of Republican voters to secure political power for the villainous manipulator. That subset of Republican voters seemed to be (1) nostalgic for an idyllic image of 1950s white American exceptionalism, (2) resentful of the election of an African American president, (3) sufficiently connected to modern American values to resist overt racism and therefore (4) receptive to politics that were legalistic in language but racist in motive, and (5) willing to ignore facts, reality, and truth in pursuit of those politics.

On June 16, 2015, Trump announced his campaign for president in a highly theatrical event, descending from the heights of Trump Tower on an escalator to a stage in the building's marble-lined atrium, where he addressed an audience that included, as later revealed, many paid actors. This is not the place for a comprehensive discussion of "The 155 Craziest Things Trump Said This Election," as *Politico Magazine* titled the aggregate of quotations it published a few days before the election,[18] but a survey will illustrate why Shakespeareans felt compelled and qualified to analyze Trump. His campaign was a treasure trove of logical fallacies and rhetorical maneuvers. There was a bewildering intersectionality among the tactics and themes employed—racism, sexism, egocentrism, authoritarianism, machismo, bullying, incitement, impunity, indecorum, indecency, irreverence, insinuation, whining, lying, coyness, and vagueness—but Trump's political persona boils down to a mixture of aggressive narcissism and jocular dishonesty reminiscent of a Shakespearean villain.

Many thought that Trump's candidacy was dead on arrival because of the bigoted characterization of Mexican immigrants in his campaign launch speech: "They're bringing drugs. They're bringing crime. They're rapists. And some, I assume, are good people." He later called for religious discrimination ("a total and complete shutdown of Muslims entering the United States") and played coy when asked about his white-supremacist supporters ("I don't know anything about David Duke, OK?"). Referring to the Hispanic American judge presiding over a legal case against Trump University, Trump complained: "He is a member of a club or society, very strongly pro-Mexican, which is all fine. But I say he's got bias." As the Republican Speaker of the House Paul Ryan stated, "Claiming a person can't do their job because of their race is sort of like the textbook definition of a racist comment." Trump claimed the opposite: "Just so you know, I am the least racist person, the least racist person that you've ever seen, the least."

Commentators sensed a connection between Trump's racism and sexism. When Megyn Kelly of Fox News questioned Trump on his penchant for misogyny ("You've called women you don't like fat pigs, dogs, slobs, and disgusting animals"), he doubled-down by suggesting that Kelly was menstruating: "You know, you could see there was blood coming out of her eyes, blood coming out of her wherever." He responded to supermodel Heidi Klum's criticism by attacking her appearance: "Sadly, she's no longer a 10." He attacked the appearance of his primary opponent Carly Fiorina: "*Look* at that face! Would anyone vote for *that?*" And he jabbed Republican primary opponent Rand Paul with *apophasis* (the rhetorical device of bringing something up by saying that it will not be brought up): "I never attacked him on his looks and believe me, there's a lot of subject matter there." He used the same strategy to return to an earlier enemy: "I refuse to call Megyn Kelly a bimbo, because that would not be politically correct." Toward the end of the campaign, when accused of sexually assaulting several women, he suggested that his innocence was obvious because his accusers were not attractive enough: "Believe me, she would not be my first choice," he said about one. "Take a look. Look at her. Look at her words. And you tell me what you think. I don't think so," about another. And he bizarrely cited his own physical appearance at a campaign rally: "Do I look a president? How handsome am I, right? How handsome?"

Trump's egocentrism is legendary. "I'm the only one," he said at a campaign rally; "I alone can fix it," at the Republican national convention. When he mocked a disabled reporter, Serge Kovaleski, it became clear that Trump was not simply racist, sexist, and ableist; he was aggressively narcissistic, his egocentrism manifesting in attacks on identities he did not hold: women, minorities, and people with disabilities. The flip side of his sexism was his machismo, displayed in his mockery of the military heroism of Senator John McCain, who had been openly critical of Trump: "He's a war hero because he was captured. I like people that weren't captured, OK?" At one rally, Trump thumped his chest by saying, of a protester, "I'd like to punch him in the face." At another, he incited violence against protesters and offered to pick up the tab: "Knock the crap out of 'em, would you? Seriously. OK? Just knock the hell—I promise you, I will pay for the legal fees." After falsely claiming that "Hillary wants to abolish, essentially abolish, the Second Amendment," he suggested violence against her: "Nothing you can do, folks. Although the Second Amendment people—maybe there is, I don't know." Perhaps the most memorable token of Trump's machismo was his obsession with name-calling: "Low-Energy Jeb," "Lyin' Ted Cruz," "Crooked Hillary." Behavior reminiscent of schoolyard bullying in the Republican primary race evolved into an almost caricatural authoritarianism in the general campaign. Trump vowed to "open up our libel laws" so that he could more easily silence bad press. Receiving negative coverage from the *Washington Post,* his campaign revoked reporters' press credentials. At the second presidential debate, he threatened to throw Hillary Clinton in jail.

Trump's egocentrism also informed his impunity, usually expressed with overtones of violence. "I could stand in the middle of Fifth Avenue and shoot somebody and I wouldn't lose voters," he boasted at one rally. "You can do anything. Grab them by the pussy," he bragged in a rediscovered recording from 2005. Why would America elect such a rogue? There were many factors, but a Shakespearean is likely to notice that Trump's success was closely bound up with his jocular dishonesty. Like a Shakespearean villain, he managed to cultivate an aversion to truth that was somehow not incriminating but rather entertaining.

He was ostentatiously politically incorrect, willing to say things traditionally considered indecorous, indecent, and offensive. He retaliated against criticism from Senator Lindsey Graham by divulging Graham's private cellphone number during a rally. When Libertarian vice-presidential nominee Bill Weld identified Trump's rhetoric as fascist, Trump responded with *apophasis:* "I don't talk about his alcoholism, so why would he talk about my foolishly perceived fascism?" And he turned the second Republican primary debate into a circus sideshow by defending his penis size against opponent Marco Rubio: "He referred to my hands: if they're small, something else must be small. I guarantee you there's no problem."

Trump's political incorrectness and irreverence provided cover—for himself and his supporters—for his dishonesty, which assumed many forms. First, he flat-out lied, as when he made up a news story about Americans celebrating Islamic terrorism. He failed to provide evidence when challenged on the authenticity of the story, and refused to acknowledge either the truth or his own fabrication. Second, he was breezily dismissive of expertise. He repudiated scientific consensus on climate change. He also disparaged the expertise of military leaders on warfare ("I know more about ISIS than the generals do") and torture ("Believe me, it works"). Third, instead of expertise, he relied on whispers. He denied statistics from government reports when they did not fit his narrative: "Don't believe those phony numbers when you hear 4.9 and 5 percent unemployment. The number's probably 28, 29, as high as 35. In fact, I even heard recently 42 percent." He repeated a bogus story from the tabloid *National Enquirer* about the involvement of the father of primary opponent Ted Cruz in John Kennedy's assassination. Fourth, Trump was a master of the manipulative use of silence. Sometimes it manifested itself in coyness, as when he was asked if he still believed that Obama was not born in the United States: "I'll answer that question at the right time. I just don't want to answer it yet." Pressed on whether he would accept the results of the election, he refused to answer: "I will tell you at the time. I'll keep you in suspense. OK?" At other times, his mastery of silence took the form of vagueness, as in his proclaimed secret plan to defeat the terrorist group ISIS: "I have a plan, but . . . if I win, I don't want to broadcast to the enemy exactly what my plan is." Trump was also adept at insinuation. He lied about immigrants and refugees, saying that our "incompetent government" was "letting 'em in by the thousands, and who knows, who knows, maybe it's ISIS." Fifth, and finally, he displayed an impudent counterfactuality, telling obvious lies that, because of their obviousness, were either ignored by supporters or celebrated as evidence of virtuosity. In bald-faced contradiction to his words and actions, Trump vowed to be the candidate of women ("I cherish women") and Hispanics ("I love Hispanics"). He had a penchant for flinging claims about him back against his opponents: "Hillary Clinton is a bigot"; "Hillary is the most corrupt person to ever run for the presidency of the United States." He repeatedly asserted that he had been "totally against the war in Iraq," long after this claim was proven to be false. He claimed to have won debates most thought he had lost.

This comic-book-villain persona extended to the big company, the big fortune, the big tower, the big airplane—all with his name on them—as well as the big ego, the big hair, the big belly, the big tie, and, he insisted, the big hands. In July 2016 Marvel Comics "officially turned Donald Trump into a supervillain—a xenophobic, orange-haired, Captain-America-hating supervillain who is obsessed with the quality of his hands."[19] Yet the American people elected him, in part, because his entertainment value, along with his populist, damn-the-system bravado, exerted a greater pull on the voting public than Hillary Clinton's more traditional political expertise and economic policies aimed at growing the middle class.

V. The Shakespearean Satirization of Trump's Language

Trump's "villainy" led most Shakespearean appropriators to critique and satirize him mercilessly—not his policies so much as his mannerisms and personality. In a February 2016 article for the *Chronicle Review*, "What Would Shakespeare Make of Trump?" the Shakespeare scholar Gary Schmidgall eulogizes political civility and elegance by contrasting recent campaign rhetoric with Shakespeare's plays and George Puttenham's *The Arte of English Poesie*.[20] Using Puttenham's definitions, Schmidgall identifies in Trump's language *sarcasmus* ("bitter taunt"), *micterismus* ("fleering frump"), *antiphrasis* ("broad flout"), *charientismus* ("privy nip"), *abominatio* ("abusive insult"), *cacemphaton* ("foul speech"), *acyron* ("uncouth speech"), and *bomphiologia* ("pompous speech"). "Trump is a master bomphiologist," Schmidgall concludes. The piece is accompanied by Katherine Streeter's illustration of Trump as a tiny-handed Falstaff (Figure 2.2).

The journalist Aryeh Cohen-Wade took a different approach in his April 2016 *New Yorker* essay, "Donald Trump Performs Shakespeare's Soliloquies,"[21] an absurdist juxtaposition of the beauty of Shakespearean soliloquies and the incomprehensibility of Trump's. Hamlet's "Thus conscience does make cowards of us all" (*Hamlet*, 3.1.82) becomes a send-up of Trump's egocentrism:

FIGURE 2.2. Katherine Streeter, illustration for Gary Schmidgall, "What Would Shakespeare Make of Trump?" *Chronicle Review*, February 7, 2016.

When people say I don't have a conscience—trust me, I have a conscience, and it's a very big conscience, O.K.? And the native hue of my resolution is not sicklied o'er, that's a lie! If anyone tells you that the native hue of my resolution is sicklied o'er, they're trying to sell you a load of you-know-what. And enterprises of great pith—listen, my enterprises are so pithy. So pithy. Fantastic pith.

Romeo's "Juliet is the sun" (*Romeo and Juliet*, 2.1.45) becomes an ode to Trump's supermodel wife and a satire of his obsession with physical appearance and dependence on unattributed hearsay: "Melania's the sun, is what a lot of people are saying. Hillary Clinton? I mean, with that face? She looks like the moon!" Antony's "Brutus is an honorable man" (*Julius Caesar*, 3.2.80) becomes a call-back to Trump's attack on Jeb Bush and obsession with innuendo: "Brutus over there—we all know he's a good guy, right? And he says Julius was low-energy. Is it a crime to be low-energy? Well, maybe it is, maybe it isn't—who knows?"

This is not citational opportunism but something more substantive: satire using the ubiquity of Shakespeare's soliloquies for a sustained critique of a modern political figure's manner of thought and speech. Jaime

Fuller adopted a similar approach for a piece for *MTV News,* "Shakespeare's Latest Tragedy: The 2016 Election."[22] She rewrote "Mitt Romney, in the style of Henry V" (he riles up Republicans against Trump: "We few, we scared few, we Establishment"); "Jeb Bush, in the style of Richard III" (Bush laments his primary loss: "Our stern alarms changed to frantic dick jokes"); and "A Democratic debate, in the style of *Much Ado about Nothing*" ("There is a kind of merry war betwixt Bernie Sanders and Hillary Clinton"). But Fuller begins with "Donald Trump, in the style of Julia in *The Two Gentlemen of Verona*":

> *[Trump deletes a tweet after the Internet complains]*
> *O lyin' hands, to delete such great words!*
> *Huge and manly paws, so big-league that you*
> *Erased my beautiful tweet without pause!*

These Shakespearean satires, like several of the examples of citational opportunism quoted above, appeared in April 2016, around the time of the 400th anniversary of Shakespeare's death (having celebrated his 450th birthday two years earlier, people were desperate for a reason for another Shakespeare jubilee). The combined forces of the 400th anniversary and the 2016 American election generated many kitschy, disposable appropriations—whether citational opportunism or Shakespearean satire—but there was also a steady stream of substantive, productive, and insightful Shakespeare-inflected political commentary.

VI. Public Shakespeare in the 2016 Election

The earliest examples came from some Shakespeare-loving philosophers in Chicago. As Trump was gaining momentum in the primaries, Andrew Cutrofello—a philosopher at Loyola University, Chicago—wrote a short essay for *Public Seminar* titled "Shakespeare and Trump: What's in a Name?"[23] It addresses several allusions to Shakespeare in Trump's books, including this reference to *Romeo and Juliet* in *Think Like a Champion*:

> I was having a conversation a few years ago with a few people when one guy mentioned that the Trump name had become a famous brand around the world and then added, "What's in a name?" He then sort of laughed and said to me, "in your case, a lot!" I noticed that one guy seemed out of the loop about the

quip. So I said "That's Shakespeare. 'What's in a name' is a famous line from Shakespeare." So he still looked perplexed and asked "From what?" And although I knew it was from *Romeo and Juliet*, I said, "Look it up. You might learn some interesting things along the way."

The final move in this narrative—claiming to have all the answers and refusing to share them—was characteristic of Trump's approach to policy during his campaign. Vagueness and coyness were covers for ignorance and emptiness. And he seems not to have actually read *Romeo and Juliet*, insofar as his answer to the question "What's in a name?" (*everything*) is the opposite of Juliet's answer (*nothing*), as is evident in Trump's *How to Get Rich*, which Cutrofello quotes next:

> Using my name on a building carries with it a promise of the highest quality available and at least a $5-million price tag. That's just for the name. . . . When I remember the line from Shakespeare's *Romeo and Juliet*—"What's in a name?"—I have to laugh. What's in a name can be far more than the Bard or I ever could have imagined.

Cutrofello uses Trump's invocations of "What's in a name?" to reflect on the value the candidate placed on his own name, but then the philosopher goes elsewhere in Shakespeare's works to perform a counter-analysis of Trump's name-branding:

> Whether Trump could imagine it or not, Shakespeare knew that it is possible to over-identify with one's name. He illustrates this in *Cymbeline*. When Cloten, the queen's privileged son, meets Guiderius in the Welsh woods, he expects his presumed social inferior to tremble at the sound of his name. . . .

> > *Cloten: Thou injurious thief,*
> > *Hear but my name and tremble.*
> > *Guiderius: What's thy name?*
> > *Cloten: Cloten, thou villain.*
> > *Guiderius: Cloten, thou double villain, be thy name,*
> > *I cannot tremble at it, were it Toad, or Adder, Spider,*
> > *'Twould move me sooner. (4.2.86–91)*

Cloten is quickly dispatched and decapitated. His headless body is buried. . . . Cloten is forgotten as Cloten.

Why is Cutrofello talking about *Cymbeline?* Trump never mentions the play. Cutrofello shifts from analyzing how Shakespeare has been appropriated to himself appropriating Shakespeare to analyze a non-Shakespearean situation. That is, Cutrofello switches from an analysis of citational opportunism to an instance of Public Shakespeare.

Two months later, a second Public Shakespearean stepped forward. Brian Leiter, a philosopher and legal scholar at the University of Chicago, published "Shakespeare on Trump: Money Made the Man" in the *Huffington Post*.[24] Leiter's progressive politics are evident in his seething takedown (Shake-down?) of "the pathetic Donald Trump":

> In Shakespeare's *Timon of Athens* (1623), Timon, a wealthy Athenian, loses his fortune, and thus his friends, his status, his reputation. When he subsequently acquires a great amount of gold, he is now rather self-conscious about the distorting effect of wealth. Speaking of his "gold," Shakespeare's Timon declares:
>
>> [M]uch of this will make black white, foul fair, wrong right, base noble, old young, coward valiant. . . . This yellow slave will knit and break religions, bless the accursed, make the hoar leprosy adored, place thieves and give them title, knee and approbation.
>
> And so has wealth served for the pathetic Donald Trump, erasing the man's actual qualities and producing a transmogrified image, in which the mediocre child of fortune appears as the epitome of competence and accomplishment, entitled to "title, knee and approbation."

Leiter then moves from Timon to Karl Marx, who (quoting this passage) made explicit the idea that Shakespeare implied: "Money is the supreme good, therefore its possessor is good." Leiter's philosophical training combines here with Marx's appropriation of Shakespeare to generate an analytical lens through which to interpret the unfolding events of the 2016 American presidential election. "Voters should remember Shakespeare!" he concludes.

Cutrofello and Leiter are philosophers by training, but formally trained Shakespeareans also took a hand in appropriating Shakespeare that election season. A cartoonist, a blogger, a journalist, or even a philosopher can cite Shakespeare to make a quick political hit; a Shakespeare scholar using his or her knowledge of the plays to elucidate an analogous political situation is something else. The Shakespearean is likely to be aware of the long history of Shakespearean appropriation and the current calls for a more activist edge in Shakespeare studies. Appropriation has been a key concern for decades, as symbolized by the creation in 2005 of a journal dedicated to the topic, *Borrowers and Lenders: The Journal of Shakespeare and Appropriation*. Books and careers are now dedicated to the interpretation of what Donald Hendrick and Bryan Cumming call "Shakespace" ("our name for the territory within discourses, adaptations, and uses of Shakespeare")[25] and what Julia Lupton calls "thinking with Shakespeare" ("think[ing] with or alongside Shakespeare about matters of ongoing urgency . . . in both their foundational framings and their contemporary unfolding").[26]

Public Shakespeareans are not studying appropriation but actively doing it. They are practicing what Terence Hawkes calls "presentism," an outgrowth of British cultural materialism, the more politically charged answer to the less activist new historicism of Greenblatt and other American Shakespeareans: "A presentist criticism's engagement with the text takes place precisely in terms of those dimensions of the modern world that most ringingly chime—perhaps as ends to its beginnings—with the events of the past. Its centre of gravity is accordingly 'now,' rather than 'then.'"[27] British presentism found its American cousin in the new Public Shakespeare that came of age in the 2016 presidential election.

A watershed moment for Public Shakespeare was the publication of Charles McNulty's May 2016 essay in the *Los Angeles Times*, "The Theater of Trump: What Shakespeare Can Teach Us about the Donald."[28] McNulty's background positioned him well for Public Shakespeare. He is the theater critic for the *Times*, a public paper, but his resume is academic: doctorate from Yale, teaching experience at universities like the New School, New York University, and the University of California, Los Angeles. He resists the urge to analogize Trump to any Shakespearean character: those who know Shakespeare best often insist on the impossibility of, or at least the need to qualify, analogies. Instead, McNulty compares Trump's voters to the mobs in Shakespeare's plays:

> What "Julius Caesar" and "Coriolanus" illuminate isn't Trump
> himself but the Trump phenomenon. Shakespeare may have no
> equivalent for the businessman who successfully transformed
> himself into a brand before redeploying his marketing acumen to
> the political arena, but the playwright understands the voters
> who are drawn like moths to the fiery glow of Trump's candi-
> dacy. . . . To anyone bewildered by the eruptions of violence at
> the Trump rallies, "Julius Caesar" and "Coriolanus" reveal just
> how easy it is to transform anxious citizens into mobs.

Where exercises in citational opportunism present a single quotation and
expect the words to interpret themselves, McNulty spends a significant
amount of time unpacking his comparisons. He cites both Shakespeare
scholars (Anne Barton, Maynard Mack, and A. D. Nuttall) and recent
Shakespearean productions (the 2005 production of *Julius Caesar* on
Broadway starring Denzel Washington, and the 2013 production of *Coriolanus* at Donmar Warehouse starring Tom Hiddleston). What is
merely implicit in Greenblatt's 2004 op-ed is the focus of McNulty's:
democracy is fragile precisely because a charismatic rhetorician can exploit and manipulate "the political immaturity of the people." In a testament to the value of "thinking with Shakespeare," McNulty quotes
A. D. Nuttall (who was citing the philosopher Karl Popper) to point out
that *Coriolanus* in particular shows the "paradox of democracy": "What
is one to do when the *demos,* the people, freely decides to resign its
power to a despot?"[29] Here a public discussion of current events is informed not only by the dramatic works of Shakespeare but also by the
academic work of Shakespeare scholars, especially those bringing Shakespeare into conversation with the pressing philosophical concerns of
modernity. This is a far cry from citational opportunism.

Two weeks later, McNulty received a response from Paul Hamilton.
An American citizen, Hamilton had received his doctorate in the U.K.
but was then (in a proto-Brexit story that attracted wide attention in
higher education) refused permission to remain in Britain to work as a
researcher. Hamilton was arrested and detained in a British immigration
removal center.[30] Written after his release, Hamilton's essay for the
Kingston Shakespeare Seminar, "Trumping Shakespeare: Donald Trump,
Boris Johnson, and the Rise of the Clown Politician," takes aim at politicians who exploit the absurd nationalism that got him arrested.[31] Like
McNulty, Hamilton is openly critical of Trump and Trumpism, but he

seeks to clarify and critique Trump's rhetorical style and success by shifting attention from tragic characters like Antony and Coriolanus to comic characters like Iago and Falstaff: "McNulty fails to give Shakespeare enough credit for anticipating the *mechanism* of Trump's rise and the advent of a new kind of political figure: the 'clown politician.'" Hamilton too provides close readings of Shakespearean passages and carefully reasoned and qualified connections to the current political situation. Pointing out that Iago's description of Cassio—"a slipper and subtle knave, a finder of occasions that has an eye, can stamp and counterfeit advantages" (*Othello,* 2.1.230–232)—actually describes Iago himself, Hamilton argues that Iago and Trump are masters of "dead-cat politics": "the trick is to 'throw a dead cat on the table' in front of reporters, and then dominate the news cycle." Iago and Trump incite racial conflict, Hamilton observes, but in a clownish way: like the Shakespearean fool, and contrary to conventional political wisdom, Trump advertises his opposition to the basic decency that makes civil society possible. His lack of principle, traditionally a liability in politics, is his greatest asset. It elicits the naughty laughter Shakespearean audiences give fools and clowns, providing cover for hateful ideas and, because substantive principles and policies are only vaguely advanced, cover for supporters whose strongest commitment is opposition to the established political order Trump is satirizing. Using the terms of literary studies for the purpose of cultural studies, Hamilton concludes that "contemporary politics is not being made by figures out of Shakespearean tragedy or history, but figures out of comedy elevated into circumstances that *produce* tragic consequences."

Publishing through the *Kingston Shakespeare Seminar,* Hamilton is perhaps a Shakespearean speaking to other Shakespeareans, but Peter C. Herman's "Shakespeare's 'Macbeth,' Donald Trump, and the Republican Party" appeared in the *Times of San Diego.* A professor of English at San Diego State University, Herman brought his expertise as a scholar of early-modern literature into the public sphere.[32] He relies on the public's general knowledge of one of Shakespeare's most popular plays but gives a specialist's reading of a key scene: Malcolm's ruse with Macduff in Act IV, Scene 3. Like other Public Shakespeareans, Herman does not try to analogize modern politician to Shakespearean character (as the citational opportunist does), but rather analyzes a modern cultural situation by presenting a comparable Shakespearean one. After summarizing, quoting, and analyzing Malcolm's claim that he is irredeemably evil, and

Macduff's declaration of continued loyalty nonetheless because it will allow them to unseat their mortal enemy, Herman suggests: "This scene nicely shows the predicament that the Republicans have found themselves in." Republicans were so opposed to Hillary Clinton, he writes, that they would do "anything, and I mean *anything*, to keep her out of office. And that means continuing to endorse Donald Trump." Herman notes that prominent Republicans like Paul Ryan, Mitch McConnell, and John McCain were openly disgusted with Trump's many indiscretions, but they, like Macduff, refused to repudiate him because he was the alternative to Clinton. "At what cost?" Herman wonders:

> If you are willing to put a sex-crazed greedhead on the throne, Shakespeare seems to ask, then maybe there isn't all that much difference between you and the criminal you want to replace. . . . By continuing to support Trump's candidacy even though they know Trump is totally unfit for the job, the Republicans demonstrate that they are now a morally bankrupt party.

Like other Public Shakespeareans, Herman analyzes Trumpism more than Trump himself. The emphasis on culture rather than character is a prominent feature of Public Shakespeare.

As noted above, Stephen Greenblatt has mastered this strategy, whereby a Shakespeare scholar crosses into mainstream media to articulate, for a nonspecialized audience, insights about modern politics developed by way of specialized Shakespeare studies. It comes as no surprise that Greenblatt returned to the *New York Times* one month before the 2016 general election.[33] Innuendo is the operant device in "Shakespeare Explains the 2016 Election," which never mentions Trump by name but criticizes him and his rise to prominence by establishing an analogy to Shakespeare's *Richard III*. On the one hand, Trump as a person and Richard as a character are, in Greenblatt's reading, both "loathsome, perverse" "sociopaths," "inwardly tormented by insecurity and rage," "haunted by self-loathing," finding "refuge in a feeling of entitlement, blustering overconfidence, misogyny and a merciless penchant for bullying," with a "weird, obsessive determination to reach a goal that look[s] impossibly far off, a position for which he ha[s] no reasonable expectation, no proper qualification and absolutely no aptitude," and offering "no glimpse of anything redeemable in him and no reason to believe that he could govern the country effectively." On the other hand, Trump's rise is analogous to Richard's: midway through his essay, Greenblatt shifts from character criticism to cultural criticism, a key move that we have seen Public Shakespeareans perform several times. He lists five ways Richard's England is "a nation of enablers." Some do not recognize the fragility of the political order; some do not believe Richard is as bad as he seems to be; some feel helpless in the face of bullying; some exploit Richard's rise for their own gain; and some take a perverse pleasure in Richard's giddy destruction of the nation. Dwelling on Richard's election in Act III—and the oddity of an election in a time of hereditary monarchy—Greenblatt emphasizes "the element of consent in Richard's rise." This reading is a twist on the "paradox of democracy" from Nuttall's reading of *Coriolanus*. In *Richard III,* the people do not actively choose to give up their freedom as much as they passively allow it to happen: "Not speaking out—simply not voting—is enough to bring the monster to power." Clearly, Greenblatt felt compelled to "speak out," using his platform as a Public Shakespearean to make sense of a modern political situation, but he turned in the final sentence from analytical interpretation to sounding the alarm: "Do not think it cannot happen, and do not stay silent or waste your vote."

The day Greenblatt's op-ed came out, the Humanities Institute at the University of California, Santa Cruz (UCSC), hosted a public conversation titled "Anger in Politics: From the Bard to the Donald."[34] Part of a series called "Questions That Matter," which brings community members together with UCSC faculty and students, the event featured Shakespeare scholar Sean Keilen in conversation with a sociologist and a political scientist. The program originated in the similarity Keilen's students saw between the anger in *Coriolanus* and that in the 2016 election. This connection sparked a wide-ranging conversation on the causes, effects, and uses of anger in politics. But Keilen also positioned the event as a response to the crisis in the humanities: "It's a clear demonstration of the importance of the arts and humanities and of open-ended conversation for our life in a free society."[35]

Greenblatt's warning, "Do not think it cannot happen," flew in the face of the widespread belief that Clinton would easily beat Trump, but it turned out to be more accurate than the polls. His prescience is unsurprising, given his thoughts on the fragility of liberal democracy, which he discussed the next month on the *Shakespeare and Contemporary Theory* podcast with Shakespeare scholar Neema Parvini (recorded before the election but released, hauntingly, after it). Parvini suggests to Greenblatt that British cultural materialists are more explicitly interested in changing the world for the better through the resources of the academy, while American new historicists are less politically activist and more academically detached. In an unsettled yet intellectually searching response, Greenblatt recounts some of his own political activism and draws attention to the virtue of liberal democracy:

> Part of the experience of Berkeley in the 1970s was to think both about the limits of civil society but also what was precious about civil society. And you felt particularly what was precious about it when the helicopters started going overhead and tear gas was being dropped on protesters. Far from feeling liberated by those moments—"Now we're seeing the real face of the fascists," blah, blah, which some of my friends were saying—I felt something like the opposite: how important it was to hold onto the basic collective understandings, however fragile and however limited and deceptive they were, of what we could allow and not allow in society. . . . There's a line, I think, between that moment of the tear gas from the helicopters and what Donald Trump is about now. It turns out that the structures of the social order and civil society are more fragile than you think they are, and they actually need some protection.[36]

One week earlier, Parvini's guest was Christopher Marlow, author of *Shakespeare and Cultural Materialist Theory.* When Parvini asked about the future of Shakespeare studies, Marlow also invoked Trump and similarly emphasized the fragility of liberal democracy:

> This year, 2016, has revealed that we're a lot less further on than we thought we were in terms of politics. I mean, if you look at what's going on in America with Donald Trump, if you look at Brexit, I think we've got to be a little bit less embarrassed about being political again. I think there was that sense in the academy that, gosh, you know, we've done this; you know, students are being bored by us being political; they don't care; all of those battles have been won. And I think, very sadly, depressingly, we've seen that those battles actually haven't been won. So, I think it would be great if we could be a bit more political again.[37]

VII. Public Shakespeareans and
Modern Dress Performances

It is a testament to Shakespeare's generic flexibility—his mixture of comedy and tragedy—that his works were appropriated in the 2016 presidential election in both comic ways (the light-hearted mockery of citational opportunism) and tragic ones (the sober analysis of Public Shakespeareans). If citational opportunism involves cultural critics using Shakespeare, Public Shakespeare is scholars doing cultural criticism. Allusions to Shakespeare in citational opportunism are decorative, but allusions in Public Shakespeare are substantive. Where citational opportunism tends to be about a line or couplet, or a character, Public Shakespeare attends to the scene or situation. Citational opportunism employs a quotation or allusion with little or no analysis, but Public Shakespeare presents sometimes extensive analysis of the text. Thus, the symbol of citational opportunism is the equals sign: it suggests one-to-one correspondences between Shakespearean lines or characters and modern politicians. Here Shakespeare's value is rhetorical: the allusion makes the writer's point fun and memorable, and the purpose is usually to mock, to satirize, to suggest absurdity, and to elicit self-satisfied laughter. In contrast, the symbol of Public Shakespeare is the lens: it identifies similar situations (and is at pains to qualify the analogy) in order to suggest similar interpretations. It exploits Shakespeare's analytical value: knowledge derived from Shakespeare studies has valuable applications in nonliterary contexts, and the purpose is to provide clarity, to make sense of the modern situation, and to critique stupidity, hypocrisy, and, usually, conservative politics, ideology, and rhetoric. In the end, the citational opportunism that attempts to establish equals signs between Shakespearean characters and modern people will always be suspect, but the Public Shakespeareans who do a close reading of a Shakespearean text in an effort to do a close reading of some aspect of modern culture have the potential to be a productive force.

In a sense, Public Shakespeareans' argumentative essays are doing what modern-dress productions of the plays do: reframing Shakespeare's texts in overtly modern terms to suggest similar interpretations of similar situations. While playing Richard II for the Royal Shakespeare Company, the actor David Tennant saw a connection between Trump and Shakespeare's highly entitled yet woefully underprepared king.[38] The RSC's artistic director, Gregory Doran (channeling Paul Hamilton), considered giving his Falstaff a comb-over, although the actor playing Falstaff, Anthony Sher, rejected the analogy.[39] In her production of *The Taming of the Shrew* for Shakespeare in the Park in New York City, Phyllida Lloyd prefaced the performance with a beauty pageant reminiscent of the Miss Universe contests run by Trump; it was emceed by a distinctly Trumpian offstage voice.[40] At a fundraising gala in support of the Public Theater, which puts on Shakespeare in the Park, actress Meryl Streep (who played Katherine in a celebrated 1978 production of *The Taming of the Shrew*) dressed up as Trump and, in his style of speech, sang "Brush Up Your Shakespeare" from *Kiss Me, Kate,* a musical based on *Taming.*[41] In her production of the first tetralogy for the Chicago Shakespeare Theater, Barbara Gaines costumed Jack Cade, the populist rebel who thinks he can become king by disrupting law and order, as Trump.[42] And one week before the general election, Michael Sexton (recalling Charles McNulty) filled his *Coriolanus* at New York's Barrow Street Theater with election-year imagery.[43]

Remarkably, all these politically inflected performances lagged behind the Public Shakespeareans. Modern-dress productions used to be the first point of contact for uncovering the ongoing resonances of Shakespeare's plays in modern society. Now, Public Shakespeare is reaching those audiences faster and, more importantly, reaching different audiences. The modern resonances of Shakespeare's plays are no longer restricted to theatergoers and those who can afford the price of a ticket. Shakespearean appropriation is being democratized.

VIII. The Villainy and Tragedy of Donald Trump

Why do Shakespeareans not only detest Trump and Trumpism but feel compelled and qualified to speak out in public forums? It is tempting to chalk the impulse up to the nature of colleges, especially English departments, as "liberal bubbles." But the 2016 U.S. election did not flood the public sphere with political commentary by Chaucerians, Miltonists, and Austenians. Shakespeare was uniquely resonant with this election, and I would like to propose two related theses: (1) Shakespeare's drama trains us to recognize immorality, and (2) Shakespeare scholars know how and why tragedies happen.

To get to the first thesis, we can ask what the characters marshaled to analyze Trump and Trumpism—Cloten, Iago, Falstaff, Macduff, Richard III, and the mobs in *Richard III, Julius Caesar,* and *Coriolanus*—have in common. It isn't stupidity: Iago, Falstaff, and the mob in *Richard III* are not stupid. It isn't buffoonery: Cloten and Macduff are not clowns. It isn't hypocrisy: the mobs in *Julius Caesar* and *Coriolanus* aren't hypocritical. The commonality is just that they act badly. Shakespeare's drama asks of us, fosters in us, an ability to recognize unethical actions, whether that immorality manifests as villainy on an individual level or depravity on a cultural level.

Studying Shakespeare makes you a better analyst of human behavior—that is my claim. Shakespeare studies enhance moral intelligence. I say this not as a celebration or defense—I hate that I sound like a Victorian moralist. But I think it is a statement that is true and supported by evidence. Most serious Shakespeareans spurn Bardolatry (Shaw's term for "the indiscriminate eulogies with which we are familiar"),[44] but I could get behind Bard-ology-olatry: a full-throated celebration of Shakespeare studies, including strands skeptical of Shakespeare worship, as a valuable training ground for skills of deep analysis.

I am not saying that Shakespeare makes you a better person, or referring to scientific studies suggesting that literature makes us more empathetic (as Scott Newstok emphasized in his June 2016 editorial for the *Chronicle Review*, "How to Think Like Shakespeare").[45] I am suggesting something less grandiose about an analytical capacity required to understand and enjoy Shakespeare's works and their afterlives, something not sought, sometimes explicitly avoided, but a byproduct of Shakespeare studies. Even more than ethical philosophy—which gives rules for living the good life—studying Shakespeare builds a capacity to identify immorality when we see it, especially in politics. Shakespeare's plays show that the way you conduct yourself personally signifies your political views and governmental desires, strategies, and talents. We can discern the political from the personal.

Shakespeareans are not better people who behave more ethically (just ask anyone who has attended the annual convention of the Shakespeare Association of America). But studying Shakespeare forces one to develop skills of moral reasoning. For all the history and theory Shakespeareans bring to our studies, moral judgments of his characters and cultures remain central to the Shakespearean experience. Determining who is in the wrong is one of the most basic acts of Shakespearean interpretation. Competing claims must be discerned. Sometimes those who seem good are, upon closer inspection, not. Shakespeare is both a moral playground and a critical training academy. Where, say, religion provides ethical clarity and strength, Shakespeare studies provide ana-lytical clarity and strength. Better interpretation leads to more under-standing, more understanding to better judgment: the ethics of intelli-gence. Because they have spent their lives studying what Shakespeare's characters do and why, Shakespeare scholars are well prepared to inter-pret human behavior, especially when it jumps from the routines of daily life into the realm of social harm. That is one explanation for the prominent presence of Shakespeareans in the 2016 election: they are professionally trained to recognize unethical actions, and electoral pol-itics were more unethical than ever.

That ethical training relates to my second thesis about the emer-gence of Public Shakespeare during the 2016 election: Shakespeare scholars are professionally trained to understand tragedy, and they saw the conditions of tragedy in the election. In Shakespearean tragedy, the only concern more prominent than the acquisition of power by unscru-pulous means is tracing the source of pain and suffering. Often they are one and the same. The highest order of interpreting the tragedies is understanding *why this happened*. Shakespeare's plays are all about the relationships between external forces working upon an individual and his or her mental processing and decision-making, leading to actions and their consequences. Shakespeare trains his audiences to ask and answer a simple question: *What is going on here?* The facts of the mat-ter are self-evident, but interpreting the plays is all about deciphering the forces—social, mental, and emotional—that bring events into exis-tence: hidden causes and manifold levels of causality. That is what life is about too, and, if you are good at Shakespeare, you will be better at life. Studying Shakespeare teaches you what villainy and tragedy are. You don't really get that knowledge from political science, because vil-lainy and tragedy have not been a part of recent politics—until Trump came along. The theatricality of Trump's politics activated the issue of villainy; the severity of his policies activated tragedy. During the 2016 election, Shakespeare scholars saw an economically anxious and angry populace variously blind to, dismissive of, and complicit in the manipu-lations of an unstable demagogue. The conditions were ripe for catas-trophe, and Shakespeareans could sense it: "Do not think it cannot happen."

3

Cultural Affirmative Action
at Penn

Protesting Trump
by Protesting Shakespeare

ON DECEMBER 1, 2016, the English department at the University of Pennsylvania held a town hall to discuss the election of Donald Trump. After the meeting, graduate students tore down a large portrait of William Shakespeare that had adorned the Heyer Staircase leading to the department for more than thirty years. In its place, they constructed a makeshift portrait on twenty sheets of copy paper of Audre Lorde, a black, lesbian, feminist, activist poet from New York.

Perhaps your initial reaction is bewilderment, since Shakespeare—artistic, humanistic, compassionate—can easily be seen as a friend of the Left. He opposed hypocrisy, hatred, and unfairness. He represented progressive identity politics, at least relative to his time and place. He showed the danger of abuse of power by government officials. From this angle, it makes no sense to oppose Trump's politics of anger, fear, and power by attacking Shakespeare. "I ponder how well those 'activists' know *Othello*," one commentator wrote when the student newspaper reported the story.[1] Shakespeare is a part of the resistance, not the enemy. It is difficult not to think of the scene in *Julius Caesar* where the riotous Roman mob kills Cinna the Poet thinking he is Cinna the Conspirator. Did students at Penn interpret white skin the way Shakespeare's Romans interpret names?

Or your first thought might be *It's. About. Time.* A shrine to Shakespeare advances the agenda of white supremacy, even if that is not the intent—not the overt white supremacy of Neo-Nazis and the Ku Klux Klan, but the assumptions, beliefs, and habits that perpetuate the connection between whiteness and cultural greatness. As illustrated by decades of work from scholars now gathered under the banner of #Shake-Race—the Twitter hashtag created by Kim F. Hall—Shakespeare's texts, their afterlives, and our scholarly field are a mixed bag of retrograde bigotry, progressive impulse, unconscious bias, and structural inequality.[2] I wonder how well the commentator quoted above really knows *Othello*.

To understand the affair at Penn more deeply, I asked three questions. (1) Why did students take down Shakespeare's portrait? (2) Why did people get so upset when they did? (3) What does the affair expose about us? Answers revealed Shakespeare to be a site of predictable disputes in twenty-first-century U.S. politics between a Right that values conservation of its vision of traditional Western culture and a Left that is pursuing its own vision of something better. But the affair also showed Shakespeare to be a site of conflicts within the Left. At Penn, younger, radical, revolutionary activists of the Left forced an older liberal establishment to act on deeply felt but poorly politicized values, ultimately realizing a long-sought vision of English literature that is forward-thinking in the way it is backward-looking. This chapter ends by theorizing this exchange into what I call *the Heyer dialectic:* the process in which Trump has activated the far Left, the far Left has activated the moderate Left, and these combined forces have created a political vision that is progressive in substance while conservative in style, constructing a platform of meaningful cultural progress that is palatable to Americans put off by radical activism. This dialectic creates a big-tent coalition that celebrates both conservation of what is best about the past and progress toward what is needed in the future.

I. Cultural Affirmative Action

The Penn incident tapped into a longstanding conflict within the Western tradition. One strand of that tradition involves the narcissistic affirmation of the self: the belief that *we* are better than *them* (however those pronouns are defined). This belief is seen variously in Christian evangelism, medieval patriarchy, European colonialism, American slavery, and German National Socialism. The second strand involves an altruistic affirmation of people who are different from the traditional wielders of power, as seen in Christian charity, modern liberalism, postmodernism, and the civil rights movements fighting discrimination based on race, class, religion, gender, disability, and sexual orientation. Both strands are present in Shakespeare's works. The heroic white, male Englishman is the ideal of humankind in his history plays, while outsiders are mocked and singled out for identity-based attacks. Shakespeare's works are filled with patriarchal fathers, rape breezily used as a plot point, anti-Semitic tropes like the greedy Jewish moneylender, virtue gendered male in plays like *Hamlet* and *King Lear*, beauty racialized in the *Sonnets*, and (by one count) a ratio of 147 female characters to 1,075 male.[3] But Shakespeare's portraits of historically marginalized identities—people with disabilities (Richard III), religious minorities (Shylock), racial minorities (Othello), oppressed women (Rosalind)—brim with curiosity about and sympathy for the experience of the other: Aaron's "black is better" speech (*Titus*, 4.2.84–102), Shylock's "Hath not a Jew eyes?" (*Merchant*, 3.1.44–60), Emilia's "Let husbands know" (*Othello*, 4.3.79–98), Edmund's "Gods, stand up for bastards" (*Lear*, 1.2.1–22), and bisexuality in the *Sonnets*.

Now, this is key: Shakespeare's altruistic exploration of the humanity of historically marginalized people was part and parcel of England's narcissistic affirmation of itself when, in the eighteenth and nineteenth centuries, he was selected as the nation's cultural figurehead. An incipient openness to others was one of the things England was celebrating about itself in canonizing Shakespeare. That canonization has its problems, discussed below, but enough has been said to suggest why Shakespeare surfaces when the big questions of the Western tradition are in dispute, especially on college campuses where the push to affirm marginalized cultures is especially strong.

The Shakespeare portrait was a lightning rod long before the 2016 episode. The five-by-seven-foot copy of the engraving from the first folio was mounted on the Heyer Staircase in Bennett Hall in the early 1980s (Figure 3.1).[4] That was before the culture wars of the 1980s and 1990s polarized the United States into conservatives (interested in the affirmation of the self) and progressives (interested in the affirmation of the other). On campuses, this conflict produced the "canon wars," where conservative literary critics looking to preserve a curriculum of classic works faced off against progressive scholars promoting a more multicultural curriculum including women and people of color. The conservative

FIGURE 3.1. Shakespeare portrait on the Heyer Staircase
in Fisher-Bennett Hall, University of Pennsylvania.
(Photograph by Mikaela Gilbert-Lurie for the *Daily Pennsylvanian*,
December 3, 2015.)

side looked back to the *Great Books of the Western World* series, published in 1952. In 1965 Shakespeare, Milton, Chaucer, Dryden, Pope, and T. S. Eliot were the most taught authors in English classes.[5] Then the political radicalism of the late 1960s swept over college campuses, bringing countercultural movements like black power and women's liberation. By the time the English majors of the sixties became the profs of the eighties, new courses emphasizing women and minority writers were sparking Stanford students to march on campus chanting, "Hey hey, ho ho, Western culture's got to go."[6] In 1988 Stanford's English faculty voted to diversify its curriculum. Conservative critics pushed back with a wave of books defending the Western canon, starting with Allan Bloom's *The Closing of the American Mind* (1987), fortified by Roger Kimball's *Tenured Radicals* (1990) and Dinesh D'Souza's *Illiberal Education* (1991), and culminating with Harold Bloom's *The Western Canon* (1994). "Today it's generally agreed that the multiculturalists won the canon wars," Rachel Donadio wrote in 2007, noting that the most popular authors in English classes in 1998 were Shakespeare, Chaucer, Austen, Milton, Woolf, and Morrison.[7]

The canon wars were a proxy for larger political battles, an exercise in what the conservative commentator Selwyn Duke calls (dismissively) "cultural affirmative action."[8] Whether educational, occupational, or cultural, affirmative action cuts to the core of philosophical debates about distributive justice. In the United States, we are taught to judge someone based not on identity, but on character, effort, talents, potential, and accomplishments. Merit—desert—is the central factor in our attitude toward the distribution of resources. But clearly identity (based on race, class, gender, religion, ability, and age) influences the social distribution of opportunities for individual development, resulting in structural inequality: discrimination written into the structure of society, rather than occurring on a merely individual level. Reparations, equality, and diversity require a structural solution. Thus, affirmative action attempts to correct for disadvantages brought on through a history of oppression and discrimination by doing what created the problem in the first place: emphasizing identity in the distribution of resources. Those harmed based on identity are helped based on identity. In the eyes of its critics, affirmative action means that more meritorious individuals are denied opportunity. In this view, institutionalized identity-based thinking perpetuates the identity-based thinking that got us into this mess.

Cultural affirmative action deliberately takes identity into account when determining whom to read, study, and celebrate as cultural figureheads. For instance, in 1994–1995, while the Shakespeare portrait was down for cleaning, Penn students pasted a collage of women writers in its place. A panoply of underappreciated, historically disenfranchised writers—defined most obviously by their identity as women—was mounted to challenge the cultural dominance of the male demigod Shakespeare.[9] The return of the refurbished Shakespeare represented the resiliency of the traditional cultural symbols of Western greatness, but the workers who rehung the portrait simply covered the impromptu collage of female writers. Underneath the conservative symbol, the progressive symbol remained; people in the know knew that it was there.

That countertradition re-emerged in 1998 when, as a prank, graduating English seniors stole the Shakespeare portrait, revealing the collage. Shakespeare reappeared at the end of the year, on Commencement Day, in the arms of the graduates, who deposited the portrait on the Heyer Staircase as their graduation procession passed Bennett Hall. It was a bit of fun; Shakespeare was remounted, and this time the women were removed. Read symbolically, the conservative tradition had responded with force, eviscerating the progressive revolution, though there were cracks in the plastic covers around the screws holding Shakespeare in place. Perhaps the conservative tradition was not as secure as it seemed.

II. Transforming Silence into Language and Action

At some point around 2012, the Penn English faculty voted to replace the Shakespeare portrait with something better representing the diversity of the authors studied in their courses.[10] Yet nothing happened. There was a vote, but no action was taken. Arguably, this reflected the state of progressive politics more generally during the Obama years: good intentions but not much action. In the absence of activist leadership, egalitarian and reformist impulses stalled.

The progressive complacency of the era was most evident in economics. After the financial crisis of 2007, the Troubled Asset Relief Program used taxpayers' money to bail out the banks with, in Massachusetts Senator Elizabeth Warren's words, "no strings attached, no accountability, no transparency."[11] Obama's attempts to regulate Wall Street via the Dodd-Frank Wall Street Reform and Consumer Protection Act were thwarted, and exorbitant executive compensation and income inequality continued unchecked. Public frustration led to collective action. On the Right, the Tea Party sought to gut government services to pay for tax cuts; on the Left, Occupy Wall Street advocated higher taxes on the ultra-wealthy and debt relief for the working and middle classes. In the 2016 Democratic presidential primary, the democratic socialist Bernie Sanders argued for an economic revolution in the United States, but Hillary Clinton won the primary, signaling a perpetuation of the center-left politics of the past twenty years—a milquetoast, complacent response to economic crisis in the eyes of the party's radical wing. The clash between the party elders, who voiced progressive sentiments but enacted them ineffectually, and the younger, more militant wing is the context in which to view the incident with Shakespeare's portrait. The controversy at Penn transposed this electoral impasse to the liberal arts curriculum. The adults at Penn who held power gestured toward a progressive agenda but, Hamlet-like, did nothing. The students felt betrayed by liberal complacency.

The spark that lit the fire was the election of Donald Trump, a politician drawn from the narcissistic strand of Western culture whose acces-

FIGURE 3.2. Audre Lorde portrait on the Heyer Staircase.
(Photograph by Julio Sosa for the *Daily Pennsylvanian*, December 23, 2015.)

sion dealt a crushing blow to the altruistic strand. Responding to this sense of disorientation, on December 1, 2016, the Penn English department held its town hall meeting. Presumably, the faculty's vote years earlier to replace the Shakespeare portrait was discussed. It was no doubt suggested that Trump was elected specifically because of the sort of progressive complacency symbolized by the department's lack of action. Students took matters into their own hands. They removed the Shakespeare portrait from the walls of Fisher-Bennett Hall, politely leaving it in the office of the department chair, Jed Esty, and replaced it with their own rendering of Audre Lorde (Figure 3.2).

Read symbolically, the portraits stand in sharp contrast: Shakespeare's large, sturdy, professionally printed and hung, meant to stand the test of time; Lorde's small, flimsy, fragmentary, twenty pieces of printer paper hung by students. One image represents the entrenchedness of the affirmation of the self in the Western tradition; one represents the nascence of the affirmation of the other. But why did emotions related to a twenty-first-century political event in the United States surface at Penn in the form of action related to a sixteenth-century English playwright?

The long tradition of seeing Shakespeare, a white male, as one of the central symbols of the narcissistic tradition in the West has its origin in the 1530s, when Henry VIII declared England an empire. The nation soon went looking for a literary figurehead, like other empires in history. Their laureates were usually epic poets—Homer, Virgil, Dante—who celebrated the self (Greece, Rome, the Holy Roman Empire). In that context, Shakespeare was an unlikely choice for England's national poet. A provincial playwright and (initially) an outsider in London's literary scene, he wrote in the more popular, less elitist medium of drama, rather than the epic verse of John Milton. Shakespeare's outside-looking-in orientation was reflected in the content of his plays, which often acknowledged and affirmed otherness. Thus, the British cultural project did not know quite what to do with Shakespeare. He was popular in his own day, but not astronomically so, receiving mixed reviews from his peers. His plays were revived forty years after his death but were often altered on the Restoration stage (including politically, to be more amenable to royalism). He became the most celebrated Renaissance dramatist only in the final decade of the seventeenth century. His fortunes continued to rise during the Enlightenment, aided by the creation of several editions of finely curated *Complete Works*. Starting midway through the eighteenth century, jubilees idolized him as the best writer England had produced. In the Romantic age, he was elevated to the very top of the English canon by critics who saw his attention to otherness as a literary symbol of the liberal politics they were promoting. *We are the best at acknowledging the other:* that sentiment, collapsing together the narcissistic (self-affirming) and altruistic (other-affirming) strands of the Western tradition, filled the air in London early in the nineteenth century. Armed with this self-assurance, the British Empire continued its imperial project in the Victorian age, with Shakespeare as a symbol for the greatness of Great Britain. As the empire lost its status during the middle decades of the twentieth century, the Shakespeare who symbolized it came to be viewed with suspicion as well. *You used him to promote the British Empire,* said many colonized peoples, *and we reject you, so we reject him.* Similarly, in the United States, the rise of countercultural civil rights movements in the third quarter of the twentieth century led to a rejection of the dominant symbols of traditional Western culture, including Shakespeare. Even if Shakespeare himself was highly critical of the traditional structures of Western power, it became possible to protest Eurocentric hegemony by protesting Shakespeare. In 2016 Donald Trump was the most recent symbol of the narcissistic tradition in the West, so, in a moment of complex but comprehensible symbolic action, anti-Trumpism surfaced as anti-Shakespeareanism.

But why Audre Lorde? Of all the possible authors to promote in an act of cultural affirmative action, Lorde was chosen, I think, because her life and work represent an activist—rather than accommodationist—attitude toward the affirmation of marginalized literature and culture. Self-described as a "black lesbian feminist mother warrior poet," Lorde was born in New York City in 1934 to Caribbean immigrants. She started publishing poetry in the 1960s, gaining an understanding of intersectional identity while navigating the contours of Greenwich Village:

> Being women together was not enough. We were different. Being gay-girls together was not enough. We were different. Being Black together was not enough. We were different. Being Black women together was not enough. We were different. Being Black dykes together was not enough. We were different.[12]

Lorde was a professor of English at John Jay College of Criminal Justice from 1970 to 1981. She wrote poetry "to make power out of hatred and destruction," her emphasis on identity sharpened with an activist edge, as in "The Black Unicorn" (1978), which she says is restless and unrelenting, but not free.[13] Scholarly attention on Lorde often focuses on the identity politics in her prose at the expense of her poetry. That legacy would have surprised her, judging from what she told a friend: "Audre Lorde informed me, as we were working one afternoon, that she doesn't write theory. 'I am a poet,' she said."[14] Most famously, Lorde fused her nuanced view of identity with fire-breathing language when dressing down a women's studies conference in an address titled "The Master's Tools Will Never Dismantle the Master's House" (1979):

> Those of us who stand outside the circle of this society's definition of acceptable women; those of us who have been forged in the crucibles of difference—those of us who are poor, who are lesbians, who are Black, who are older—know that survival is not an academic skill. It is learning how to take our differences and make them strengths. For the master's tools will never dismantle the master's house. They may allow us temporarily to beat him at his own game, but they will never enable us to bring

about genuine change. And this fact is only threatening to those women who still define the master's house as their only source of support.[15]

Lorde also addressed strategic outrage in the work of education in "The Uses of Anger: Women Responding to Racism" (1981): "Anger is loaded with information and energy. . . . Focused with precision it can become a powerful source of energy serving progress and change."[16] Clearly, students at Penn were compelled by her blend of poetic expression, identity politics, and political activism when they adopted her image as a counterpoint to the Shakespeare-Trump configuration.

The students placed to the right of Lorde's portrait a quotation from her essay "The Transformation of Silence into Language and Action" (1980): "We share a commitment to language and to the power of language, and to the reclaiming of that language which has been made to work against us."[17] Here language—explicitness, outspokenness—is the symbol of courage as an antidote to complacency. As much as the students presented Lorde as a countersymbol to Shakespeare, therefore, they were citing their sources for their disruptive action: she voiced the logic behind the need to act against silence. On the left side of Lorde's portrait, students placed another quotation as a rejoinder to Trump: "It is not our differences that divide us. It is our inability to recognize, accept, and celebrate those differences." As far as I can tell, Lorde never said these words. On the internet, they are often credited to her *Our Dead Behind Us: Poems* (1986), but they do not appear there. The quotation does, however, closely resemble a passage from "Age, Race, Class and Sex: Women Redefining Difference" (1980):

> Certainly there are very real differences between us of race, age, and sex. But it is not those differences between us that are separating us. It is rather our refusal to recognize those differences, and to examine the distortions which result from our misnaming them and their effects upon human behavior and expectation.[18]

A hostile reading would say that this misquotation reflects poorly on the Penn activists, leaving the impression that they were better versed in BrainyQuotes.com than Lorde's actual writings, which in turn reflects poorly on the way the Penn English department trains students in research methods and the responsible use of sources. A more charitable reading would, instead, focus on how the misquotation associates Penn protestors with youth culture—with the internet, with imprecision, with rapidity. While vices from the perspective of scholarship, these are the features of youthful urgency that the faculty had lost touch with. And the protestors proved, like good academics, open to revising their work; the misquotation was later taken down. As the tape on the patchwork portrait lost its grip and fell to the floor, the large-scale image was replaced by a small picture of Lorde on a single piece of paper, accompanied by the quotation about reclaiming language.

Thus, in Fisher-Bennett Hall, Trump's election sparked not identity politics but, rather, a revival of a dormant activism as young progressives agitated where complacent adults had not. After the election, progressive U.S. politics saw a changing of the guard and the most powerful surge of activism on the Left in decades. People who had never been activists hit the streets, including white, middle-class, suburban mothers and grandmothers. A diverse set of Americans found common ground in opposition to Trump. What were once basic norms and morals of American society were now political causes. Donations to nonprofit groups soared. Protesters gathered night after night outside Trump Towers and the Trump International Hotel. The week before Trump took office, protesters occupied the area outside the headquarters of Goldman Sachs. On the day after the inauguration, the Women's March flooded the streets of Washington; one-third of the participants had never protested before.[19]

Crucially, protesters also gathered outside the home of Senate minority leader Chuck Schumer to steel him to resist the new administration on all fronts. These protests were not organized by the Democratic Party; they arose from grassroots movements designed to galvanize Democrats as much as to oppose Republicans. Many of the protesters were reading *The Indivisible Guide,* a manual by former congressional staffers explaining how the Left could co-opt the political strategies that the Tea Party rode to success against Obama. "We don't view ourselves as an arm of the Democratic Party," said Ezra Levin, one of the authors. "If we were, it would be difficult to apply pressure to make Democrats stand up for progressive values."[20] Grassroots movements, such as Swing Left, Sister District, Run for Something, Action Together, and Our Revolution, sprang up and matured, often taking aim at Democratic moderates rather than the Right. Our Revolution, according to its president, Nina Turner, sought to support "Democrats who really stand up for what it means to be a Democrat."[21] Organizing agencies like Daily Action made sure that congressional offices were flooded with phone calls. Members of Congress found their town halls packed, often with constituents eager to create viral news clips by dressing down their elected officials. And it worked. As Harvard political scientist Theda Skocpol put it, "When you see Charles Schumer out there calling for 'resistance,' you realize something's happening. That's not his natural state."[22]

III. Controversy and Cultural Justice

On December 8, department chair Jed Esty emailed the Penn English faculty and students to inform them of the incident involving the Shakespeare portrait and its backstory and to state that Lorde's image would remain in place until a "collective solution" was reached. Reported on December 12 by the *Daily Pennsylvanian*, the story received national attention. Representatives of the university tried to defuse the controversy, repeating that Shakespeare's portrait was not being replaced but relocated, but the outrage machine was in full swing. By the end of the same day, undergraduate chair Zachary Lesser (also a Shakespeare scholar) had to tweet a request for civility: "Dear concerned readers of conservative websites calling in outrage about Shakespeare at Penn: please do not hurl abuse at our staff. Thx."[23]

Why were people so upset? Because the incident tapped into tensions between the competing policy differences of the two American ideologies: a Republican Party wanting a strict meritocracy in which each individual determines his or her own destiny through talent and hard work, and a Democratic Party insisting that meritocracy does not work unless there is a level playing field, exposing the limitations of individualism by pointing out that the deck is stacked.

In other words, the portrait incident imported the debate about affirmative action in the United States wholesale. Use of the term "affirmative action" dates back to at least 1834, but the policy of encouraging employers, colleges, and organizations to provide special opportunities for minority groups who have historically suffered discrimination emerged only in the middle of the twentieth century.[24] In 1941 President Franklin Roosevelt's Executive Order 8802 declared it "the duty of employers and of labor organizations . . . to provide for the full and equitable participation of all workers in defense industries, without discrimination because of race, creed, color, or national origin."[25] After *Brown v. Board of Education* (1954) said that "separate but equal" has no place in public education, President John F. Kennedy's Executive Order 10925 (1961) reaffirmed Roosevelt, using the term "affirmative action" for the first time in a major policy document. The Civil Rights Act of 1964 gave fuel to both the antidiscrimination cause and the charge of "reverse discrimination" that emerged later. The following year, President Lyndon B. Johnson used a powerful metaphor in support of affirmative action in his commencement address at Howard University (1965):

> You do not take a person who, for years, has been hobbled by chains and liberate him, bring him up to the starting line of a race and then say, "You are free to compete with all the others," and still justly believe that you have been completely fair. This is the next and the more profound stage of the battle for civil rights. We seek not just freedom but opportunity. We seek not just legal equity but human ability, not just equality as a right and a theory but equality as a fact and equality as a result.[26]

Johnson's Executive Order 11246 (1965) reaffirmed Kennedy's earlier call for "affirmative action," and President Richard Nixon's Revised Order No. 4 (1971) expanded affirmative action to include women.

The concept has always been divisive. As early as 1965, a *Wall Street Journal* article said that the "zeal" for affirmative action "sometimes obliterates good judgment."[27] The following year, Anthony Rachal addressed critics in a speech that invoked "true merit": "The intent is to make the merit system whole—a true merit system, one which recognizes that all groups . . . are competent and worthy and that their inclusion . . . is essential to the mandates of the merit system."[28] These competing viewpoints informed the first major challenge to affirmative action, a lawsuit by a white student who claimed to be a victim of discrimination based on his race. The Supreme Court ruling in *Regents of the University of California v. Bakke* (1978) deemed quotas in the pursuit of affirmative action unconstitutional but also acknowledged cultivating diversity to enhance the educational experience of the student body as a legitimate practice.

More than most hot-button issues of the culture wars, the affirmative action debate is complex because it challenges good-faith convictions on both sides of a fundamental question of justice and equality. The Right and Left both pledge allegiance to the ideal of fairness. The campus Left has held rallies, conducted marches, and occupied administration buildings in support of their vision of inclusiveness. Counterprotests from the Right include bake sales charging white males $1.00, white females 75 cents, and black people 25 cents for the same item, and scholarships designated only for white heterosexual males. Critics claim that these counterprotests embrace a naive vision of liberalism that uses the rhetoric of freedom, equality, and individualism but ignores the concrete reality of racism on the ground. The controversy about Shakespeare's portrait was ready-made.

When the portrait switch became a national news item, the predictable grenades were lobbed. The *Daily Pennsylvanian* quoted a Penn English major who described the episode as "a cool example of culture jamming."[29] Generic opposition to white male hegemony was an accessible position for young, energetic progressives, recently exposed to countercultural theories and traditions, whose politics were somewhat inchoate. Such students were derided as "dumb ass snowflakes" by the far-right traditionalists, whose aggressive mentality was variously redneck, military, and masculine. These traditionalists wanted meritocracy and saw calls for social and racial equality as whiny claims of victimization. Any modification of strict meritocracy, based on identity or anything else, was a form of discrimination: "You're bigots—plain as day—who want to purge white history/culture," one told Penn students. Another wrote, "It's time to burn these schools down and start from scratch." But this aggressive reaction elicited countercharges of snowflakiness: "Why is whiteness so fragile?" The far Right's reactionary identity politics exhibited precisely the oversensitivity they complained of in the Left. From a different angle, one leftist commentator asserted that "unless you are black you can't comment on this matter," claiming that a history of being oppressed conveys an exclusive license to interpret.

A more interesting debate about the Shakespeare portrait arose from less extreme positions, based in principles and values but open to reason and willing to have sincere discussions. Some argued that Shakespeare is more important than Lorde in the history of the English language. Cultural meritocracy means that honor and prestige should be assigned to those who earn them through talent, effort, and accomplishment. This position rejected the logic of affirmative action in the literary canon: the way we have been teaching English is the right way. Such traditionalists do not know or are not convinced that canons are cultural constructs that need to be deconstructed. "Never heard of her," one wrote of Audre Lorde. "The fact that you don't know her is exactly the point," was one progressive's response. Without deliberate efforts to increase the diversity of our commemorative cultural symbols, Western white male celebrity culture is a self-perpetuating system in which we study the writers we have always celebrated, and celebrate those we have always studied. Others added that Shakespeare has enough portraits on enough walls. White male hegemony need not be toppled today, but we should be more inclusive with our symbols of cultural greatness. The response from the Right was: "I know when I want to be inclusive, I eliminate things. Because that's what 'include' means: to get rid of stuff." The incident at Penn was indeed an act of both negation and affirmation: negation of the white-skinned tradition in the removal of Shakespeare, and affirmation of the black-skinned tradition in the placement of Lorde. Does diversity mean the erasure of white culture?

No, of course not, yet historically identity politics often feels like a zero-sum game, and one that the Left has been losing. One of the most interesting responses at Penn came from liberals with a focus on economic equality, who worried that identity politics would inevitably result in losses for the Left because such campaigns alienate conservatives and independents. One commentator was "very sad to see aspects of 'regressive liberalism' taking root": that is, an emphasis on social equality rather than economic regulation. In the words of another: "This is exactly why the short-fingered oompa loompa won. Liberals never seem to get it—political correctness isn't the answer." Even some liberals associate progressive identity politics with a victim complex and entitlement baggage that comes across as weak and whiny to independents and conservatives who value meritocracy. Is there a form of identity politics that affirms the other without threatening the self?

IV. Mutual Recognition

African American writers like James Baldwin and Maya Angelou provide models for mutual recognition, affirmation, and celebration in their readings of Shakespeare. In "Why I Stopped Hating Shakespeare" (1964) Baldwin says that he first saw Shakespeare through the prism of identity: "In my most anti-English days I condemned him as a chauvinist ('this England' indeed!) . . . as one of the authors and architects of my oppression."[30] *Julius Caesar* brought about an epiphany. Cassius's resistance to tyranny—a precursor to the resistance in our time—lessens his nobility: "This single-mindedness, which we think of (why?) as ennobling, also operates, and much more surely, to distort and diminish a man—to distort and diminish us all, even, or perhaps especially, those whose needs and whose energy made the overthrow of the State inevitable, necessary, and just." Hostile resistance has its own liabilities.

At the same time, the murder of Cinna the poet reveals, to Baldwin, the tyranny of a mob mentality. The mob in *Julius Caesar* is not a grassroots populist movement, he recognizes; it is an arm of the tyrannical state. If we follow this analogy to Penn, the mob is not made up of student protesters but of Trump voters—the students are Cinna being shredded. Here an act of close reading sparks a vision of Shakespeare both confirming Baldwin's progressive politics (his opposition to oppression) and challenging them (via his newfound opposition to a form of resistance that cedes the moral high ground through its principled yet short-sighted hostility). Shakespeare could sustain Baldwin's politics if read charitably rather than with a preconceived animus. The English language symbolized by Shakespeare, Baldwin writes, "might be made to bear the burden of my experience if I could find the stamina to challenge it, and me, to such a test." Shakespeare becomes valuable to Baldwin as a platform for raising his voice in and against a tradition Shakespeare himself stood in and against: "My relationship, then, to the language of Shakespeare revealed itself as nothing less than my relationship to myself and my past."

As a black child in Stamps, Arkansas, Maya Angelou had a similar experience with Shakespeare.[31] At twelve she wanted to recite Portia's speech on mercy from *The Merchant of Venice* to her church: "The quality of mercy is not strained. . . . It blesseth him that gives and him that takes" (4.1.182–185). The young Maya memorized the speech and choreographed her recitation. It spoke to her experience as a disabled child—a traumatic experience left her mute from age seven to twelve— shown mercy by a woman who gave her books and sparked her love of literature, while most of the people in Stamps snickered behind her back. "Mama asked," writes Angelou, "Now sister, who is this very Shakespeare?"

I had to tell her that Shakespeare was white. And Mama felt the less we said about whites, the better, and if we didn't mention them at all, maybe they'd just get up and leave. I couldn't lie to her, so I told her, "Mama, it's a piece written by William Shakespeare who is white, but he's dead. And has been dead for centuries." Now, I thought then she would forgive him that little indiosyncracy. Mama said, "Sister, you will render a piece of Mister Langston Hughes, Mister County Cullen, Mister James Weldon Johnson, or Mister Paul Lawrence Dunbar. Yes ma'am, little mistress, you will."

Maya did. But as she grew up, she found herself coming back to Shakespeare. Sonnet 29 especially spoke to her: "I all alone beweep my outcast state." Shakespeare strengthened her, Angelou writes; he "puts some starch in my backbone." His works were useful for the life she wanted to live: "That is the role of art in life." Shakespeare is "for me," she says of Sonnet 29, "because I use it." "Of course he wrote it for me; that is a condition of the black woman. Of course, he was a black woman. I understand that. Nobody else understands it, but I know that William Shakespeare was a black woman."

These readings involve, on the one hand, a jubilant, even aggressive, celebration and affirmation of the best we in the West have accomplished and, on the other hand, an identification of our accomplishment as a deep and abiding commitment to otherness. That is what makes us great: our attention to the marginalized, vulnerable, and powerless. That altruism is too seldom celebrated as the virtue it is. In theory, America is great precisely because it is committed to the historically disenfranchised. In practice, that is not always the case. But Baldwin's and Angelou's Shakespeare affirms both the self and the other in a stance that can appeal to both conservatives and progressives.

Like Baldwin, Angelou, and most twenty-first-century Shakespeare scholars, I view bardolatry with suspicion, balancing sincere enjoyment of the texts with uneasiness about what Shakespeare has come to represent. "You are never ever only you," says Keith Hamilton Cobb in *American Moor*, an adaptation of *Othello*. This, to me, is also the thesis of twenty-first-century identity politics, capturing the tension between who we are as individuals and the cultural histories and identities we carry with us.[32] As I see it, the only image of Shakespeare worth celebrating is one including refractions of the author in modern culture and around the world, including voices, both artistic and scholarly, that speak back to him, sometimes hostilely: the Shakesphere that creates a contact zone for conversations spanning the centuries between the early-modern era and today. As the students at Penn knew, the image of the man from the first folio does not capture that Shakespeare.

V. The Heyer Dialectic

The controversy over Shakespeare's portrait at Penn might seem to symbolize a split in the Left—between a more moderate Left committed to its dated image of the Western tradition (represented here by Shakespeare) and a radical Left opposed to it (represented by Lorde). But in January 2017 the English department replaced the makeshift Lorde portrait with a professional collage portraying eighty-eight writers. From Thomas Mallory and Christine de Pisan to Zora Neale Hurston and Zadie Smith, and including Shakespeare and Lorde, they represent authors from the department's "Fifty Book List," works covered by the examination taken by second-year Ph.D. students (Figures 3.3 and 3.4).[33] This resolution offers a dialectic involving a thesis (Shakespeare), an antithesis (Lorde), and a synthesis (the collage).

As symbolized by this collage, a unified Left emerged from the Penn affair. Activists and centrists happily coexist, united by a strong, diversified, and celebratory cultural symbol, but only because the young and angry post-Trump progressives mobilized the complacent elders, who still hold the levers of power on the Left, to enact policies long supported in voice but not deed. The collage presents a vision of politics that is progressive in substance but conservative in tone, creating a political space welcoming to everyone from the far Left to the Center-Right. It appeals to both self-affirming and other-affirming traditions of Western culture by proudly celebrating what is great about the past, and identifying that greatness as the diversity and openness of our cultural heritage. In this collage, being white and male does not disqualify one from cultural celebration, but that identity emphatically does not constitute the

---

Facing page, top: Figure 3.3. Collage of writers on the Heyer Staircase. (Photograph by Julio Sosa for the *Daily Pennsylvanian*, December 23, 2015.)

Facing page, bottom: Figure 3.4. Detail of the collage of writers on the Heyer Staircase. (Photograph by Julio Sosa for the *Daily Pennsylvanian*, December 23, 2015.)

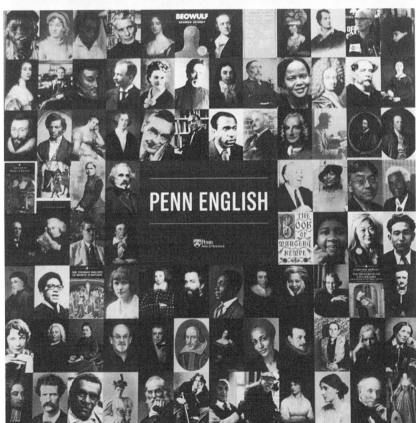

entirety of what we value. Western greatness as traditionally defined thrives side by side with Western greatness as progressively imagined. By working through this dialectic, the Penn English department arrived at a cultural stance that was broadly supported and, in a word, effective. This collage has satisfied the competing interests in the portrait controversy.

I want to conclude by thematizing the *Heyer dialectic,* the strong and nimble center-left movement created through negotiation between pre-2016 establishment complacency and post-2016 revolutionary activism. Trump's election activated a radical progressive politics in the United States that, in turn, activated those Democrats who had become, in the Obama years, tepid in their pursuit of cultural progress. In return, establishment Democrats have moderated the more aggressive and alienating aspects of the radical Left, resulting in a left-of-center political position that is progressive in policies yet moderate in politics, and thus appealing to centrists, independents, and even moderate conservatives. It is not a radical coalition, but it was made possible because the radical Left forced action on progressive values long held but weakly politicized. The coalition includes under its umbrella the moderate and radical Left, as well as political independents underwhelmed by both major parties. That is because the coalition is positive, not negative, promoting both tradition and change, leaving aside the alienating features of tradition and the alienating strategies of change.

I am not trying to police tone here. "Oppressed peoples are always being asked to stretch a little more," Lorde writes. "Black women are expected to use our anger only in the service of other people's salvation or learning. But that time is over."[34] In fact, an argument against tone policing could be inferred from the Heyer dialectic, but my goal is not to advocate a course of action. I am trying to discern what makes a political posture successful. When asking that question, both politicians and analysts need to consider the importance many Americans attach to tone.

The synthesis achieved through the Heyer dialectic is diverse and inclusive, but proud and celebratory, filled with joy, not anger. It stands *for* something, not *against* something. It embraces affirmative action, for example, but not by attacking American institutions and Western traditions. Those tactics turn away independent and right-of-center people who are otherwise allies in the fight for equality and prosperity. The position achieved by the Heyer dialectic seeks to celebrate human talent and achievement in all their diversity, without casting aspersions on the forces that have prevented us from doing so in the past. It invites good-faith political opponents to debate as part of a collage of voices, not by retreating to isolated parties. The Heyer dialectic encompasses the whole range of citizens who believe in both principles proclaimed by Shakespeare's canonicity, ideas sometimes presented as paradoxical but in fact entirely compatible: (1) the Western tradition is glorious and deserves to be celebrated, and (2) the most glorious part of the Western tradition is its openness to others. These two tenets, which in Shakespeare and America alike exist in shades and gradations open to qualification, not as absolutes, create a middle space between those who think the Western tradition is a purveyor of evil that must be rejected and those who think it can only be celebrated, never critiqued.

The Heyer dialectic's stance toward the Western tradition resembles political theorist Yascha Mounk's "inclusive patriotism."[35] As Mounk shows, an exclusionary nationalism is resurgent around the world, not only in the United States. Defining nation through ancestry, this form of nationalism is aggressive, repressive, suspicious, jealous, resentful, xenophobic, and culturally isolationist, against cosmopolitanism, against integration, against liberalism, and against regional blocs like the North American Free Trade Association and the European Union. It prompts discrimination and becomes a tool for authoritarian leaders. In Mounk's telling, the Left often responds by rejecting patriotism, meaning that it has "vacated the space of nationalism altogether—and allowed the right to occupy it on its own terms" (208). Mounk's answer is to embrace an "inclusive patriotism" that reclaims the meaning of the term. It is multiethnic; defines nation in terms of geography, not ancestry; emphasizes the ties that bind beyond race and religion; thus appreciates racial and religious diversity; values liberty; seeks community among those with shared ideals; is open to immigration but attentive to, not dismissive of, concerns about it; and embraces American values while redefining which ones matter most. As Mounk concludes, "The best chance for bending the arc of history toward justice is to make shrewd use of the symbolism of the American republic, not to reject patriotism altogether" (207). Our desire—our obligation—to critique the reality of America is not incompatible with our opportunity to define the America we want to live in. Lord(e) knows anger can be useful. Consider the inclusive patriotism of Nikole Hannah-Jones's description of *The 1619 Project*, an initiative from the *New York Times* observing the four hundredth anniversary of the start of slavery in America: "It is black people who have fought more than any other group to make the ideals laid out in the Constitution a reality."[36]

Since the portrait incident at Penn, the Heyer dialectic has repeatedly surfaced in both campus controversies and America at large. At Reed College, the liberal arts school in Portland, Oregon, with one of the most progressive student bodies in the United States, students protested that the syllabus for Humanities 110, *Introduction to Humanities: Ancient Greece and the Mediterranean,* was too white and Eurocentric, elevating Europe over other areas, erasing the history of people of color. Protesters' tactics included more than sixty silent sit-ins surrounding lecturers with signs reading "We cannot be erased" and "Fuck Hum 110," among other slogans, alienating many, on campus and off.[37] Reed students were condemned as the political-correctness police in national media. In April 2018, however, the college announced changes to the Hum 110 syllabus. A new four-module system features ancient Near Eastern civilizations, Athens, Mexico City, and Harlem. Again, the result is a collage, and we can see the Heyer dialectic at work. The Hum 110 faculty are the liberal adults holding progressive beliefs but lax in enacting them; the Reed students are the young and energetic progressives whose disruptive tactics were obnoxious but who spurred the establishment into making policy changes; and the new Hum 110 syllabus is the synthesis: progressive in substance yet traditional in temperament. The new syllabus stands for something, not against something. Its content is palatable to the radical youth; its tone, to older traditionalists.

Consider also the politics that popped into the National Football League. In 2016 Colin Kaepernick and a handful of other players knelt during the national anthem to protest police violence against African Americans. Many Americans, seeing the protest as expressing disrespect for the flag, could not move beyond the symbolic means of the statement to engage with its substance: they might agree with Kaepernick's sentiment but could not get past his strategy. Contrast the take-a-knee protests with Lady Gaga's performance at the halftime of the 2017 Super Bowl, a flag-waving show of inclusive patriotism that segued from "God Bless America" to Gaga's catalogue of songs celebrating social diversity and nonbinary sexuality. Even ideologues on the Right, like Mike Huckabee and Marco Rubio, celebrated her performance. I am not saying that Kaepernick's protest was bad politics and Gaga's performance was good. Kaepernick paved the way for Gaga. Her more understated act was effective only because it came in the context of his more radical and disruptive one. Kaepernick and Gaga are on the same team, but he is a blocker and she is the ball-carrier. Gaga gets credit for the touchdown, but she could not have scored without Kaepernick doing the real work of leading the way and clearing a path. Far from arguing against political activism, the Heyer dialectic suggests that radicalism creates the conditions in which polite progressivism is appealing to Americans.

When the owner of the Red Hen Restaurant in Lexington, Virginia, refused service to White House press secretary Sarah Huckabee Sanders, many saw the act as uncivil, but it cleared a path for moderates, such as CNN reporter Jim Acosta, to articulate a more palatable critique of Sanders's complicity. Sasha Baron Cohen's television show *Who Is America?* duped far-right ideologues into making jackasses out of themselves. His deception may be deemed ethically repugnant, but it cleared a way for moderate Democrats to call for the resignation of politicians with retrograde beliefs. Morally, many judge the radical incivility and the moderate response differently; analytically, we need to see them as stages in a single process.

Above all, the Heyer dialectic informed the 2018 midterm elections. Riding a wave of postelection anger and protests, Democratic primary voters chose younger and more progressive candidates. Sometimes there was only the first phase of the Heyer dialectic, as in New York's deep-blue Fourteenth Congressional District, where the young activist Alexandria Ocasio-Cortez upset the progressive incumbent Joe Crowley. Sometimes there was the full process, as in red-state Kansas's Third Congressional District, where Sharice Davids—a lesbian Native American lawyer whose platform was, basically, "Midwestern values"—beat the incumbent Republican. A record-breaking number of women were elected. The Democratic caucus got younger and more diverse; Ocasio-Cortez and Davids posted squad photos on Instagram with fellow first-years like Ayanna Pressley, Rashida Tlaib, and Ilhan Omar. White men like Joe Biden, Sherrod Brown, and Beto O'Rourke still have a place in this progressive vision. They are not the enemy because of their identity, but they had to make room for other identities so that Congress can better reflect who we are as a culture. Not coincidentally, headshots of the new class of Democratic representatives recall Penn's collage of writers: 64 percent female, 37 percent people of color. Contrast that with the image of the new Republicans, all white, all but two male, evoking the image of Western culture conveyed by the Shakespeare portrait.

The new progressives were tough but not angry. They stood for something, not against something. And the problem was not that establishment progressives held unpopular beliefs. It was that they were complacent. As at Penn, the young rebels never wrested power from the party elders. That is not what the struggle was about. Instead, the midterms forced establishment progressives who still held the levers of power to act upon the values long espoused yet long deferred. Through a series of back-room deals, Nancy Pelosi secured support for her re-election as Speaker of the House in exchange for key committee appointments for the new representatives and attention to new policy priorities such as campaign finance reform, voting rights, climate change, gun control, and White House ethics. The Heyer dialectic suggests that the odds are good that this class of representatives can produce a plan for America—as progressive in policy as possible, as positive in tone as possible—appealing to citizens across our current political divisions.

4

Villainy and Complicity in Drama, Television, and Politics

Shakespeare's Richard III, House of Cards, *and the Trump Administration*

IN FALL 2016, I taught *Richard III* alongside the Netflix show *House of Cards,* which adapts Shakespeare's early-modern story of radical political villainy in medieval England to a twenty-first-century American setting. When assigning texts, I figured that the class would overlap with election season, and everyone would want to talk politics. Then the election happened, and no one wanted to talk politics: Donald Trump rode to the presidency on a campaign of lies and manipulations. Our class now had to navigate three parallel realms, (1) *House of Cards* bridging (2) the early-modern Shakespearean tragedy and (3) the twenty-first-century American politics that Stephen Greenblatt and other Shakespeareans saw as analogous.[1]

The insight emerging most clearly from our discussions was that *Richard III* and *House of Cards* help us identify and dissect the problem of political complicity in Trump's campaign and presidency. Complicity, first defined in 1656 as "a consenting or partnership in evil," arises in three different ways—the same three different ways—in each of these three cases.[2] There is the *conscienceless complicity* of the henchmen and -women without scruples who help a diabolical villain execute his plots; *conscientious complicity,* where people want to resist villainy but are afraid to speak out; and *unconscious complicity,* in which audiences are hypnotized into support for a villain whose comic vitality eclipses his obvious immorality. After stepping away from Trump to establish these categories in readings of *Richard III* and *House of Cards*, this chapter returns to him at the end, applying political theories developed from literary studies to life today. At present, however, it is unclear whether the tragic fate of the villain who cultivates complicity in *Richard III* and *House of Cards* also awaits the protagonist of our other story.

I. From Vice to Villain

Shakespearean complicity originates in the Tudor Vice. A character in sixteenth-century moral comedies, an allegorical personification of an abstract sin like Iniquity, Lust, Greed, or Riot, the Vice fights against various personified virtues (Good Deeds, God's Law, Temperance) for the soul of the Everyman character. Henchman of the devil, the Vice is complicit in Satan's corruption of humankind, an agent of evil, exhibiting *conscienceless complicity*. But the more elusive *unconscious complicity* also appears in these plays. Authors made audiences complicit in the temptation of the Everyman by having the Vice speak directly to them. He detailed his schemes to seduce the Everyman before their interaction and celebrated his talents of seduction afterward, in both cases addressing the audience with a wicked verve that exploited the naughty excitement we feel when knowingly throwing caution to the wind and bucking the rules in pursuit of pure pleasure. Because the Vice made sin appealing, English audiences enjoyed and applauded him, rather than denouncing him. By leading the audience to enjoy the Vice more than the virtuous character, the early English moral comedies (1) represented the allure evil presents in everyday life, (2) made the audience complicit in the production of evil in the drama, and (3) recreated the choice of evil that inspired the moral comedies in the first place. At the same time, the plays showed the Vice conquered and punished by the representatives of Christian virtue, suggesting that audience members who succumbed to sin would be punished by the same forces.

Richard III cultivates a similar dynamic. The title character, explicitly associated with the Vice (3.1.82), draws audiences into the excitement of evil. His first speech thrusts us into his topsy-turvy world of villainy by lamenting his physical deformity and exclusion from the joys of love now that his country has emerged from civil war, his family the victors:

> *Why, I, in this weak piping time of peace,*
> *Have no delight to pass away the time,*
> *Unless to see my shadow in the sun*
> *And descant on mine own deformity.*
> *And therefore, since I cannot prove a lover,*
> *To entertain these fair well-spoken days,*
> *I am determined to prove a villain*
> *And hate the idle pleasures of these days. (1.1.24–31)*

This is not a soliloquy that offers a glimpse into the mind of the protagonist or shows him thinking out loud. It is an address to the audience. Richard knows that we are there. He is speaking not as a literary character usually speaks, remaining within the illusion of the story, but as a politician speaks: to an audience from a stage to secure their support. It is a political rally, as the scene is memorably played in Richard Loncraine's film, which sets the story in 1930s Europe to suggest an analogy between Richard and Hitler (Figure 4.1). This chapter is about the surprising transferability of tyranny under a monarchical form of government in medieval England to demagoguery in a modern democratic context, but we can approach that issue only by recognizing that *Richard III* is profoundly democratic in spirit. By that, I mean that we the people in the audience have all the power—the power of moral judgment. That power to throw our support behind the characters and ideas we like most is why Richard begins with an appeal to us. He covets and secures support from other characters and the audience alike through a series of virtuoso performances and underhanded stratagems. We do not realize that he is doing to us in the audience the very same thing he is doing to the characters on the stage.

Hearing of Richard's pain and suffering because of his deformity, we tend to sympathize with his plight while admiring his resolve in refusing to let forces beyond his control dictate his course in life. Even though he is born into a royal family, Richard is the original underdog in English literature (he is compared to a dog eight times in the play). We always root for the underdog, whose display of individual will, talent, and resistance toward the contingencies of life appeals to audience members who feel similarly defiant. Richard is a fighter, and we cheer for him as we cheer for any fighter pitting his courage, effort, and resolve against the pure power of a more dominant opponent, which in Richard's case is nature and culture. We find ourselves attracted to him,

FIGURE 4.1. Ian McKellen as Richard in *Richard III*, dir. Richard Loncraine
(United Artists, 1995).

even though he explicitly and unapologetically pledges himself to villainy and hatred. Our emotional relationship with Richard leads to an
affinity that even the most basic logical or ethical thought would instantly abhor.

But Richard does not simply get an A for effort; he has real talent. He wants to be king of England, which is next to impossible under
the country's system of hereditary monarchy, where the crown passes
from eldest son to eldest son. Richard's oldest brother, Edward, is the
king; were Edward to die, the crown would pass to Edward's oldest son,
also named Edward; were the younger Edward to then die, it would pass
to his younger brother, Richard, Duke of York; were both boys to die, it
would pass (since they have no children) to their uncle, George, Duke of
Clarence, Richard and the older Edward's middle brother. If and only if
all of these people were to die or become unable to take the crown would
the protagonist of our play, Richard, Duke of Gloucester, become
king. Those massive odds do not stop Richard from trying, and succeed-
ing, through a series of lies, manipulations, and crimes.

You would think that these evil acts would make us despise Richard,
but they do not, because he brings us in on them. He tells us exactly how
he is going to con his way to the crown: "Plots have I laid, inductions
dangerous . . . To set my brother Clarence and the King / In deadly hate
the one against the other" (1.1.32–35). Our willingness to go along with
Richard's conspiracy is only enhanced by its sheer ludicrousness—*Is the
King of England really going to believe a prophecy about someone with*

the letter G in his name plotting to kill his children?—and by Richard's excitement. He turns his disregard for everyday ethics from a liability into an asset by proclaiming it unapologetically, presenting himself as the embodiment of our unchecked desires. He actually does what we would all do in the name of stony-hearted self-interest were we not held back (thank goodness) by our consciences and our concerns about how our actions might harm others. Richard's scheme comes across not as sociopathy, as we might expect, but as bravery. He presents himself as a hero who must play the villain, with the audience as his constituency and benefactors. In the pleasure we take from watching him destroy a series of stupid, entitled, undeserving nobles—an entire system of government corruption—we reap the rewards of his villainy without getting our own hands dirty.

We align ourselves with Richard because of his energy and the thrill it creates in us, and because he speaks directly to us and takes us into his confidence. Here's how the con works: you tell someone who might be inclined to resist you exactly what your evil plan is. "I am subtle, false and treacherous," Richard boasts (1.1.37), later smiling that he uses "lies well steel'd with weighty arguments" (1.1.147). When the con man explains the con outright, it imparts the illusion of value and power to someone who might otherwise be an opponent but who, when brought in on the con, instead becomes an accomplice. We all want to be part of something. We want to be on the winning team. It provides a sense of achievement and validation. By turning politics into a game, Richard makes winning a greater good than virtue. And by drafting us onto his team, he ensures that our commitment to the team, the game, and the win exerts a greater pull on our sensibilities than everyday morality. When he says that he is going to kill his own brother—"Simple, plain Clarence, I do love thee so / That I will shortly send thy soul to heaven" (1.1.118–119)—it is like hearing a football coach pumping up his team before the game: *We're gonna rip their heads off!* No one is actually going to decapitate the people on the other team; everyone knows that the hyperbolic aggression is metaphorical. But we allow, even celebrate, that sort of hostile bravado because we have shifted from everyday life into the game, where winning is everything and the coach motivates us through violent imagery and metaphors. The virility cultivated here leads to sexually perverse images, as when the coach says, *We're gonna slaughter 'em on the field and then take their wives and daughters home with us!*—the rough equivalent of what Richard says about his second victim, Lady Anne Neville, whose husband and father-in-law he has killed in pursuit of the crown:

> *For then I'll marry Warwick's youngest daughter.*
> *What though I killed her husband and her father?*
> *The readiest way to make the wench amends*
> *Is to become her husband and her father. (1.1.152–155)*

Whenever I see *Richard III* in the theater, the audience has the same response: first they groan and purse their lips as if to say, *That's so disgusting,* then they turn to their friends and start smiling, partly because Richard's statement about becoming Anne's father-husband is extremely uncomfortable, partly because they cannot believe that someone is actually saying that, and partly because Richard says the unsayable with such gumption that it impresses us as much as it disgusts.

The successful wooing of Anne is the first clear demonstration of Richard's talents of persuasion. After persuading the widow of the man he just murdered to marry him, Richard again turns to us to celebrate: "Was ever woman in this humor wooed? / Was ever woman in this humor won?" (1.2.213–214). His excitement is infectious. He is as impressed with his success as we are. With excitement and talent comes confidence and, with confidence, an ability to ease the anxieties of others and emerge as a leader, rendering others into followers. That is the real con game here: not just that Richard takes us into his confidence, but that he displays so much confidence that we trust and follow him without paying much attention to what he is actually saying and doing. Wowed by his will, talent, and charisma, we follow him into his schemes, allowing his apparent command of the situation to impress us more than the obvious immorality of his actions.

Once Shakespeare has spent the first scenes of *Richard III* cultivating this unconscious complicity in the audience, the next few acts dramatize a different kind. First, Richard hires two Murderers to kill Clarence. When the Second Murderer expresses "some certain dregs of conscience" (1.4.108), the First reminds him that they get paid only if they kill Clarence. "Where is thy conscience now," the First asks. "In the Duke of Gloucester's purse," the Second responds (1.4.112–113). Legally speaking, Richard is complicit in the crimes carried out by his minions. Morally speaking, it is Richard's henchmen who are complicit in his tyranny. While the audience may be lulled into an unconscious complicity with Richard, the Murderers are fully aware of their situation. They just care more about money than morality. Similarly, co-conspirators Buckingham and Catesby, who covet status and power more than they worry about their consciences, exhibit a conscienceless complicity in the killing of Hastings, who stands in Richard's way. "What shall we do if we perceive / William Lord Hastings will not yield to our complots," Buckingham asks Richard (3.1.188–189). First comes Richard's usual bravado—"Chop off his head, man" (3.1.190)—but then quickly a bribe: "And look when I am king, claim thou of me / The earldom of Hereford" (3.1.191–192).

Beyond this conscienceless complicity, the plot against Hastings reveals another kind. When it becomes clear that Hastings will not join them, Richard trumps up a preposterous charge of treason. With all the English nobles gathered together to decide the future of the country, Richard presents them with a clear falsehood so outlandish that no one knows quite what to say:

> RICHARD *I pray you all, what do they deserve*
> *That do conspire my death with devilish plots*
> *Of damnèd witchcraft, and that have prevail'd*
> *Upon my body with their hellish charms? . . .*
> [HASTINGS] *I say, my lord, they have deservèd death.*
> RICHARD *Then be your eyes the witness of their evil:*
> *Look how I am bewitch'd. Behold, mine arm*
> *Is like a blasted sapling withered up. . . .*
> HASTINGS *If they have done this deed, my noble lord—*
> RICHARD *"If"? Thou protector of this damnèd strumpet,*
> *Tell'st thou me of "ifs"? Thou art a traitor:*
> *Off with his head! (3.4.64–71)*

Everyone in the room knows that Richard was born physically deformed, as Shakespeare's source, Thomas More's *History of King Richard the Third,* makes clear: "No man was there present but well knew that his arm was ever thus since birth."[3] So what is going on here? Obviously, Richard is lying when he says that his arm was deformed by witchcraft. It is equally obvious that no one believes him. But Richard does not expect anyone to believe his story. Instead, he is saying, effectively, that he has the power to determine reality. Believe what he says is true, rather than what is obviously true based on what you see with your own eyes. No one believes Richard, but no one other than Hastings opposes him, either because supporting his lies is their way of indicating political allegiance or because they are afraid of ending up beheaded like Hastings. Richard does not need people to believe his preposterous lies; he only needs people to support them.

This conscientious complicity—practiced by those who want to oppose Richard but are afraid to do so—is theorized in a subsequent scene. A random Scrivener enters with the order to indict Hastings, which is to be publicly displayed. He has noted a problem with the timeline. The indictment took at least twenty-two hours to produce: eleven to write it out, another eleven for the printer. But the scene leading to Hastings's indictment only happened five hours ago. Shakespeare borrowed this shady indictment from Thomas More, who writes, "Every child might well perceive that it was prepared before" (137). Shakespeare adds a coda conceptualizing conscientious complicity: "Why, who's so gross / That sees not this palpable device? / Yet who's so bold but says he sees it not?" (3.6.10–12). The Scrivener knows perfectly well that Richard is a liar and manipulator. Unlike Richard's henchmen, the Scrivener laments this fact. He does not want Richard to succeed. He despises Richard and wants to resist, but cannot. He is afraid and feels powerless. He is just a newsman. He does not want to editorialize. It is not his job to critique public figures. He could get fired. And, anyway, everyone already sees what is going on. Knowledge of the duplicitous politician's lies is not what is lacking. What is lacking is the public will to oppose the evil that everyone claims to disapprove of.

This conscientious complicity reappears in the next scene, with the election of Richard as king of England. It begins with Buckingham narrating his failure to generate public support for Richard, an oddly proto-democratic moment of representational government. Buckingham has tried to clear the way for Richard's claim to the throne by implying the illegitimacy of the rightful heir, Prince Edward, but "the citizens are mum" (3.7.3). No one bought Buckingham's lies:

> *And when my oratory drew toward end,*
> *I bid them that did love their country's good*
> *Cry, "God save Richard, England's royal king!"*
> RICHARD *And did they so?*
> BUCKINGHAM *No, so God help me, they spake not a word,*

But like dumb statues or breathing stones
Stared each on other and looked deadly pale. (3.7.16–21)

Buckingham's "No" is an important moment in *Richard III:* it cuts down to size a mounting Richard who has been brimming with energy. It is the first time Richard's talents of manipulation fall flat on their face. The people cannot believe what they are hearing. They see through Buckingham's political maneuvering, and they refuse to support it. A frustrated Buckingham reprehends them, but the Mayor of London asks to speak on Richard's behalf:

When he had done, some followers of mine own
At lower end of the hall hurled up their caps,
And some ten voices cried, "God save King Richard!"
And thus I took the vantage of those few:
"Thanks, gentle citizens and friends," quoth I.
"This general applause and cheerful shout
Argues your wisdom and your love to Richard." (3.7.29–35)

Buckingham and his followers are what we have come to call campaign surrogates. They applaud an argument to induce others to support it: when we hear others clapping, we often mindlessly clap ourselves. They are clearly conscienceless. But those citizens who stood firm in silence against Buckingham find themselves experiencing their own complicity as the scene unfolds.

The Mayor and the citizens head to Richard's house. Buckingham and Richard plot out the next step, in which Buckingham will court Richard, pressing him to take the crown, but Richard will "play the maid's part" (3.7.45) and demur like a chaste virgin. The scene is explicitly theatrical: Buckingham, the director, instructs Richard, the actor, on props (a prayer book) and blocking (standing between two clergymen). When the audience arrives, Richard pretends to be concerned that he has offended them; Buckingham pretends to be offended that Richard will not take the crown. The Mayor furthers Buckingham's plea. Whether he does so out of conscienceless complicity (as someone who is in on the plot) or unconscious complicity (as someone who has been deceived by the theatrics of the campaign) is left unclear. It is also unclear what the gathered crowd does when Buckingham proclaims, at the end of his plea, "Long live Richard, England's royal King!" (3.7.220). The citizens have no lines in this scene. Do they recognize that they are being manipulated but go along out of fear? In that case we are dealing with conscientious complicity. Or do they zealously chant along with Buckingham because they have been duped into supporting Richard—an instance of unconscious complicity?

Shakespeare left the question open, although More clearly thought it was conscientious complicity. Everyone knew what Richard and Buckingham were doing, but no one could or would stop them. They all remained silent:

> There was no man so dull that heard them but he perceived well enough that all the matter was already made between them. Howbeit, some excused that again, and said all must be done in good order now. And men must sometimes for the manner's sake not seem to know what they know. . . . In a stage play all the people know right well that he that plays the Sultan is perchance a shoemaker. Yet if one should know so little, to show out of season what acquaintance he has with him and call him by his own name while he stands in his majesty, one of his tormentors might hap to break his head, and rightly for marring of the play. So they said that these matters be Kings' games, as it were stage plays, and for the more part played upon scaffolds, in which poor men be but the lookers on. And they that wise be, will meddle no farther. For they that sometimes step up and play with them, when they cannot play their parts, they disorder the play and do themselves no good. (145)

Using the theater as a metaphor, More gives a stunning account of the form of conscientious complicity in which someone pretends not to believe what he or she really believes. Everyone knew that Richard and Buckingham had conspired to proclaim Richard as king of England. Their performance was not politics but theater. If so, the "willing suspension of disbelief" (to use Coleridge's well-known phrase) we exercise when we go to the theater also has a political manifestation. Just as no one thinks that the actor is the character—that Gary the shoemaker is the Sultan—and yet everyone in the audience ignores this obvious reality, politics can involve actors on stages transparently lying while onlookers both easily recognize and entirely ignore those lies to allow the performance to continue. Standing up at the theater and indignantly shouting *Gary is not really a Sultan!* would not only tell everyone something they already knew but would also ruin the performance and get one thrown out of the theater. Thus, the audience sits in silence. And in politics, as in theater, "men must sometimes for the manner's sake not seem to know what they know."

Here's how Shakespeare's *Richard III* works. Audiences love Richard at the opening of the play; they sympathize with him, take a visceral pleasure in his unrepentant wickedness, his comic vitality, and his talent for manipulation and deceit. We go along with Richard, even though he does horrible things, because of the confidence he exudes and the pleasure he provides—until, just after his coronation, he orders the execution of two small children. That marks the point in the play when he stops speaking to us in the audience. His naughty addresses and asides transform into nervous soliloquies spoken to himself, revealing the limits of his talent and his lack of control.

The difference between the murder of the two young princes and the murder of Clarence is not simply that they are innocents. It is that Richard does not confide in us. He does not address us directly, share his plan in advance, or revel in the delightful wickedness of the act. Earlier it was us and him against the world; now, because he does not address us directly, we are aligned with the others against him. The murder of the princes is heinous enough, and Richard's personality diminished enough, that we in the audience are shocked back to our senses. We are disgusted by our earlier intimacy with a man who is transparently evil according to the most obvious ethical standards. *How did I allow myself to get wrapped up in this bad man's ruse? Why would I derive pleasure from crime and deceit? Why did I so easily abandon my core ethical values?* Like the English moral comedies before it, Shakespeare's *Richard III* draws us into an unconscious complicity with an evil character, then draws back the curtain on him, and us, forcing us to confront the meekness of our proudly proclaimed moral compass. *Richard III* shows the depths of evil we are willing to explore, test out, turn a blind eye to, excuse, allow, justify, rationalize, enfranchise, and perform when a charismatic man short-circuits our most basic moral capacity.

Because of his villainies, Richard's reign comes crashing down. Buckingham turns against him when Richard does not make good on the promised earldom of Hereford. Other conspirators abandon Richard for the Earl of Richmond, who goes on to defeat Richard at the Battle of Bosworth and become King Henry VII. Richard tries to marry his niece to consolidate his claim to the English crown, but his attempt to become her uncle-husband has none of the absurdist verve of his earlier courtship of Lady Anne. His plotting is anxious and unhinged: "I must be married to my brother's daughter, / Or else my kingdom stands on brittle glass" (4.2.60–61). And the plan fails: he is outplayed by Queen Elizabeth, who promises her daughter to him but turns around and marries her to Richmond, enhancing his claim to the throne. Richard is not as confident, as entertaining, or as talented in the second half of the play as he was in the first, symbolized by his decreased interaction with the audience.

The Richard of Acts IV and V is a pathetic man, not in the sense of pitiable, but weak and embarrassing. His downfall and death are not sad—we are glad to see him wiped from the earth. Henry VII is a joyless person who offers none of the excitement of the early Richard: we do not love Henry. But by this point in the play we are prepared to value the boring stability he offers over the exhilarating chaos surrounding Richard. Henry offers the safety, security, and civility we need to recover from the unhinged theatrics of the unapologetically villainous Richard. Thus, we move from the childish pleasures of entertainment with Richard to the adult pleasures of good government with Henry.

II. From Stage to Screen

While it updates *Richard III* to twenty-first-century American politics, the Netflix *House of Cards* dates back several decades. In 1989 Michael Dobbs, a former chief of staff of the Conservative Party in Great Britain, wrote the novel *House of Cards,* whose main character, Francis Urquhart, is based on Shakespeare's Richard III and shares his habit of directly addressing the audience (in this case, the reader). Eventually a trilogy of Francis Urquhart books put Richard's early-modern political villainy in a modern parliamentary setting. The novels were adapted between 1990 and 1995 into an acclaimed BBC series. In March 2011 Netflix announced an American version, staring Kevin Spacey (Figure 4.2).[4] It was the first major original program produced by Netflix. To prepare for the role, Spacey played Richard III in a production at the Old Vic in London, where he was artistic director; it toured the world,

FIGURE 4.2. Kevin Spacey as Frank Underwood in *House of Cards*
(Netflix, 2013–2018).

as recorded in the documentary *Now: In the Wings on the World Stage*
(2014). The Netflix *House of Cards* started filming in June 2012, and
the entire first season was released on February 1, 2013, all at once, to
encourage binge watching.[5]

Like Shakespeare's play, *House of Cards* begins with the protagonist
addressing the audience directly. Car tires screech, a crash is heard, a
dog yelps: Kevin Spacey as Frank Underwood emerges onto a residen-
tial street in Washington, DC, explaining to his Secret Service agent that
it was a hit-and-run. Frank crouches down over the whimpering dog,
then glances up at the camera and, with a charming southern drawl,
explains his philosophy of life: "There are two kinds of pain. The sort
of pain that makes you strong, or useless pain. . . . Moments like this
require someone who will act, who will do the unpleasant thing"
(1.1). With that, he strangles the dog: "There, no more pain" (1.1). So
House of Cards begins by turning the table on the dogs that barked at
the halting Richard III. Where Richard is demonized by being compared
to a dog, Frank is villainized, now that dogs have become man's best
friend, by killing one. But it is a mercy killing, so Frank is heroicized as

well. Thus, *House of Cards* begins with Frank as an antihero who does bad things but for good reasons, whereas Richard is an antivillain who does evil things in entertaining ways. We never see Frank cackle and revel in his own demonic wickedness.

The next scene contains Frank's second audience address. In the manner of a bubbly host introducing guests at a party, he identifies the key characters in his story. President-Elect Garrett Walker: "Do I like him? No. Do I believe in him? That's beside the point." Vice President Jim Matthews: "They're about to put him out to pasture." Chief of Staff Linda Vasquez: "She's as tough as a two-dollar steak." Frank himself is a Democratic congressman and majority whip in the House of Representatives: "I keep things moving in a Congress choked by pettiness and lassitude. My job is to clear the pipes and keep the sludge moving" (1.1). The necessity of these introductions emphasizes that *House of Cards* is a fictional, not historical, story. Whereas *Richard III* is real history told as myth, *House of Cards* is an imagined story told with gritty realism. Richard is dedicated to villainy; Frank, to power: "Money is the McMansion in Sarasota that starts falling apart after ten years," he tells us. "Power is the old stone building that stands for centuries" (1.2). Richard is radically strange and unnatural; Frank is a typical American male climbing the social ladder.

Unlike Richard, Frank has no deformity to descant upon. Instead, we sympathize with him because he is passed over for a promised job as secretary of state. Frank associates that most American of pitiable events—losing a promotion—with the most common concern of classical tragedy: "Hubris, ambition," he says to his wife, Claire, explaining why he did not see the betrayal coming (1.1). Then, like Richard, Frank starts plotting and scheming. Very much unlike Richard, however, he shares his schemes with his wife: "I know what I have to do," he tells her. "We'll have a lot of nights like this, making plans" (1.1). The next day, his right-hand man, Doug Stamper, asks if Frank is thinking about the second-most-common concern of classical tragedy: "Retribution?" (1.1). Our only hint that Frank is planning a Richard-like extermination of everyone who stands between him and the pinnacle of power comes when Doug points to the man who got the job instead of Frank—"Kern first?" (1.1). Thus, the first few scenes of the very first American television show designed specifically for the digital age hark back to the two central concerns of classical Greek and Roman tragedy: ambition and revenge.

Although the setting and the specifics are radically altered, *House of Cards* is remarkably faithful to the structure and logic of *Richard III*, especially in the first two seasons. As with Richard, we admire Frank's resolve, confidence, and talent. We find him affable, charming, and charismatic. We appreciate his damn-the-system irreverence. His addresses to the audience are shorter and more frequent than Richard's, a sustained relationship constantly cultivated, sometimes with as little as a nod to the camera. Because *House of Cards* is a serialized television show, not a play meant to be enjoyed in one sitting, the mutual affection of protagonist and audience is continually affirmed—by the protagonist with the increased number of addresses to the audience, and by the audience each time we choose to watch the next episode, which Netflix cleverly makes happen automatically. The audience's unconscious complicity is deeper and more elemental here than it is with Richard. A serialized streaming television show meant to be binge-watched, on a platform that automates the viewer's choice to continue watching, has unconscious complicity built into its very form. *House of Cards* adds to *Richard III* the unconscious complicity of the viewer who keeps coming back to the warming glow of the screen.

As Frank's plots unfold, Doug becomes a textbook case of conscienceless complicity. Typical henchman stuff. A more gripping example is Claire. "We do things together," she scolds Frank, livid that he did not call her after losing the secretary of state post (1.1). Frank and Claire have crafted his political career together over years. After their fight, he spends all night scheming, telling Claire in the morning that he has hatched a plan. Her satisfaction comes across as both cold-blooded and warm-bodied. Frank turns to the camera: "I love that woman. I love her more than sharks love blood" (1.1). This oddly violent metaphor captures the ruthless pursuit of power at the core of the Underwood marriage.

The show's central source of tension is the clash between the Underwoods' maneuvers against their enemies and against each other. After Frank demands that Claire reject a quid pro quo gift to her nonprofit organization because he does not want to be beholden to the donor, she, clearly upset, reconnects with a former lover. We soon learn that the Underwoods have an open marriage. Frank starts his own affair with a young reporter at the *Washington Herald* named Zoe Barnes. They begin as professional allies, Frank leaking politically advantageous stories to Zoe, Zoe using access to Frank to advance her career, in another example of conscienceless complicity. But their relationship soon becomes sexual, clearly recalling the creepiness of Richard's father-husband relationship with Lady Anne. The perverseness of their partnership is a running theme. To establish trust, Zoe has Frank take "pictures, the kind I wouldn't want my father to see" (1.5). Frank goes down on her as she talks with her dad on the phone, saying "Happy Father's Day" as she orgasms (1.7). *Ewww.* When their relationship turns sour, Zoe shames Frank's weird daddy fantasies:

> ZOE You're almost twice my age.
> FRANK You said that didn't bother you.
> ZOE I lied. If you had a daughter, she'd be older than me. In twenty years, I'll still be younger than you are now. . . . Why do you need this? You don't seem to get any pleasure out of it? . . .
> FRANK A great man once said that everything in life is about sex, except sex. Sex is about power. (1.9)

"Sex is about power" is from Oscar Wilde, not Shakespeare, but it certainly applies to *Richard III*: marriage is a purely political tool that Richard uses, in both the wooing of Lady Anne and the wooing of Princess Elizabeth, to consolidate his power. On this point, the difference between *Richard III* and *House of Cards* is that in the modern text, women also use sex to accrue power, as represented by Zoe's work/play relationship with Frank and Claire's attitude toward it.

Frank's thesis about sex is shown to underwrite the Underwood marriage when he comes home on the morning after his first night with Zoe. Claire is not angry, merely concerned about how much of an asset Zoe can be. Frank and Claire clearly love each other, but their marriage is a political rather than emotional partnership. The romance comes from the power, rather than the intimacy, they achieve together. Claire says this explicitly when a longtime friend confesses his love for her:

> You know what Francis said to me when he proposed? I remember his exact words. He said, "Claire, if all you want is happiness, say no. I'm not going to give you a couple of kids and count the days until retirement. I promise you freedom from that. I promise you will never be bored." (1.6)

Claire then gives the man a hand job, asking, "Is this what you want-ed?" (1.6). His world turned upside-down, the distraught man begs her to stop. As with Frank, sex is meaningless to Claire; rather, "sex is about power."

Obviously, Claire is no docile queen who simply stands by her man. Women have as much agency—villainous or otherwise—as men in *House of Cards*, a status best captured at the end of Season 4 when Claire joins Frank in breaking the fourth wall to acknowledge the audi-ence. They work in unison, their teamwork memorably captured in the opening shot of Season 2, which shows them jogging together in perfect rhythm. Claire is deeply complicit in Frank's lies and crimes.

Claire is no Lady Anne. She is more of a Lady Macbeth, a co-con-spirator as cruel and cunning as her husband. Zoe Barnes is more like Anne, a young lover drawn into a perverse sexual relationship with the protagonist, but this upstart political journalist who enters into an affair to advance her career, later tries to investigate and expose Frank's cor-ruption, and is eventually killed by him also has elements of Shake-speare's Queen Elizabeth (a female opponent) and of Buckingham (aide-turned-enemy, betrayed and killed by the protagonist). Doug Stamper is clearly a Buckingham. Young Congressman Peter Russo is a Hastings (the pawn killed off after his usefulness expires). Secretary of State Mi-chael Kern is Clarence (the first victim), but so is Vice President Jim Matthews (the man blocking the line of succession). President Walker is Edward IV (the rightful ruler whose fall clears the way for the protago-nist's rise to power). In Season Four, after Frank has become president and is running for re-election, his Democratic primary challengers, Jack-ie Sharpe and Heather Dunbar, are the two young princes in the tower (threats who must be eliminated to legitimate the protagonist's author-ity). Arguably, the media (Zoe and her colleagues at the *Herald*, Janine and Lucas) come to represent the same force as Shakespeare's queens (Anne, Elizabeth, and Margaret). Where the medieval queens articulate their opposition to Richard in curses, publicly proclaiming his crimes and asking God to punish them, the modern media does so through in-vestigative journalism, hoping that the highest power in America, the people, will punish Frank.

These minor characters exhibit the varieties of complicity. In Peter Russo, we see conscienceless complicity (he does Frank's bidding) but also conscientious complicity when, to appease Frank, he closes the shipyard he was elected to protect. The decision rips him apart, but Frank has leverage over him. Peter's job is more valuable to him than his commitments or his conscience. This is not the conscientious complicity of Shakespeare's Scrivener, a helpless citizen: Peter is a politician who wants to resist Frank on moral grounds but cannot, because it would be politically damaging, a form of conscientious complicity specifically suited to American democracy. Janine is the show's Scrivener. She wants to resist the villain but feels powerless. "You know what? I'm really fucking scared this time," she cries. "He's got power. He's got a lot to lose. And right now he's winning" (2.1).

Frank, like Richard, repeatedly uses his winning personality to deceive and manipulate other characters while the audience, like Shakespeare's, does not realize that he is doing the same to us. The first crack in our relationship with Frank comes during his nationally televised debate with union lobbyist Marty Spinella. Up to this point in the show, Frank has been utterly charming in his audience addresses and wildly successful in his plots against his enemies. During the debate, however, a distracted Frank flubs a witty retort, becoming the butt of late-night comedians' jokes and internet memes. This is the *House of Cards* equivalent of Buckingham's failure to persuade the London crowd to support Richard, or Queen Elizabeth's outmaneuvering him. But the scene in *House of Cards* illustrates even more clearly what happens when we see failure from the villainous protagonist whose charm and talent have hypnotized an audience into unconscious complicity. We are willing to go along with the virtuoso, even if he does horrible things, as long as he is successful in his manipulations. The moment his talent is shown to have limits, we awake, shocked back to our senses, and begin our divorce from the villain who seduced us into his plots. Significantly, after Frank's failure he talks to the audience less frequently.

Frank addresses the audience an average of 8.75 times per episode in the first four episodes of the show (Figure 4.3). In the remainder of Season 1, he addresses the audience an average of 4.11 times per episode. The show drew attention to this trend at the end of the first episode of Season 2. Frank does not address the audience for the entirety of the episode, but then turns to the camera and asks, "Did you think I forgot about you?" (2.1). The line reminds us that this is a show where the protagonist speaks directly to us—but not lately. It also reminds us that Frank is someone we used to like. We once found him fun and exhilarating, but, as he lost his grip on the situation in Season 1, he confided his plots and plans less often, leading us to like him less and less. The delicious master-planning of Season 1 transforms, in Season 2, into quick glances at the camera that convey Frank's annoyance at the resistance he encounters as he claws his way up the line of succession, becoming president at the end of the season. Bizarrely, Richard, under a system of hereditary monarchy, becomes king through a public election, while Frank, under a system of representational democracy, becomes president without ever receiving a vote.

Figure 4.3 also shows Frank addressing the audience a total of 129 times in Seasons 1 and 2, but only 52 times in Seasons 3 and 4. In Season 3, directors often juked as if Frank were going to talk to the audience: after others leave the room, Frank would exhale and pause—as he often does before addressing the audience in Seasons 1 and 2—and then walk out of the frame without acknowledging us. Audience addresses fell off further as the show started exploiting other narrative devices, such as a flash-forward to Frank and Claire renewing their wedding vows (3.7), competing voiceovers by writers Thomas Gates and Kate Baldwin (3.8), and Frank's guilty-conscience nightmares (4.1, 4.6). Many episodes in these later seasons have no audience addresses at all (3.7, 3.13, 4.1, 4.4, 4.5, 4.6, 4.10). There are times in Seasons 3 and 4 when watching *House of Cards* feels like a chore. In Season 5, the energy of the audience address comes not from Frank but from the will-she-or-won't-she relationship between Claire and the camera. In Season 6, Frank is gone, and Claire has none of his playfulness when she speaks to us. She is more a Macbeth anxious about the security of her power than a Richard.

It is tempting to think that this design is deliberately modeled on *Richard III*, where Shakespeare all but eliminated interaction with the audience in the second half of the play. If the creators of *House of Cards* picked up on that dynamic, it was a profoundly good reading of Shakespeare's play. Recreating it in *House of Cards* would be a risky move, involving a concerted effort to get the audience to dislike the character that the show spent enormous energy getting them to like. Yet there is a precedent in the other show to usher in the age of streaming television, *Breaking Bad,* whose creators asked, "Wouldn't it be interesting to have a show that takes the protagonist and transforms him into the antagonist?"[6] That change disrupts the audience's enjoyment of *House of*

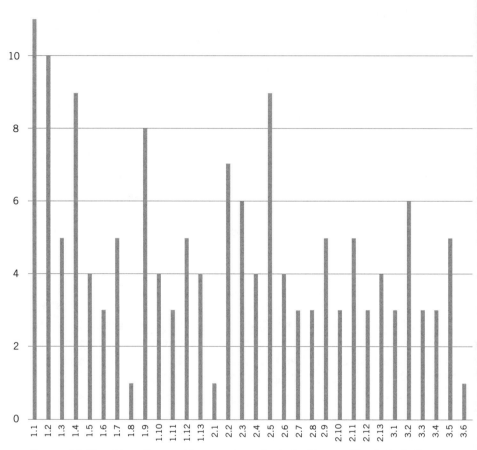

FIGURE 4.3. Frank's audience addresses, per episode, in *House of Cards* (including

Cards. Without his remarks to the audience, Frank becomes just another villain, and the show just another political drama. We might just click away when Netflix asks, "Continue watching?"

III. Theorizing the Kinds of Complicity

Let's step back to formalize the varieties of complicity in *Richard III* and *House of Cards*. The easiest version to identify is the conscienceless complicity of the evil henchman or -woman who does the villain's bid-

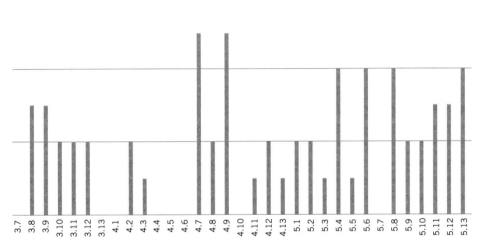

nods, smiles, and other nonverbal acknowledgments). (Created by the author.)

ding in exchange for money or status: the Murderers, Tyrell, Bucking-ham, and Catesby in *Richard III,* and Claire, Doug, and Zoe in *House of Cards.* This complicity is a two-way street: the villain is legally com-plicit in the crimes of his lackeys, while they are morally complicit in the schemes of the villain. But the fate of the accomplice complicates this form of complicity. Does the accomplice remain loyal to the villain or turn against him? Does the villain remain powerful or lose his grip? Answers to these questions reveal three permutations of conscienceless complicity. First, if the accomplice remains loyal, and the villain remains in power, the accomplice continues to enjoy the benefits—wealth and status—of the villain's power: this is the case with Claire and Doug. Second, if the accomplice betrays the villain, and the villain remains in power, the accomplice is killed: this happens to Buckingham, Zoe, and Peter. But perhaps the most interesting permutation of conscienceless complicity is the third: if the accomplice remains loyal, but the villain loses his power, the accomplice simply fades into the night, as with the Murderers, Catesby, and Tyrell in *Richard III*. We never hear from them again or learn their fates. As long as audiences get to see the main villain fall, they don't need to see his accomplices punished.

In cases of conscientious complicity, a villain wielding enormous power, displaying a vindictive personality, and performing awful crimes secures the support of someone who recognizes his depravity and wants to resist but is afraid to do so. The conscientious accomplice may fear bodily harm, like the English nobles in *Richard III*, who do not want to end up like Hastings, or like Janine in *House of Cards*, who does not want to end up like Zoe. Or, like Peter, the conscientious accomplice fears that the villain will take away his or her livelihood. As the Scrivener in *Richard III* says, everyone knows what the villain is doing, but everyone is also afraid to acknowledge it. Resistance is suppressed.

With unconscious complicity, an obviously evil villain secures support from a mass audience by speaking directly to them from a stage; drawing attention to the artificiality of the phenomenon in which he is involved; speaking irreverently, and with energy, wit, and humor, about that discourse; taking great joy in seeking to destroy a political system that the audience also despises; displaying an irrepressible will; exhibiting remarkable talents and success (even if that is only being good at being bad); speaking with a confidence that persuades hearers that he can do whatever he wants; and establishing with them an us-against-the-system dynamic. With its serial form, *House of Cards* additionally offers the binge-watching audience as a version of unconscious complicity specific to the digital age. But in *Richard III* and *House of Cards*, the audience's support for the villain lasts only until one of three things (or some combination of them) happens: (1) the villain commits a heinous crime against defenseless innocents who are not a part of the system the villain is seeking to destroy, as when Richard kills the princes, or Frank and Claire allow the hostage Jim Miller to die at the end of Season 4; (2) the villain's talent for manipulation is shown to be less powerful than he claims, as when Buckingham fails to persuade the citizens or Frank stumbles in his debate with Marty Spinella; (3) the villain stops talking to the audience, cutting them off from his charisma and leaving them to look at his actions alone, as happens in the second half of *Richard III* and in *House of Cards* beginning in the second half of Season 1. In both texts, these three developments come in conjunction with each other, coordinated with the villain's attainment of the power he has so vivaciously sought. The conclusion is straightforward: it can be fun to watch a wicked yet charismatic villain obtain power, but it is not much fun to watch an anxious criminal try and fail to keep it, especially if he cuts his audience off from his gleeful verve.

IV. From Literature to Life

The terms developed in this chapter allow us to identify conscienceless complicity in the Trump campaign and administration, conscientious complicity in the Republican Party, and unconscious complicity in the American public. To be sure, there is a huge difference between the murders committed by Richard III and Frank Underwood and the lies told by Donald Trump. It is not illegal for Trump and surrogates to lie to the American people. But if the villainy of Richard and Frank (crime) is seen as a metaphor for the villainy of Trump (dishonesty), the structures of complicity surrounding these three figures bear some striking resemblances.

The most obvious example of complicity in the Trump administration is that of Ivanka Trump and Jared Kushner. During a campaign that bounced from one asinine comment ("They're rapists") to another ("Grab 'em by the pussy"), Ivanka appeared to be a reasonable, ethical, and civilized daughter who held some sway over her father. She came to represent his conscience, the moderating force checking his immoral impulses. Critiquing this characterization, *Saturday Night Live* aired a skit in March 2017 called "Complicit," a parody of a glamorous perfume ad featuring Scarlett Johansson as a clear-eyed Ivanka Trump who enables rather than softens her father: "She's beautiful. She's powerful. She's *Complicit*. . . . *Complicit,* the fragrance for the woman who could stop all of this, but won't. Also available in a cologne for Jared."[7] Kushner, a one-time Democrat, has also been silent in the face of Trump's unethical behavior (in another *Saturday Night Live* skit, Jimmy Fallon plays a mute Kushner). Ivanka claimed not to understand the critique, demonstrating its validity in her attempt to dismiss it: "If being complicit is wanting to be a force for good and to make a positive impact, then I'm complicit. . . . I don't know what it means to be complicit."[8] She got a sense of what it means a couple weeks later when she was loudly booed at a summit on women's entrepreneurship after claiming that her father was a champion for women. The open question is whether Ivanka Trump and Jared Kushner's complicity is conscienceless (they knowingly stifle their beliefs about Trump in exchange for wealth and status), conscientious (they want to speak out but do not, out of fear), or unconscious (they were taken in, like many others, by his dazzling personality).

The most obvious example of conscienceless complicity in the administration is press secretary Sean Spicer, who had the unenviable job of defending Trump's repeated lies. Shortly before the inauguration, Spicer attested to the existence of a conscience when he drew a distinction between spinning and lying, observing that a spokesperson loses credibility if he or she lies: "The one thing, that whether you're a Republican, a Democrat, an Independent, you have your integrity. . . . You can spin the way you want, but I think to go out and tell an all-out lie is just not acceptable."[9] Yet Spicer lied to America in his very first press briefing. The day after the inauguration, the president claimed that the media were underreporting the size of his inauguration crowd. Later that day, Spicer aggressively shouted at the press corps: "This was the largest audience to ever witness an inauguration—period—both in person and around the globe."[10] Several media outlets determined the claim to be false, and commentators were baffled that Spicer would compromise his integrity and undermine his credibility on his first day. According to Ari Fleischer, former press secretary for President George W. Bush: "This is called a statement you're told to make by the President. And you know the President is watching."[11] It was only the first of a series of lies and dissimulations. Spicer went on to claim that Trump's proposed ban on Muslims was not a ban, even though Trump described it as one, and that Trump's charge that Barack Obama "wiretapped" him was not meant to be taken literally, because "wiretapping" was in quotes. Trump lied, then made Spicer lie, stifling the conscience and integrity earlier trumpeted, becoming complicit.

The following month, after Trump claimed that massive voter fraud was the only reason he had lost the popular vote to Hillary Clinton, his surrogate Stephen Miller went on the Sunday talk shows and aggressively defended the president's charge. Pressed by George Stephanopoulos of ABC News, he offered no evidence but only spoke louder: "I'm prepared to go on any show, anywhere, anytime, and repeat it and say the president of the United States is correct, 100 percent."[12] Arguably, conscienceless complicity was the unifying feature of Trump's chaotic presidential campaign. His ascendency was orchestrated by a series of political spin doctors turned campaign managers—Corey Lewandowski, Paul Manafort, and Kellyanne Conway—who sold to Trump their abilities to put a shiny gloss on his unpopular policies and statements. That is what political operatives do, of course, but Trump's surrogates did not simply advocate on his behalf in an open marketplace of ideas. Instead, they were forced to defend his lies and to lie on his behalf. The motto of the first campaign manager, Corey Lewandowski, was "Let Trump be Trump": his deceitful, demagogic tendencies should not be stifled but nurtured. The second campaign manager, Paul Manafort, defended Trump's false claim that Hillary Clinton wanted to abolish the Second Amendment, dismissed Trump's veiled incitement of violence against her, and created a diversion by inventing a story about a terrorist attack against a NATO base in Turkey (which never happened). The third campaign manager, Kellyanne Conway, was a blisteringly effective media figure who lied and misled on nightly cable news without compunction. After the election, she became a White House aide, abetting Trump's lies by using the phrase "alternative facts" to describe Spicer's trumped-up evidence for the claim that Trump's inauguration was bigger than Obama's.

Significantly, each operative disappeared from view as soon as his or her media appearances started to hurt rather than help Trump. Lewandowski was replaced by Manafort, Manafort by Conway. When Conway became ineffective, she was sidelined from media appearances, leading *Saturday Night Live* to satirize her with a "Where in the World is Kellyanne Conway?" skit. We saw this in *Richard III*: an audience is willing to go along with a politician's lies if he is an effective and successful liar. He loses support not by lying but by failing to lie successfully. As long as a politician can advance the candidate, the party, and the ideology, his or her truthfulness is, for a significant portion of the populace, irrelevant. Those seeking to oppose politicians like Richard, Underwood, and Trump might want to focus on better performances rather than better policies.

If some conscienceless Trump accomplices were motivated merely by money, like the Murderers in *Richard III*, others had Buckingham-like aspirations for political positions. Early supporters during the campaign, such as Michael Flynn and Jeff Sessions, went on to receive high-profile positions in the Trump administration. Mike Pence brought his Christian credentials to Trump's clearly un-Christian campaign and became vice president. Others threw their support behind Trump but failed to secure positions. Chris Christie, a fierce critic during the primaries, dropped out of the race, saw which way the wind was blowing, and endorsed Trump, hoping for a role in the future president's administration. Rudy Giuliani was the only Trump supporter to go on the Sunday talk shows to defend the candidate after the release of the infamous *Access Hollywood* tape, in which he bragged about being able to sexually assault women with impunity. Both Christie and Giuliani were, like Buckingham, denied any position. It remains to be seen whether the high-profile Trump supporters who did not receive the financial and professional rewards they expected in return for their service will, like Buckingham, join the opposition. It also remains to be seen whether the American public will view conscienceless complicity as a two-way street: Trump complicit in the daily lies of his surrogates, the surrogates complicit in his villainy. The analysis earlier in this chapter suggests that audiences do not need to see accomplices punished if they get to witness the downfall of the villain at the center of it all.

Whereas the Republicans in Trump's inner circle exhibited varying degrees of conscienceless complicity, those outside his campaign—establishment Republicans—displayed conscientious complicity. Paul Ryan, Ted Cruz, and Reince Priebus despised Trump as a person and disagreed with many of his policies. On the surface, this bloc of Trump supporters were practicing shrewd *realpolitik*: they rationalized that any Republican, no matter how flawed, would be better than Hillary Clinton, so they held their noses as they voted for Trump. I would suggest, instead, that they were afraid of not supporting Trump, felt powerless to resist, and feared the consequences of speaking out. In contrast to the conscientious accomplices in *Richard III* and *House of Cards*, who feared bodily harm and political revenge from the villain himself, the conscientious Republicans in the 2016 election feared Trump's supporters. As establishment Republicans, their power, money, and status did not flow from Trump, yet his following in the party was so strong that they judged that their future political careers might be contingent on their support for him. So what initially appeared to be conscientious complicity in the Republican Party (a desire to resist Trump but a fear of doing so) turns out to be old-fashioned conscienceless complicity (doing Trump's bidding in exchange for wealth and status). I think it is fair to say that there is a crisis of consciencelessness in the current Republican Party.

I would even suggest that the Republican Party as a whole was complicit in Trump's rise, not just because it supported him and voted for him, but because it cultivated the divisive brand of partisan politics that made a transparently immoral man into a viable candidate for half the country. Democrats are just as partisan as Republicans, but the twenty-first-century version of party-first politics is a product of an oppositional Republican strategy passed on from Newt Gingrich to Mitch McConnell. Only when the political game is defined as such—as a competition between political parties—and winning is the greatest good, can the simple fact of belonging to the Republican Party be an *ipso facto* qualification for the presidency. When the choice came down to *Support Donald Trump* versus *Republicans Lose the Election*, Republicans wanted to be on the winning team more than they wanted to elect the best person for the job. Because they wanted to win so badly, Republicans heard Trump's immoral statements not as disqualifying but as legitimating: he was willing to say anything to get elected. Republican voters admired Trump's gumption in saying the unsayable more than they despised the substance of what he said.

Since Trump's political support flowed almost entirely from his popular support, we arrive at the issue of unconscious complicity. *Why did the American people like Donald Trump?* Like Richard and Frank, Trump gave the people every reason to hate him. Why did voters throw their support behind a transparently immoral man? For starters, because his personality exerted a greater pull upon his audience than his actions and policies. He addressed them directly, as it were. Just as Richard and Frank do not speak as literary characters usually speak, Trump did not speak as politicians usually speak. He spoke directly to the people in a way that drew attention to the artificiality of other politicians. He broke the illusion of conventional political discourse. He spoke irreverently about politics. His genuine joy at firing one broadside after another at Washington corruption was infectious. Supporters clung to this "authenticity": seven in ten Republicans thought Trump "tells it like it is," despite his demonstrable dishonesty.[13] And Trump did not hide his self-interest and self-aggrandizement. It must be remembered, going all the way back to the Vice in early English drama, that wickedness is fun.

Second, like Richard and Frank, Trump displayed just the right mixture of victimization (drawing sympathy) and heroism (inspiring followers). Where Richard was a victim of nature, and Frank of politics, Trump presented himself as a victim of the media. Like Richard, Trump was born into privilege, yet both characterized themselves as underdogs willing to scrape and claw for success. People were mesmerized by Trump's work ethic. Voters admired his resolve and fighting spirit, as audiences admire the same qualities in Richard and Frank. But, like Richard and Frank, Trump did not simply work hard; he was successful, both in the private sector and in his improbable assent through the ranks of the Republican primary. And, like Richard and Frank, Trump's confidence reconfigured the discourse from ethical questions of *right versus wrong* into a more animalistic situation in which the herd got behind the alpha male who promised protection. As *Richard III* illustrates, the way someone speaks to us can exert more of a pull than the content of what he says.

Like Richard, Trump told obvious lies, not because he expected people to believe them, but because he expected people to show their support by perpetuating them. Contrary to much political commentary, I do not think that Trump lived in a fantasy world where he sought to determine his own reality; instead, he employed a manipulative version of politics where loyalty was tested and affirmed via adherence to transparent lies. He did not believe that all Mexicans are rapists, that he won the popular vote, or that Obama wiretapped him. His lies were things that, to quote Thomas More, "every child might well perceive." Everyone saw those "palpable devices" for what they were. "There was no man so dull" that he did not recognize Trump's lies as lies, but "men must sometimes for the manner's sake not seem to know what they know." So Trump's voters dismissed his lies as "King's games, as it were stage plays." One study even revealed that, when shown side-by-side images of Obama's heavily attended inauguration and Trump's lightly attended one, and asked which photo had more people, some Trump supporters were willing to make a clearly false claim to indicate their allegiance, a phenomenon theorized as "expressive responding."[14]

Like the Scrivener in *Richard III* and Zoe Barnes in *House of Cards,* the media in the 2016 presidential election experienced conscientious complicity. They clearly wanted to resist Trump's rise, but for three reasons they did not. First, many saw their job as reporting the news, not critiquing the candidate, especially because—this is the second reason—

the lies and manipulations that Trump promulgated as a presidential candidate were completely obvious to everyone. The third reason the media did not denounce Trump (a factor too large to consider here in any depth) is that he was a boon for ratings: morally disgusting but financially rewarding. As with the Murderers in *Richard III,* money exerted a greater pull upon the media than morality. That puts the media in the realm of conscienceless complicity. Yet Trump's media ratings were fueled by *House of Cards*–style binge watching of news coverage, even by people who detested him but could not turn away from the screen, raising the possibility of unconscious complicity from those most opposed to Trump.

As president, Trump has proved to be less successful and less talented than his campaign led supporters to believe he was. The small crowd at his inauguration clearly irked him. The FBI investigated Russia's efforts to sway the election in Trump's favor. Trump was forced to fire his national security advisor, Michael Flynn; his attorney general, Jeff Sessions, had to recuse himself from the Russia investigation. Trump's attempt to ban Muslims from entering the United States was blocked by the courts, twice. His pledge to repeal and replace Obamacare stalled in the House of Representatives. His promise to build a wall on the southern border and have Mexico pay for it was not fulfilled. A Quinnipiac University poll found most Americans (58 percent) describing his first 100 days as "mainly a failure"[15]—an extended version of Underwood's bumbling performance in the debate with Marty Spinella. It would be reasonable to conclude that Trump's underperformance might cause voters once allured by his talent and success to turn away in the next election.

As a result of his failures and flubs, Trump became rather reclusive. His campaign-style rallies continued, but he stopped speaking directly to the public. In his first 100 days, he held only one solo press conference. He was not having fun: he said he missed his old life. During the campaign, when Trump was constantly holding forth to his admirers with energy and wit, their support was strong. During his presidency, when he cut himself off from them, their support diminished. His approval ratings fell to near-record lows.[16] If the logic of *Richard III* holds true, there may soon come a moment when, cut off from his verve, Trump's supporters are shocked back to their senses. At that point they will have to ask themselves how they got wrapped up in his ruse, and why they so easily abandoned their most basic ethical values.

V. The Genre of the Trump Presidency

Richard III suggests that civil war and violent overthrow are the only way to overcome the chaos created by a political villain at the middle of intertwining webs of conscienceless, unconscious, and conscientious complicity. Surely we have progressed enough in the four centuries since Shakespeare that a political solution can triumph instead.

Let us conclude, then, with a return to the realm of literature and the terms of literary studies. The question at the moment is one of genre. Will the Trump presidency be a tragedy like *Richard III*, which ends in a downfall? Or will it be a serial show like *House of Cards,* where we all just keep watching?

5

Twenty Questions about
the Public Theater's Trump-Themed
Julius Caesar

CHARACTER COSTUMED as President Donald Trump was assassinated night after night on stage in New York in a June 2017 performance of Shakespeare's *Julius Caesar*. The show was run by the most established and respected Shakespearean company in the United States, the Public Theater, which does Free Shakespeare in the Park each summer at the Delacorte Theater in Central Park. Controversy erupted. Corporate sponsors fled. Protesters stormed the stage. Shakespeareans were threatened with death. Apart from the Astor Place Riot of 1849—when twenty-two people died in a dispute about *Macbeth*—there has never been a more dangerous production of Shakespeare.

This chapter asks twenty questions about the Public's *Caesar*. Many were answered in a July 2018 interview I did with Oskar Eustis, director of the show and artistic director of the Public. Eustis and I do not always read *Julius Caesar* the same way; in the pages that follow, I note where our readings diverge. But we both believe that at a time when a consequential social problem had become acute, literature worked as it is supposed to. The Public Theater's *Julius Caesar* created a venue for a proxy conversation about the viability of violence against the president of the United States. It provided a space for thinking and talking through the issue that was one step removed from the gritty reality. It pressed people to scrutinize their attitudes toward a concrete situation by asking them to formulate a generalizable principle for the question at hand. The production both acknowledged the fantasies of radical political violence that many on the Left were harboring and refused to let them fester in silence. In doing so, the Public Theater's *Julius Caesar* led audiences and commentators not to imitate the harmful act it represented, but to purge themselves of passions harmful to society. Tragedy worked as planned: in observing the fictional representation of thoughts and actions that cause harm to society, audiences found release from the pull to do those things. At a time when tensions were running high, art proved its social value through its ability to provoke and enlighten.

I. How Can One Person Be Another?

This first question is more of a riddle. Born in July 100 B.C.E. into a patrician Roman family aligned with revolutionary plebeian politicians against a corrupt dictatorship, which sought to centralize power in the Senate and lessen the power of popular assemblies, Julius Caesar became a political fugitive at the age of 18, then a soldier, and then, at 22, an attorney for the plebeian cause back in Rome. He was a student of oratory at 24, military tribune (commanding officer) at 27, quaestor (financial administrator) at 30, aedile (overseeing temples, buildings, markets, and games) at 34, pontifex maximus (chief priest) at 36, praetor (elected magistrate) at 37, governor of Spain at 38, consul of Rome and military general at 40. As general, he led a war for land in Gaul and later a civil war against his former ally Pompey. At 51 he was Cleopatra's lover in Egypt. At 53 he was appointed temporary dictator of Rome and, at 55, dictator for life. Later that year he was assassinated by a group calling themselves the Liberators.

For his part, Donald Trump was born to a real estate mogul in New York City in 1946, started working for his family's business at 16, dodged the draft and service in the Vietnam War in his twenties, and graduated with a bachelor's degree in economics from the University of Pennsylvania at 22. He became president of his family's company at 26, launched his own business with a million-dollar loan from his father in his thirties, and opened Trump Tower in Manhattan at 37. He co-wrote and published *The Art of the Deal* at 41 and filed for bankruptcy for the first time at 44. He started running the Miss Universe and Miss USA beauty pageants at 50, founded a modeling agency at 53, launched the NBC reality show *The Apprentice* at 58, started dabbling in politics at 63, and announced his presidential campaign as a Republican at 69. Exploiting populist politics in the 2016 campaign, he was elected forty-fifth president of the United States on November 8, 2016.

There are certainly similarities: born into wealth; thrice-married; shrewd, successful, and celebrated in his chosen career; engaged, though a member of the upper class, in aggressively populist politics; insatiably hungry for personal power and glory; variously fearless and shameless in the pursuit of fame; flaunting a glamorous style; habitually referring to himself in the third person; megalomaniacal; open to flattery; closely attentive to the entertainment industry; able to leverage his life's work into political success; adept at consolidating support in order to cut through a gridlocked political culture; and wildly offensive to traditional norms. Among the differences—Caesar a soldier, Trump a draft-dodger; Caesar a politician, Trump a businessman—the biggest one, possibly fatal to the analogy, is that Caesar was sincere and dignified, while Trump is a circus clown. So how can Donald Trump be Julius Caesar?

Our riddle has an answer: when two people are the same character. Trump is not the Caesar of Shakespeare's main source, *The Lives of the Noble Greeks and Romans* by Plutarch (born c. 46 C.E.). Plutarch was sharply critical of Caesar—"this was a plain tyranny"—but praised him as a capable and magnanimous leader, always concerned with the quality of life of soldiers and citizens, especially during the war with the Gauls. Plutarch's Caesar had an "excellent natural gift to speak well before the people" and was "excellently well studied"; no one had ever seen "as valliant a soldier and as excellent a Captain"; he was "entirely beloved of his soldiers"; "very commendable." "After he had ended his civil wars, he did so honorably behave himself, that there was no fault to be found in him," to the point that he was "heavy and sorrowful" when people tried making him king, refusing the honor.[1]

Shakespeare gave us none of this dignified Caesar. His Caesar, in William Hazlitt's description, "makes several vaporing and rather pedantic speeches, and does nothing."[2] He is "little better than a grand, strutting piece of puff-paste; and when he speaks, it is very much in the style of a glorious vapourer and braggart, full of lofty airs and mock-thunder," as Henry Hudson put it.[3] That is why G. B. Shaw looked with "revulsion of indignant contempt at this travestying of a great man as a silly braggart."[4] Ignoring Plutarch's dignified Caesar, Shakespeare adapted the character into the "ranting tyrant" of Middle English religious drama. Tyrants like Lucifer, Antichrist, Herod the Great, Pilate, and Augustus Caesar (Julius's successor) were played as fools reminiscent of the boaster or "braggart soldier" of classical comedy. Being able to laugh at them neutralizes the political threat they pose. Similarly, Shakespeare's Caesar is a grandiose, blustering gull, full of obtuse braggadocio, an inadequate dupe susceptible to flattery and manipulation. He is neither handsome nor sympathetic. Shakespeare meant for his lines—such as "Danger knows full well / That Caesar is more dangerous than he" (2.2.44–45)—to be delivered more in the style of Monty Python's tyrants than Cecil B. DeMille's, more Dr. Evil than Voldemort. If that sounds nothing like the Julius Caesar you remember, that is the point: the Caesar of history and the character of modern Shakespearean performance are serious and formidable men. Self-serious actors play him with gravitas, but Shakespeare's Caesar is a joke. The punchline is that everyone—the author, the audience, the other characters, and (given the Christianity informing Shakespeare's vision of Rome) God too—knows that Caesar is not as great as he claims, as loved as he seems, or as safe as he feels.

The most remarkable quality of Shakespeare's Caesar is his lack of definition. He is almost completely empty: the play provides no specific details about his life, about plebeian politics, about military brilliance or generosity to his soldiers. Depersonalizing Caesar by cutting away his biography before 44 B.C.E., Shakespeare steered attention away from Caesar's tyranny to the abstract question of tyrannicide in general. Put differently, Shakespeare turned history into tragedy by replacing particulars with abstractions. Audiences must supply the specifics of Caesar's life, allowing Elizabethans to plug their sixteenth-century politics into the play, and modern Americans to do the same with Trump.

Costuming Caesar as Trump reveals who Shakespeare's Caesar is as much as it helps us understand Trump. Eustis was able to find the comedy in *Julius Caesar* because Donald Trump acts with the absurd bluster of the Middle English stage tyrant. Consider Trump in *The Art of the Deal* advising readers to be braggarts: "Key to the way I promote is bravado. . . . A little hyperbole never hurts. People want to believe that something is the biggest and the greatest and the most spectacular. I call it truthful hyperbole. It's an innocent form of exaggeration."[5] As he entered politics, Trump's "truthful hyperbole" veered from salesmanship to egotistical boasting on absurd topics: "My fingers are long and beautiful, as, it has been well documented, are various other parts of my body."[6] "The only difference between me and the other candidates is that I'm more honest and my women are more beautiful."[7] "Sorry losers and haters, but my I.Q. is one of the highest, and you all know it! Please don't feel stupid or insecure, it's not your fault."[8] "It's very hard for them to attack me on looks, because I am so good looking."[9] That's why, when Trump announced his candidacy, the *New York Daily News* ran a cover with him in clown makeup.[10] During the campaign, Trump was more of a braggart than ever: "I'm very highly educated. I know words. I have the best words."[11] "I know more about ISIS than the generals do. Believe me."[12] "Do I look like a president? How handsome am I, right? How handsome?"[13] After he won, he promoted his presidency like a parody of himself: "We are going to have an unbelievable, perhaps record-setting turnout for the inauguration, and there will be plenty of movie and entertainment stars. All the dress shops are sold out in Washington. It's hard to find a great dress for this inauguration."[14] Commentators said that he would pivot to become more presidential, but he spent his first year in office retweeting videos of himself as a World Wrestling Federation fighter assaulting CNN. When his goofiness led to questions about his mental health, he tweeted with truthful hyperbole, "Throughout my life, my two greatest assets have been mental stability and being, like, really smart . . . not smart, but genius . . . a very stable genius at that!"[15] In an absurdly clownish tweet of July 2018, he misspelled "pore": "After having written many best selling books, and somewhat priding myself on my ability to write, it should be noted that the Fake News constantly likes to pour over my tweets looking for a mistake."[16]

Trump can be Caesar because his political persona performs the clownish character Shakespeare gave to Caesar. That is how Eustis found the comedy in the play, as he told me:

> Once you start thinking of the analogy between Trump and Caesar, the comedy's kind of inevitable. Hegel said, "History repeats itself"; Marx said, "And the first time it's tragedy. The second time it's farce." Caesar is maybe a tragic character, but Trump is a farcical one. In a way, you could sum that up by saying Caesar had some of the greatest achievements in the history of the planet as a military genius, and Trump has had no real achievements whatsoever his entire life, except for bluster and faking. So in a

way, Trump himself is a parody of Caesar, just as he's a parody
of a leader. He's not somebody like Caesar who accrues power
through tremendous achievement. He's somebody who accrues
power through lying and self-promotion and bluster and playing
on the resentments and anger of a scared and embittered population. So it felt to me like the draw to comedy was powerful. You
can see in Trump something people did not report about the
historical Caesar, which is a reveling in the vulgarity of wealth,
a reveling in the cheapest and shoddiest appearances of luxury
and power. That's not something that one associates with the
historical Caesar at all: this was a guy who slept on the ground
with his men. But it is something that one associates with Trump.
So in that way the Caesar I portrayed was more influenced by our
president than by the Roman general.

II. Why Didn't Anyone Care
When Obama Was Assassinated?

Shortly after the assassination in *Julius Caesar,* imagining dramatic re-
enactments echoing through history, Shakespeare describes what he
was doing at that moment, and what future generations would do with
his play: "How many ages hence / Shall this our lofty scene be acted
over / In states unborn and accents yet unknown!" (3.1.112–114). As
Stanley Wells told the *New York Times* during the *Julius Caesar* controversy, the line points "to times when people will also see this his-
toric event as relevant to their own times."[17] During the controversy,
people often cited a 2012 Obama-themed *Julius Caesar* with financial
support from Delta Airlines and the National Endowment for the Arts.
Why wasn't there controversy and corporate backlash then?

Because drawing an analogy between Caesar and contemporary
politics is not a controversial move; it is the oldest trick in the book.
Julius Caesar is and always has been an instrument enabling a closer
look at something else. Plutarch paired Caesar with Alexander the Great
to present ambition as a chronic political problem. When Shakespeare
opened the newly constructed Globe Theatre with *Julius Caesar* in 1599,
audiences thought of Queen Elizabeth I. Censorship made direct critique
impossible, but Shakespeare used Caesar to gesture toward one of Elizabeth's favorites, the Earl of Essex. He did this explicitly in *Henry V,*
where Essex, "the General of our gracious Empress," is compared to

"conqu'ring Caesar . . . Bringing rebellion broachèd on his sword, / How many would the peaceful city quit / To welcome him!" (5.Ch.28–34). Shakespeare shaded Essex more deeply in *Julius Caesar:* both were ambitious, self-aggrandizing warriors, influential with aristocrats, yet popular among the people. Refocus the lens, however, and Essex looks different. If one sees Elizabeth herself as a power-hungry Caesar, Essex is a regicide Brutus. Look in a different direction a few years later, and an endangered King James I is promoting Shakespeare's play as a caution against regicide.

Similarly, political allegory was a feature, not a bug, of the afterlife of *Julius Caesar* in America. The first American production—at the Southwark Theater in Philadelphia in 1770—depicted "the noble struggles for liberty by that renowned patriot, Marcus Brutus."[18] John Adams repeatedly invoked Caesar during the fight for American independence: "The same great spirit which once gave Caesar so warm a reception . . . is still alive and active and warm in England; and that the same spirit in America, instead of provoking the inhabitants of that country, will endear us to them forever and secure their good will."[19] Adams roused his colleagues by quoting Shakespeare: "Cassius from Bondage shall deliver Cassius."[20] The historian Michael Kauffman's *American Brutus,* about John Wilkes Booth and southern Democrats, states that "Lincoln, to them, was Caesar in need of a Brutus."[21] After the assassination, Booth—who played Mark Antony in *Julius Caesar,* delivering the eulogy for Brutus at the end of the play—complained that he was hunted "for doing what Brutus was honored for."[22]

Using Caesar for veiled critique is not politicizing a literary figure; that is what the literary figure is designed to do and has always done. Because Shakespeare depersonalized Caesar, the play is open to analogies beyond Republican Rome and Elizabethan England. In 1937 Orson Welles mounted the first modern-dress production of *Julius Caesar,* subtitled *Death of a Dictator,* at the Mercury Theatre in New York. Caesar was Mussolini. He was also a fascist on British television in 1938, on the London stage in 1939, in Berlin in 1941, and on U.S. television in 1949. He was Charles de Gaulle in John Barton's 1968 production for the Royal Shakespeare Company; a Latin American dictator in Minneapolis in 1969 and in Stratford, Connecticut, in 1979; Anwar Sadat in Belfast in 1981 and again (with a touch of Che Guevara) at the Oregon Shakespeare Festival in 1982; Fidel Castro in Miami in 1986; Boris Yeltsin in London in 1992, and then Margaret Thatcher there in

1993; George W. Bush in London in 2005; Dick Cheney in Chicago in 2013; and Hillary Clinton in Providence, Rhode Island, in 2015.

Director Rob Melrose, a Eustis mentee, cast the African American actor Bjorn DuParty to play a tall, charismatic, confident, basketball-playing Obama Caesar who was stabbed by right-wing conspirators in 2012 at the Guthrie Theater in Minneapolis. "The Tea Party was in full effect," Melrose recalls, "the birther movement well underway, and Mitch McConnell had stated that his main goal was to deny Obama a second term. It wasn't hard to imagine one of these groups pushed to the point where they would consider violence."[23] Most of the scheming conspirators were white men reminiscent of Representative Paul Ryan, but Brutus was the African American actor Will Sturdivant. As a model for his Brutus, Melrose cited "any number of smart, serious African-American conservatives." The Obama Caesar was assassinated, and corporate sponsors and the National Endowment for the Arts had no reaction. Why wasn't the Obama Caesar controversial? And why, if President Caesar is an established trope, was the Trump Caesar so shocking?

It was not simply because the Public's production was clearly personalized—that also happened with Mussolini, de Gaulle, Sadat, Castro, Yeltsin, and Thatcher. Not simply because it was an American Caesar on an American stage—that also happened with Bush, Cheney, and Clinton. Not simply because the Public's production was about a sitting American president—that happened with Obama. What was new about the Public's *Caesar*? Was it the national stage, given that other President Caesars died on local stages? The size, scope, and significance of the Public Theater surely contributed to the controversy but, put in the context of the literary history surveyed here, it is clear that the mode of Shakespearean theater did not change. Instead, society had changed—both the sovereign and the citizens.

First, Trump was actually more tyrannical than Obama or Clinton, tightening the correspondence with Shakespeare's Caesar, lessening the ability to dismiss the conceit connecting politician to character as a cute cliché, increasing the likelihood that audiences would see a viable comparison, reflecting the increased likelihood that Trump's political opponents might actually pursue violence against him. Second, the Public's *Caesar* was staged after the disastrous and demoralizing first 100 days of the Trump administration; the Right was desperate for an opportunity to seize the moral high ground after two years of Left-based grievances about Trump's incivility. Third, political commentary was shifting from trained professionals at centralized outlets to partisan magazines, blogs, and social media, becoming less informed and more inflammatory. In this context, fantasies of radical political violence violating the social contract became much more plausible and realistic. In short, the Public's Trump Caesar generated controversy because, for the first time since Welles's Mussolini, assassination seemed to fall within the realm of something that might actually happen.

III. Why Did the Public Theater Stage a Trump-Themed *Julius Caesar*?

A little background on Oskar Eustis. His politics are best described as congenial radicalism. His mother, a professor of English and women's studies at the University of Minnesota, and his stepfather were proud members of the Communist Party. His father was an official in the Minnesota Democratic Party, his stepmother a sociologist at the university. I asked Eustis about his own ideology:

> I think the simplest thing to say is that I'm a socialist. What I believe is that there's an inherent principle behind capitalism, which is about the individual appropriation of collective creation, that is fundamentally wrong. The wealth of the world is created by the people of the world as a collective. It is not created by individuals. Therefore, individuals should not appropriate the fruits of that. How that works out in practice in a political system, I've had many different points of view over the years, but that's one underlying principle that informs me.

Born in 1958, the young Eustis had a precocious intellect, graduating from high school at the age of fifteen. He attended New York University but dropped out to enter the politically charged experimental theater scene in New York. An anti-establishment, countercultural iconoclast, Eustis co-founded an avant-garde theater troupe called the Red Wing Company that took him to Switzerland before he was twenty. In 1980, longing to reconnect with a proletarian audience, he joined the Eureka Theatre in San Francisco, which viewed theater as an instrument of social change. There he discovered a gift for dramaturgy; he liked bringing new plays into existence, most famously Tony Kushner's *Angels in America* (1991) and later Lin-Manuel Miranda's *Hamilton* (2015). In

1989, losing interest in opposing mainstream American culture and opting instead to change it by infiltrating it, Eustis joined the Mark Taper Forum in Los Angeles, where he became associate artistic director. He moved on to the Trinity Repertory Company in Providence, Rhode Island, in 1994, and became artistic director of the Public Theater in 2005. At a 2010 panel on the history of the Public, Eustis put a stamp on his unique vision of institutional radicalism: "The best thing about America is that there is a penumbra of democracy around our institutions that keeps insisting we are not yet democratic enough."[24]

Eustis did a modernized *Caesar* once before—staging it for Eureka in 1988, for Trinity in 1990, and for the Taper Forum in 1991.[25] Set against a 1960s White House evoking Kennedy's Camelot, archival newsreels ran before the show, while eavesdropping Secret Service agents evoked the paranoia of the Nixon era and banks of television monitors figured the rise of media in politics, showing police sirens flashing and Rodney King–style beatings in the streets. Eustis's production turned Caesar's Rome into the twilight days of Golden Age America. I asked him to look back on it in the light of his 2017 version:

> My intentions at that point were much less directly political because they didn't have to do with our political moment, right then. They actually, to me, very much had to do with the image of "the best and the brightest"—of what happened with the arrogance of a group of really entitled, smart guys who feel like they have the ability to control the fate of the world. And I made one change in the text, back then: after the assassination, Brutus says, "Then walk we forth, even to the marketplace, / And, waving our red weapons o'er our heads, / Let's all cry, 'Peace, freedom, and liberty!'" [3.1.109–111]; and Cassius says, "Brutus shall lead, and we will grace his heels / With the most boldest and best hearts of Rome" [3.1.122–123]. I just couldn't resist, and I changed it to "the best and brightest minds of Rome." And that image of these guys, who all looked like Robert McNamara, with their bloody hands, walking through the streets shouting "Freedom!" felt very evocative. It is evocative, but obviously of a much less headline-producing, of-the-moment type of political resonance. It was more finding a historical analogy, even though it was recent history, whereas this time around the urgency felt really timely, of-the-moment.

Tony Kushner praised the earlier production as "a particular kind of political tragedy, one that troubled the minds of Shakespeare's audience and ought to be troubling the minds of Americans today."[26] Dressed in a dark business suit, Stephen Markle's Caesar was not a specific individual but, to Kushner, "a deliberately composite demagogue, equal parts Huey Long, Lyndon Johnson, Kennedy—noble and dangerous all at once." Standouts included Lise Hilboldt's Calpurnia as Jackie Kennedy, and Delroy Lindo's Cassius, culled from the Black Power movement. The funeral orations after Caesar's death became a press conference, reporters forming the angry mob, which transformed into rioters in street clothes. Seeing "a wild lamentation for the failures of progressive people to stop Octavius Caesar from ascending to power," Kushner loved that Eustis "takes sides": "Eustis' production declares, in a bold and moral voice, solidarity with Brutus and Cassius—the choice is between a monarchy or a republic, and Eustis' preference is clear."[27] Kushner concluded, triumphantly, "I live in the America of Ronald Reagan and George Bush, and this 'Julius Caesar' feels very painfully to me to be the tragedy of my time."

Eustis's sympathy for Shakespeare's conspirators explains why he returned to *Julius Caesar* in 2017. He wanted, first, to critique Trump as a tyrant, as he recalled to me:

> The decision to do *Caesar* happened, literally, immediately after the 2016 election—a couple of days after. I had been planning to do *Richard II,* but I just felt the overwhelming need to tell this story. And in looking back on it now, I feel like I was telling exactly the story that needed to be told: this is a story of a republic or democracy that is threatened to its very core by a populist charismatic leader who has clear aspirations to dictatorship. That's the dilemma that faced the conspirators in *Julius Caesar.* And I feel it's, unfortunately, a very exact analogy to the dilemma that we're in as Americans. And I wish it wasn't. I wish I could say that, now, looking back, it seems like a hysterical overreaction, but that's not how I feel. I feel like those points remain dramatically effective.

Eustis never critiqued Trump this explicitly when the show was running. Especially after controversy struck, he maintained a conciliatory posture. In the playbill, he wrote, ambiguously: "*Julius Caesar* is about how fragile democracy is. The Institutions that we have grown up with, that we have inherited from the struggle of many generations of our ancestors, can be swept away in no time at all."[28] More definitively, he added on the theater's website: "*Julius Caesar* can be read as a warning parable to those who try to fight for democracy by undemocratic means. To fight the tyrant does not mean imitating him."[29] On opening night, Eustis told the *New York Times* that the show was "a progressive's nightmare vision of [resistance]."[30] His second motive, therefore, was to warn the Left against violence.

This *Caesar* about the pitfalls of radical political violence feels like an about-face from Eustis's earlier production. I asked if he still sided with the conspirators:

> While my sympathy remains with the conspirators, my judgment is pretty harsh. And it was in the production as it is in my mind, namely that these are people who attempt to preserve democracy by undemocratic means and, as a result, bring about the exact opposite of what they set out to do. You know, the theater operates in a realm, not so much of literal fact, as in a realm of imagination, fantasy, and catharsis. And what I felt, and what many, many other people who saw the production told me, was that the production acted out a fantasy that people had, that somehow, if they could just get rid of Trump, everything would be OK. And the production, as the theater is supposed to do, acted out impulses that none of us really feel committed to acting out in real life, that we could fantasize. And to me it functioned exactly as catharsis is supposed to function, which is: many of us fear and loathe the person who is now president of the United States. And watching that fear and loathing acted out in the form of murder purged many of those emotions. It made me—it made many in the audience—feel, "Oh, right, this is absolutely not the way to go. This is not an effective or appropriate solution, whatever fear and disagreement we feel." So, in the most quotidian ways, I hoped the production would allow everybody to focus on the 2018 midterms, to focus on trying to battle tyranny with democracy, and not battle tyranny with violence.

Thus, Eustis mounted a Trump-themed *Julius Caesar* for two layered, competing reasons: first, to act out his liberal desires for the ultimate resistance against tyranny, and, second, to act out his own suppression of those desires based on a reasoned consideration of the costs of pursuing them. Eustis both wanted and did not want to see President Trump violently removed from power, and—this is key—his familiarity with Shakespeare allowed him to recognize that tension in himself, make sense of it, proceed in an ethical manner, and, crucially, magnificently, create a venue for others experiencing similar emotions to think them through. That is how he responded when I pressed him on the divide between the anger he must have felt on the night of Trump's election and the reasoned restraint he later claimed for the Public's *Caesar*:

> I can't tell you I had my fully formulated elevator pitch for why killing Trump on stage was a cathartic thing as opposed to a revolutionary thing formed at that moment. But I make theater for a living, and it's all I've ever done. And what I felt really strongly that night was that we were facing what I thought was an unprecedented situation, at least since the Civil War, where the very existence of our democracy was on the line, and I needed to do something to respond to that. *Caesar* was the most immediate response I could have. So for me that was the equivalent of a rapid reaction. That was the quickest I could get a show up dealing with this. And it felt to me, even though the initial impulse was not intellectual but was sort of a visceral impulse, that we have to tell the story of trying to defend democracy from a latent dictator. And then, as I kept working on it, I think the thoughts became a little more subtle.

This tension between liberal desire and liberal restraint was widespread in the months after the 2016 election. Ultimately, therefore, Oskar Eustis and the Public Theater staged a Trump-themed *Julius Caesar* because the dialectic of interpretation in response to Shakespeare's play— first aligning oneself against tyranny, then aligning oneself against tyrannicide—paralleled the dialectic of interpretation in response to Trump during his first year in office. "Exactly right," Eustis said:

> In a way, it was immediately debating the tactics of resistance— because as soon as he was elected, the question was, "How do we resist this?" And the great thing about producing Shakespeare and directing Shakespeare is that you know, if you pick a

Shakespeare play to produce, you're not going to get a simple-minded answer to anything. He's just so complexly human in how he weaves drama that he's going to force you into subtlety; he's going to force you into complexity.

IV. Is Shakespeare's Caesar Donald Trump?

Fresh off playing a caricature of Trump on Shonda Rhimes's ABC show *Scandal,* actor Gregg Henry was cast as Eustis's Caesar (Figure 5.1). "I did not hire Gregg because he could imitate Trump," Eustis told me, "but he turned out to be really good at it. And I kept expecting that there would be hand gestures or intonations which were clearly modeled on Trump that would feel too much to me, but they fit so seamlessly into the story." Corey Stoll, the actor playing Brutus (Figure 5.2), did not know that the production would be Trump-themed when he signed on. The cast found out after four weeks of rehearsal, when they moved from the rehearsal room to the theater. Stoll later wrote that he was "disappointed by the literal design choice" because he was "worried that the nuanced character work we had done in the rehearsal room would get lost in what could seem like a *Saturday Night Live* skit."[31] That erasure of nuance was purposeful, Eustis said: "I thought this production should be a very blunt instrument. I kept waiting to feel like I was being too literal in rehearsal. And I never felt that way. I always felt, the more Gregg Henry looked like Trump, the more I went, yeah, that's *exactly* what I want to do. Because it felt to me like it was exactly the situation we were facing." Eustis never hid what he was doing from the Public Theater, its board of directors, or its trustees, and he never sought permission from corporate donors: "It would be dreadful if we allowed anybody to preapprove or censor what we do."[32] I asked him about the atmosphere at the Public during the early stages of production: "You know, it was interesting. Until things went south, there was very little anxiety from anybody. I had one staff member, who will remain nameless, who was a Trump supporter, and he was unhappy."

On May 23, 2017, previews of the trim, two-hour production began at the Delacorte, a few dozen blocks from Trump Tower. Before the performance, a recorded announcement from Eustis explained that only one line in the play had been changed, and audiences would know it when they heard it. The stage was set to look like a modern-day Wash-

FIGURE 5.1. Tina Benko as Calpurnia, Gregg Henry as Caesar,
Teagle F. Bougere as Casca, and Elizabeth Marvel as Mark Antony
in *Julius Caesar*, dir. Oskar Eustis
(New York: Delacorte Theater in Central Park, 2017).
(Photograph by Joan Marcus.)

FIGURE 5.2. Corey Stoll as Brutus and John Douglas Thompson
as Cassius in *Julius Caesar*, dir. Oskar Eustis
(New York: Delacorte Theater in Central Park, 2017).
(Photograph by Joan Marcus.)

ington, DC. Banners depicting the Capitol, national monuments, and the U.S. Constitution were framed by a large gear evoking a mechanistic totalitarianism. Audience members were invited to add their own graffiti to the walls onstage, which held prompts like *I mourn for* and *I hope for.* People mourned for "innocents lost," "Manchester," "Brett," and "Apathy, Enemy of Democracy"; they hoped for "Paris accord," "a better life for my sister," and "unconditional love, including self-love."[33] The dark business suits of the actors stood out against the ivory white set. Faceless police officers lined the back of the stage. Gregg Henry played an orangish, vulgar, blustery, coarse-voiced, pussy-grabbing Julius Caesar with a blond coif, expensive suits, unbuttoned overcoat, and too-long red tie. Tina Benko as Caesar's wife, Calpurnia, wore slender designer dresses and stilettos and spoke with an Eastern European accent, evoking First Lady Melania Trump (see Figure 5.1). The audience cheered with liberal euphoria when Caesar and Calpurnia first appeared to the sound of patriotic electric guitars and screaming hicks in Make America Great Again hats. Henry's Caesar made triumphal hand gestures, grabbed Calpurnia's crotch, and harangued a Fake News reporter in the audience: Shakespeare's "Who is it in the press that calls on me?" (1.2.15), referring to a mob of people, was effortlessly transferred to a press conference.

The line Eustis changed came in Casca's account of Caesar's devout supporters: "But there's no heed to be taken of them; if Caesar had stabbed their mothers, they would have done no less" (1.2.268–269) became "if Caesar had stabbed their mothers *on Fifth Avenue,* they would have done no less." Eustis told me he "couldn't resist": "That analogy was so exact. What Trump was saying is *exactly* what Casca was saying about Caesar's supporters: if he had killed their mothers, they would have done no less. It's the exact thing. I'm not stretching the analogy. I'm just changing the words a little to drive home with a blunt instrument what this connection is." In the scene where Calpurnia begs Caesar not to go to the Capitol, she joined him in an obnoxiously gold-tiled bathtub, where Caesar soaked, a cigar in one hand, typing on his phone with the other. After their exchange, he emerged from the tub stark naked: "Give me my robe, for I will go" (2.2.107).

Does Donald Trump really resemble Shakespeare's Caesar? The opening of the play dwells on the difference between the reputation of Caesar and the reality. Amid a lavish festival welcoming the triumphant Caesar back to Rome after his victory over Pompey, the plebeian tribune Murellus scoffs that Caesar does not deserve it: "Wherefore rejoice? What conquest brings he home?" (1.1.31). Caesar is a celebrity, but he isn't worthy of his status, Murellus claims, like many of Trump's detractors. Trump isn't as rich as he claims. He isn't as tough as he claims. And he isn't as talented in business as he claims. But Trump will "leave no ceremony out," as Caesar instructs Mark Antony (1.2.11): recall Trump's descent on the escalator to announce his candidacy. And Caesar's ceremoniousness is directly tied to his thirst for personal power: "When Caesar says, 'Do this,' it is performed," a servile Antony responds (1.2.10).

That discrepancy between Caesar's reputation and his reality—much more than some love of liberty—is what launches the conspiracy. That divide is the point of Cassius's story about Caesar at the start of the second scene: "Honor is the subject of my story," he says (1.2.92), and Caesar should not have so much. He's no better than Cassius and Brutus. Why celebrate Caesar? This indignant envy fills Cassius's story about the stormy day when a boastful Caesar dared Cassius to swim the Tiber River. Cassius dove head first into danger, a sign, he thinks, that he should be first in honor. Caesar followed, but struggled. He was not as strong a swimmer and started drowning, calling for help. In an epic simile comparing himself to Aeneas, the founder of Rome, Cassius says he saved Caesar and arose on the shore, the damaged man on his back. This is the first in a string of moments where Shakespeare, *contra* Plutarch, characterizes Caesar as weak in body. Shakespeare's mounting tyrant is a middling man who has achieved a mythological stature. With an outsized reputation based on his success, but rather weak according to those who know him personally, Trump provides a solid inlet for someone representing Shakespeare's Caesar.

How does the man make himself myth? Caesar and his cronies are skilled actors on the political stage, crafting effective public spectacles, such as the fake coronation related in the second scene: "There was a crown offered him; and being offered him, he put it by with the back of his hand, thus, and then the people fell a-shouting" (1.2.220–222). Critics usually see here a Roman ritual whereby the ambition of leaders was kept in check. If it seems like a stretch to treat it, instead, as a master class in political manipulation, keep in mind that Shakespeare staged exactly that a few years earlier in *Richard III* when Buckingham begs Richard to become king and Richard "play[s] the maid's part" (3.7.50).

The coronation ritual in *Julius Caesar* is staged political theater—

that is what Casca means when he calls it "mere foolery"—but it does not go as Antony and Caesar planned:

> It was mere foolery; I did not mark it. I saw Mark Antony offer him a crown—yet 'twas not a crown neither, 'twas one of these coronets—and, as I told you, he put it by once; but for all that, to my thinking, he would fain have had it. Then he offered it to him again; then he put it by again; but to my thinking, he was very loath to lay his fingers off it. And then he offered it the third time; he put it the third time by, and still as he refused it the rabblement hooted and clapped their chopped hands, and threw up their sweaty nightcaps, and uttered such a deal of stinking breath because Caesar refused the crown that it had—almost—choked Caesar, for he swooned and fell down at it. (1.2.234–246)

Antony and Caesar had hoped that when Caesar refused the crown, the crowd would shout for him to take it, allowing them to say that Rome's shift to monarchy was the people's will. But as Plutarch makes clear, the people are glad when he refuses the crown. They are not shouting for him to take it; they do not want him to be king; they are not in his pocket; and they are not the easily manipulated mob usually associated with Shakespeare's crowds. In this moment the people, with a firm democratic voice, are standing up to the political elite—for democracy, against monarchy. Casca gives voice to that sense of a populace exercising judgment—deliberately, effectively—against politicians trying to manipulate public sentiment, invoking the agency of audiences at the theater: "If the tag-rag people did not clap him and hiss him, according as he pleased and displeased them, as they use to do the players in the theater, I am no true man" (1.2.255–257). This is democracy on the brink, about to get outmaneuvered by a master manipulator who, having failed in his planned performance, must, like an actor, resort to improvisation: "When he perceived the common herd was glad he refused the crown," Casca reports, "he plucked me ope his doublet and offered them his throat to cut" (1.2.259–261). Caesar risks everything. He realizes that the crowd does not support him, and so he tests them: *You may not love me enough to make me king, but do you hate me enough to want me gone?* We never hear what Casca did. I imagine him frozen by the absurdity of the request. The crowd is also paused. They do not clamor for Caesar to commit suicide. They don't hate him; they just don't want him to be king. Caesar hopes that they will cry out against suicide, reverse course, and get behind him. It is not clear that they do, but, sensing an opening, Caesar pulls off one of the all-time great political stunts.

He fakes an epileptic fit—on stage, in front of everyone. Historically, Caesar had epilepsy, and Shakespeare may have meant to show a moment of acute stress triggering a seizure (as happens in *Othello*). But that explanation does not accord with Shakespeare's emphasis on "the players in the theater" in this scene. Having epilepsy does not prevent a person from using a seizure for political advantage, but it does help him to feign one, which is (I think, though this was not present in Eustis's production) what Caesar does. He shrewdly calculates that he can win over the crowd by making himself radically vulnerable. Not even Donald Trump, king of the counterintuitive political maneuver, would take such a risk. For Caesar, it pays off:

> And so he fell. When he came to himself again, he said if he had done or said anything amiss, he desired their worships to think it was his infirmity. Three or four wenches where I stood cried, "Alas, good soul!" and forgave him with all their hearts. But there's no heed to be taken of them; if Caesar had stabbed their mothers, they would have done no less. (1.2.263–269)

To date, Trump has not faked a seizure at a campaign rally. But the ratings-obsessed reality television veteran is an accomplished performer of scripted drama presented as spontaneous. In June 2017, at the height of the controversy about the Public's *Caesar,* cameras were brought into the first full cabinet meeting of his administration for a bizarre kiss-the-ring moment in which each suppliant cabinet member praised Trump's election victory and leadership—"We thank you for the opportunity and blessing to serve your agenda"—earning comparisons to the opening of *King Lear*.[34] In his first year Trump teased policy proposals with "stay tuned," and timed announcements to peak television hours. He sent Vice President Mike Pence to an Indianapolis Colts football game so that when Colts players took a knee during the national anthem, as everyone knew they would, Pence's walkout could be filmed for television. To quote Casca, "There was more foolery yet, if I could remember it" (1.2.280).

Caesar's other core characteristic is arrogance, registered through repeated dismissals of warnings about impending danger. He disregards the Soothsayer's "Beware the Ides of March" (1.2.18), scoffing, "He is a dreamer" (1.2.24). Wrong. He disregards his suspicions of Cassius—"I fear him not" (1.2.197)—based on his own absolute greatness: "I rather tell thee what is to be feared / Than what I fear; for always I am Caesar" (1.2.211–212). With the same illogical self-regard, he spurns Calpurnia's fears: "Caesar shall forth. The things that threatened me / Ne'er looked but on my back. When they shall see / The face of Caesar, they are vanishèd" (2.2.10–12). His refusal to read Artemidorus's letter changes the dynamic a bit, since it is motivated not by arrogance but by a commitment to attend to matters of state before personal affairs—adding a touch of humanity, even nobility, as his tragedy approaches: "What touches us ourself shall be last served" (3.1.8). Before that climactic moment, however, the arrogant, egotistical, self-willed, and self-satisfied Caesar reappears. "I am constant as the Northern Star" (3.1.61), he pronounces. "I do know but one / That unassailable holds on his rank, / Unshaked of motion; and that I am he" (3.1.69–71). Eustis cited these lines when asked how Caesar resembled Trump:

> The narcissism, the grandiosity, the unstoppable ambition—famously in *Caesar,* he gives the best justification for his assassination seconds before he's assassinated when he describes himself as "constant as the Northern Star." You could stick "I alone can fix this" into that last speech of Caesar's, and nobody would notice. So there are personality characteristics—which, by the way, don't have much to do with the historical Caesar, who's a much wilier, subtle, and sophisticated character, but do have to do with Shakespeare's Caesar. But the contempt for democratic norms, the belief that there are no rules that should apply to him—that feels to me not only very much like Trump; that feels very much like what an incipient dictator looks like. It's so shockingly obvious with our president that he just has no belief whatsoever that he should be accountable the way other people are accountable. It's just an absent category in his thinking.

Yes, Donald Trump resembles Shakespeare's Caesar—in his clownish bravado, his mythological reputation, his meager reality, his skillful use of political theater, and his arrogance. These multiple parallels, in light of Caesar's status as one of history's most infamous tyrants, lead to our next question.

V. Is Trump a Tyrant?

Timothy Snyder certainly thinks so. His field guide for resistance, *On Tyranny* (2017), released shortly after the 2016 election, was the first academic book to respond to the Trump phenomenon.[35] It did not argue that Trump is a tyrant; it took that for granted and provided lessons for resistance drawn from the twentieth century. But that sidesteps the first-order question that the Public's *Caesar*, basing its frame of reference in classical political theory, helps us ask: *Is Trump actually a tyrant?*

Derived from a Greek term for any lord, master, or sovereign, the word "tyrant" evolved to refer to those who came to power through usurpation, without a legitimate warrant.[36] Trump is not a tyrant according to the early definition from the Greek tragedian Euripides:

> *Nothing means more evil to a city than a tyrant.*
> *First of all, there will be no public laws*
> *but one man will have control by owning the law,*
> *himself for himself.*[37]

We certainly have "public laws" in the United States today. In Trump's first year, the courts were the biggest check on his policies. Nor is Trump a tyrant according to Socrates's definition:

> Kingship and despotism [*tyrannida*], in his judgment, were both forms of government, but he held that they differed. For government of men with their consent and in accordance with the laws of the state was kingship; while government of unwilling subjects and not controlled by laws, but imposed by the will of the ruler, was despotism.[38]

Again, Trump is controlled by laws, though the issue of consent is admittedly less certain. There are questions about the integrity of the 2016 election, including Russian interference and an Electoral College vote that did not reflect the popular vote, but no one has advanced a serious argument that, given the electoral system in place, U.S. citizens did not consent to elect Donald Trump. As the Athenian statesman Solon says in one of the oldest observations on tyranny, "The people fall through ignorance under the slavish rule of one man."[39]

Trump is implicated, however, in Aristotle's definition: "Tyranny is a kind of monarchy which has in view the interest of the monarch only."[40] Trump is not a monarch, but he exercises political power for his own benefit rather than that of the public: self-enrichment seems to be his top priority. Aristotle identifies three kinds of tyranny. In the first, a usurper gains and keeps power by force—that is not Trump. The second category consists of "elected monarchs who exercise a despotic power" (1295a)—that is closer. Aristotle's "third kind of tyranny, which is the most typical form," does and does not apply to Trump: "This tyranny is just that arbitrary power of an individual which is responsible to no one, and governs all alike, whether equals or better, with a view to its own advantage, not to that of its subjects, and therefore against their will" (1295a). Aristotle is not suggesting that the tyrant is above the law and indifferent to class; he is saying that regardless of the situation at hand, the ruler thinks first and foremost about himself, and what will profit him personally. I am convinced that this is the case with Trump, who is also implicated in the tactics of tyranny Aristotle lays out: "(1) he sows distrust among his subjects; (2) he takes away their power; (3) he humbles them" (1314a). Trump's administration fits none of the characteristics of tyranny in ancient Greece described by political theorist Roger Boesche, except the last: "rule by one person, rule over an unwilling population, arbitrary rule unrestrained by constitutional bodies, arbitrary rule unrestrained by an independent judiciary or a well-defined legal code, and rule in the interest of the tyrant and not for the general good."[41]

Boesche's last characteristic proved to be the most important in the early modern age because it was central to debates about tyrannicide. In 1556, John Ponet's *A Short Treatise of Politic Power* conveyed a Christianized Aristotelian view of tyranny in presenting "the reasons, arguments, and law that serve for the deposing and displacing of an evil governor," including Biblical examples and natural laws "not written in books, but grafted in the hearts of men," that determined that "it is lawful to kill a tyranny."[42] In 1649, John Milton's *The Tenure of Kings and Magistrates*—subtitled *Proving, That it is Lawful, and hath been held so through all Ages, for any, who have the Power, to call to account a Tyrant, or wicked KING, and after due conviction, to depose, and put him to death; if the ordinary MAGISTRATE have neglected, or denied to do it*—also presented a Christianized Aristotelian argument (through Saint Basil) defending the execution of Charles I:

> A Tyrant whether by wrong or by right coming to the crown, is he who regarding neither law nor the common good, reigns only for himself and his faction: Thus St. *Basil* among others defines him. And because his power is great, his will boundless and exorbitant, the fulfilling whereof is for the most part accompanied with innumerable wrongs and oppressions of the people, murders, massacres, rapes, adulteries, desolation, and subversion of cities and whole provinces; look how great a good and happiness a just king is, so great a mischief is a tyrant; as he the public father of his country, so this the common enemy.[43]

The royalist Thomas Hobbes scoffed, "They that are discontented under *Monarchy,* call it *Tyranny.*"[44] But John Locke pressed on in his *Second Treatise on Government* (1690):

> Tyranny is the exercise of power beyond right, which nobody can have a right to. And this is making use of the power any one has in his hands; not for the good of those who are under it, but for his own private, separate advantage. When the governor, however entitled, makes not the law, but his will, the rule, and his commands, and actions are not directed to the preservation of the properties of his people, but the satisfaction of his own ambition, revenge, covetousness, or any other irregular passion.[45]

In the Miltonic and Lockean strand, tyranny continued to be a useful concept in the shift from monarchy to democracy in the modern age.

What about the definition James Madison gave at the dawn of America in the Federalist Papers? "The accumulation of all powers, legislative, executive, and judiciary, in the same hands, whether of one, a few, or many, and whether hereditary, self-appointed or elective, may justly be pronounced the very definition of tyranny."[46] Under Madison's description, Trump is not a tyrant. Ultimately, I would say that he both is and is not. He is a tyrant in personality but not in policy. Legally, he is not a tyrant, but morally he is. Or, to put it differently, Trump is not a tyrant, but he acts like one. That makes him a good referent for Shakespeare's Julius Caesar, who (in contrast to the historical Caesar) is all personality and no policy.

VI. Are Shakespeare's Conspirators Our Politicians?

In the Public's *Caesar*, the politicians were led by *House of Cards* alumni: Corey Stoll's Brutus and Elizabeth Marvel's Mark Antony. During the assassination, the stage was set to look like the U.S. Senate chamber. Caesar, American flag on one side, presidential flag on the other, lorded over the rest of the cast from a podium, which Casca climbed to strike the first blow. Others rushed in, with Stoll's Brutus wavering off to the side, frozen in uncertainty. Henry's Caesar was pulled from the podium and thrown to the ground, where a flurry of knife strikes ripped off his suitcoat. Blood soaked his white dress shirt. Old white politicians reacted with horror in off-set balconies, helpless to stop the attack. The race- and gender-conscious casting of the conspirators led to Caesar being murdered by a group of young black men, pulling knives from their finely tailored suits, and successful career women in high heels. As Eustis explained:

> I wanted the conspirators to look and feel like the Obama coalition. They didn't really have a good idea of what to do. They didn't know how to handle this. They had a very tentative unity about how to resist. And they then make a series of disastrous choices. Something that's very much there in the play—it's not got to do with my production at all—is the repeated trope of Cassius suggesting something, and it clearly being the right thing to do, Brutus rejecting it, and Cassius saying, "OK, I'll do what you say." That happens with the question of leaving Antony alive; it happens with the question of getting Cicero on their side; it happens with letting Antony speak; and it finally happens when they decide to take the battle to Philippi. Each time, Cassius says, "Don't do this," and each time Brutus says, "No, we have to do this." And they do with disastrous consequences. And for me, the lesson there, and part of the story in the second half of the play, is about what happens when the resistance isn't unified.

Are there meaningful parallels between Shakespeare's politicians and the resistance against Trump in our time?

In the first scene, absolutely. The tribunes of the people, Flavius and Murellus, oppose the tyrant openly, wary of his mounting power. Crowns are being placed on statues of Caesar around Rome, indicating support for a campaign to elect him king; Eustis represented this campaign with graffiti and posters. Flavius and Murellus mount a counterinsurgency to "disrobe the images / If [they] do find them decked with ceremonies" (1.1.63–64). As tribunes of the people, set off against the patrician Senate, these two are ideologically aligned to the lower class, yet they are oddly condescending toward those they represent. Flavius vows to suppress the common voice, adopting a politics of hostility, partisanship, and secretive maneuvers in place of representation, education, and debate: "I'll about / And drive away the vulgar from the streets" (1.1.68–69). Caesar's supporters respond in kind: "Murellus and Flavius, for pulling scarves off Caesar's images, are put to silence" (1.2.278–279). In making Flavius (played by Chris Myers) and Murellus (Natalie Woolams-Torres) young activists of color, male and female, dressed in relaxed business-casual attire, Eustis asked the audience to see them—not implausibly—as progressives: of the people, radical lovers of liberty, fighting in the streets against demagoguery, yet still detached from and condescending toward the working-class people enthralled by the strongman celebrity turned politician.

Where the tribunes pursue open opposition, and fail, the conspirators in the Senate publicly signal support for Caesar while working behind the scenes to bring him down. Cassius is the most passionate Never Caesarer. I have argued that his hatred stems not from ideological differences but from envy. Cassius hates Caesar cause he ain't Caesar. The latter's physical weakness—the reality that contradicts the reputation—is the basis for Cassius's revulsion, hostility, and conspiracy. That is why he ends the story about Caesar's failure on the Tiber by complaining:

> *And this man*
> *Is now become a god, and Cassius is*
> *A wretched creature and must bend his body*
> *If Caesar carelessly but nod on him. (1.2.105–118)*

Cassius then alludes to Caesar's epilepsy: "How he did shake. 'Tis true, this god did shake" (1.2.121). A disgusted Cassius views Caesar "as a sick girl" (1.2.128). Shakespeare even invents another disability: his Caesar is deaf in one ear (1.2.213). How could such an unworthy man gain such status, Cassius wonders, perhaps like the Republican candidates Trump defeated in the primaries:

> *Ye gods, it doth amaze me*
> *A man of such a feeble temper should*
> *So get the start of the majestic world*
> *And bear the palm alone. (1.2.128–131)*

Repulsed by his status as "underling" (1.2.141), Cassius traces his resentment not only to Caesar's meager reality but to his own:

> *Why, man, he doth bestride the narrow world*
> *Like a Colossus, and we petty men*
> *Walk under his huge legs and peep about*
> *To find ourselves dishonorable graves. (1.2.135–138)*

If Trump resembles Caesar in the void between man and myth, his Republican primary opponents resemble Cassius in their absolute hatred of him—not because he stood against liberty but because he gathered up honor and acclaim they thought were theirs. That is why, in the all-time greatest reading of Cassius's first major speech, Tina Fey, in the film *Mean Girls,* had a petulant Valley girl paraphrase him in the middle of a high-school popularity contest:

> Why should Caesar get to stomp around like a giant? While the rest of us try not to get smushed under his BIG FEET. What's so great about Caesar? Hmm? Brutus is just as cute as Caesar. Okay, Brutus is just as smart as Caesar. People totally like Brutus just as much as they like Caesar. And when did it become okay for one person to be the boss of everybody???!? Huh!? Because that's not what Rome is about! WE SHOULD TOTALLY JUST STAB CAESAR![47]

Cassius's mean-girl quality leads me to take issue with Eustis's casting of John Douglas Thompson in the role (see Figure 5.2). Not only does the incomparably talented Thompson give Cassius more dignity than he deserves, but casting a black actor aligns Cassius, and the rest of the

Obama-coalition conspirators, with the similarly cast tribunes, as if Cassius hates Caesar for the same reason Flavius and Murellus do. If the tribunes are left-of-Caesar in their principled and open opposition to his tyranny, the conspirators, as represented by Cassius, are slightly to the right: jealous would-be Caesars threatened by his rise. I want to see the far-right conspirators of Melrose's 2012 Obama-themed production next to the Trump-themed Caesar of Eustis's version. The real parallel between Shakespeare's text and the first year of the Trump presidency was this question: *Will the senators who hate Trump in private but support him in public ever turn on him?*

Caught in the middle is Brutus, a senator from the aristocratic class, yet concerned—sincerely, thoughtfully—with the preservation of liberty and the common good, not personal glory. As someone who does "aught toward the general good" (1.2.85) and "love[s] / The name of honor" (1.2.88–89), Brutus has been "vexèd . . . / Of late" (1.2.39–40) and "with himself at war" (1.2.46) because he "fear[s] the people / Choose Caesar for their king" (1.2.79–80). Corey Stoll was perfectly cast as Brutus: he has the aura of a bright-eyed red-state Republican, born in middle America, with a schoolyard toughness, maybe educated at an Ivy League school, serious and sincere, not flashy, a little low-energy, and clearly out of his depth amid the conscienceless power politics of the capital. Brutus is easily manipulated by Cassius, who emerges as a scheming Machiavel at the end of the second scene:

> *Well, Brutus, thou art noble. Yet I see*
> *Thy honorable mettle may be wrought*
> *From that it is disposed. . . .*
> *For who so firm that cannot be seduced? (1.2.301–305)*

Eustis and I read Cassius differently. To me, he chimes so perfectly with the early modern Machiavel—resentful and conniving—that I cannot see him as a hero. "But he can equally be seen as the pragmatist of the group, far more willing to see clearly what needs to be done to succeed than Brutus is," Eustis replied. His production cut the above soliloquy because the lines in which Cassius describes a plan involving fake letters made to look like entreaties from the citizens of Rome make him sound like the cackling Vice of the morality plays. The planted letters will glance upon Caesar's ambition, but ambiguously, because Cassius knows that Brutus will be spurred to complete the thoughts and feel personal ownership over ideas hostile to Caesar. The plan is more improbable than Hamlet's *Mousetrap,* but, symbolically, it suggests that scheming aristocratic senators, publicly praising yet privately hating the tyrant, are the origin of the conspiracy to unseat him. Those far-right radicals are savvy enough to harness the cultural authority of their center-right colleagues to lend legitimacy to their scheme. Luckily for them the sincere centrists—like Brutus—are weak-minded enough to be blown around as needed. We have strayed from Eustis's conceit here, but I think that the most rigorous reading of *Julius Caesar* as applied to the Trump presidency is a hypothetical: what would happen if, after an acrimonious election, with the Democrats defeated, decimated, and silenced, corrupt and self-serving Never Trumpers on the Right sought to convince well-intentioned establishment Republicans to mount a campaign against him?

Brutus's sincerity masks his stupidity. His famous soliloquy, "It must be by his death" (2.1.10–34), is filled with what-ifs, abstractions, and confirmation bias. *There's no reason to kill Caesar,* Brutus reasons, *but a reason might someday emerge—possibly—even though I like him and trust him, so I should assume a worst-case scenario and respond in the most extreme way possible.* He replaces evidence and logic with a series of questionable metaphors. "It is the bright day that brings forth the adder." "Lowliness is young ambition's ladder." "Think him as a serpent's egg." "Fashion it thus," he says: think of it as something different from what it actually is. He convinces himself the "cause" of the conspirators is just enough "to prick [them] to redress" (2.1.122–123), using the rhetoric of patriotism to declare—quite incorrectly—that "the even virtue of [their] enterprise" (2.1.132) means that they "shall be called purgers, not murderers" (2.1.180). Whetting his knife on this vague and unconvincing patriotism—"pity to the general wrong of Rome . . . Hath done this deed on Caesar" (3.1.172–174)—Brutus does not realize that he was masterfully manipulated into political violence by conscienceless and self-serving aristocrats.

In sum, there are meaningful parallels between Shakespeare's conspirators and modern American politicians, but the Public could have handled this connection differently. First, it could have recognized that the conspirators parallel the *Republican* Party and its intraparty turmoil as it negotiated the primaries and the Trump presidency; the Democrats, an openly hostile opposition, are represented in *Julius Caesar* only by the relatively minor characters Flavius and Murellus. Costumes and casting could have more clearly reflected those alignments to indicate that the central political question of 2017 was *Will the Republicans turn on Trump?*

Second, the Public could have performed assassination as impeachment. The goal here would not be to insulate the production from controversy; rather, impeachment is the structurally parallel concept if one follows the America-as-Rome conceit. This was, in fact, the approach taken in a one-night-only romp called *Trumpus Caesar,* performed in August 2017 at the University of California, Santa Barbara, and written by theater professor Carlos Morton: "The comic premise is that Trumpus Caesar, having recently been elected Emperor by the plebeians, is impeached by a Chorus of Republican satyrs who then fight over the crown."[48] We can imagine a serious production where, during the assassination scene, instead of pantomiming a criminal act against the president of the United States, the conspirators start impeachment proceedings. Nothing in the text would need to be altered. Both before and after the assassination, the conspirators could still talk about Caesar's "death": an impeachment conviction is political death. The "O Caesar" from Cinna that starts the assassination (3.1.74) could be a disappointed Republican Speaker of the House initiating articles of impeachment. Caesar's indignant response—"Hence. Wilt thou lift up Olympus?" (3.1.75)— plays just as well in this context. Decius sorrowfully apologizes, "Great Caesar" (3.1.75), as he casts his vote for impeachment; Casca casts his vote with "Speak, hands, for me" (3.1.77). As the stage direction says, *"They stab Caesar"* (3.1.77sd) with each vote; "Et tu, Brutè?" (3.1.78) is no less powerful as the decisive vote is cast. Eustis hated this idea—"I can promise you plays bitterly resist changing their core action"—and perhaps it works better as thought experiment than performance. But if you are turning togas into business suits, nothing is stopping you from pursuing that conceptual update and turning physical death into political oblivion.

VII. Is Shakespeare's Rome Trump's America?

At early performances, according to Stoll, "isolated audience members would scoff or even applaud during the bloody, awkward, and ugly assassination scene. Two weeks in, once we refined our performances to neutralize the laughter, you could hear a pin drop."[49] Eustis recalled to me:

It was really important, as we began the show—the first 45 minutes of the show—that people would respond to it as comedy because I knew I wanted to turn it completely at the midpoint. And so Caesar's first appearance at the Lupercalia is funny because people are just laughing at the fact that he looks like Trump. Caesar's second scene in the bathtub—that's funny because I'm making it funny and, basically, it's a story about a guy being flattered into going to his own death, and that seemed to me to have a comic element. Once we were in the Senate, it ceased to be funny at all, and once the knives came out in the third act, there was just dead horror in the audience. And I can so remember, on the second preview—obviously we had a very anti-Trump audience, people laughing at Trump, applauding, feeling great about how we were sticking it to Trump—and then we got to the murder, in the second preview, and when Gregg collapsed dead, one person in the audience started to applaud, then realized that nobody else in the audience was, and just stopped. It was, to me, the perfect realization of the fact that this audience thought this was just an anti-Trump spectacle, but it's going to go someplace much darker. It's going to go someplace much more complex. And after that, once the knives came out, the show turned into a horror show; it was not a satire anymore.

Marvel's Mark Antony started out as a hard-drinking political spin artist with a southern drawl, proudly wearing an obnoxious American-flag track suit. She changed into a respectable business suit for the assassination scene. During Brutus's and Antony's orations, actors planted in the audience at the Delacorte cheered the politicians onstage, creating a sense of immersion for the actual audience. In the streamlined second half of the play, banners and graffiti proclaimed "Resist." Shakespeare's Roman mobs, portrayed as Brooklyn hipsters in Anonymous masks, squared off against Caesar's supporters in Make America Great Again hats. Thompson's Cassius donned a pussy hat. A massive cast of extras toppled over trash barrels, chanting, "No justice, no peace!" Actors playing protestors ran through the aisles; actors playing police in riot gear fired automatic weapons toward the audience. It was the police who murdered Cinna the Poet. In the battle of Philippi, the anti-Caesar resistance fought against pro-Caesar forces in tactical gear, led by Marvel's militarized Antony (Figure 5.3). Her firing squad shot

FIGURE 5.3. Elizabeth Marvel as Mark Antony in *Julius Caesar*, dir. Oskar Eustis
(New York: Delacorte Theater in Central Park, 2017).
(Photograph by Joan Marcus.)

the conspirators one by one. Then she handed off power to the new emperor of Rome, Octavius, played by Robert Gilbert as a slick young upstart, his blazer covered with a flak jacket and sunglasses, an outfit recently worn by presidential son-in-law Jared Kushner.

Are there meaningful parallels between the Roman mobs in *Julius Caesar* and recent U.S. political activists? After being called "you blocks, you stones, you worse than senseless things" at the start of the play (1.1.34), the crowd is shown to be a fickle mess. They support Pompey, then Caesar. They celebrate Caesar joyously, then skulk away meekly when chastised by the tribunes. They oppose Caesar becoming king, then embrace him. They cheer Brutus's defense of the assassination, then swing to Antony's side.

At the Public, there was no Shakespearean mob lurching from side to side. Instead, there were two deeply divided subcultures equally entrenched in their own ideologies. To Eustis, making part of the mob stand against the senators was key:

You know, Yeats's quote "The best lack all conviction, while the worst are full of passionate intensity" definitely applies to the relationship between the conspirators on the one hand and the mob on the other hand. And, of course, that was one of the big reasons I was attracted to the play. It wasn't just Trump as an individual political figure. It was the fact that Trump had brought the mass campaign rally back into our political toolkit. What I think Trump understood is that, in this era, when so much of our stewing happens in the monad isolation of the internet, bringing a group of people together so they can feel the power of being part of a crowd is a hugely galvanizing force. I just think he got that in a way that progressives didn't get at all.

In the end, to put it as bluntly as possible, the logic of Eustis's production was this: in a deeply divided country, where the Right loves and the Left hates an arrogant celebrity turned strongman politician who is, paradoxically, a member of the urban elite yet populist in self-presentation, dispossessed and vengeful radicals on the far Left manage to enlist centrist lovers of liberty in a coup to remove the mounting tyrant. The ugliness of this revolt, lingering love for the celebrity, and the power vacuum left by his removal allow a bizarre far-right coalition of upper-class plutocrats and resentful lower-class revolutionaries to turn the defeated celebrity into a martyr. This rightist coalition campaigns to end corrupt politics-as-usual by replacing representative democracy with a permanent monarch, whose harsh law-and-order policies deprive individual citizens of their liberties and right to participate in government.

That leads to the big question everyone was asking.

VIII. Does *Julius Caesar* Argue For or Against Tyrannicide?

The answer many Shakespeareans would give is *No.*

Trained in the classical rhetorical strategy of argument *in utramque partem,* "on both sides," playwrights in Shakespeare's world wrote works that pose questions rather than answers. This attitude toward art is distilled in the poet Philip Sidney's claim, in the most important literary treatise of the Elizabethan age, that literature "nothing affirms."[50] It is bold to say that literature makes no claims about the world, but that is also the idea underwriting Hamlet's statement about "the purpose of playing, whose end both at the first and now was and is to hold as 'twere the mirror up to nature" (*Hamlet*, 3.1.19–20). Literature reflects reality; it does not argue politics. Thus, citing Shakespeare, John Keats said that the best literature identifies for us the questions that need to be asked, then allows us to answer them ourselves. Keats called this Shakespeare's "Negative Capability": "that is, when a man is capable of being in uncertainties, Mysteries, doubts, without any irritable reaching after fact and reason."[51] Eustis views theater the same way: "That's what people who don't understand or attend the theater don't get: the theater isn't a place where you make logical arguments. The theater isn't good at reporting facts or headlines, and the theater really isn't good at presenting positive role models. That's not what it's there to do. The theater is a place where you act out impulses, act out desires and visions in order to see what becomes of them."

Accordingly, most Shakespeareans see *Julius Caesar* as politically ambiguous—not partisan, not ideologically driven, allowing different readings. Arguably, Shakespeare's entire dramatic strategy is encapsulated in one key moment, Brutus's and Antony's funeral orations, where the onstage audience wrestles with competing—mutually compelling yet mutually exclusive—interpretations. But critics make a mistake, I feel, when they defiantly proclaim that Shakespeare has no political agenda. Yes, *Julius Caesar* makes tyrannicide both appealing and disgusting, advocating neither for nor against it. But we should not jump from that observation to the claim that the play is ambivalent or open to all sides—make of it what you will—because it has no substantive political message. The play fiercely affirms a political message, but it is an analytical message about what happens in certain circumstances and why, not a polemical message about how we should lead our lives. It is a message about the causes and effects of radical political violence.

IX. What Are the Causes and Effects of Radical Political Violence in *Julius Caesar*?

At the beginning of the play, before we even get to the conspiracy, *Julius Caesar* shows two things that emerge in the aftermath of civil war: a strongman hero and a populace ready to worship him. Women are sidelined and ignored. An impoverished working class becomes a nebulous mob, light-hearted and excitable, pathetically abject and fickle. They are desperate for a hero to lift their spirits, servile and submissive when chastised by the elite. Thus, the talented, successful, and heroic general who has defeated his opponent comes home to find himself a celebrity. He starts believing his own hype and acting like the demigod of the people's imagination—a self-willed, self-assured, self-satisfied, and self-aggrandizing persona that quickly becomes absolutist, arrogant, proud, and reckless. Those who know him best feel that the reputation does not match reality. He is actually weak in body and mind; he has no political values; his only commitment is to his own greatness. Anxious to squash doubters, eager to make reputation reality, he hires political operatives who understand, much better than he does, how to orchestrate political theater and manufacture public sentiment. He is a good actor. Once his minions set the scene, he can play to the people. He is thirsty for power, authority, and recognition, but able to feign nobility and humility.

Although the people do not want him as king—all they really want is food in their bellies and a good time—they are fragile enough to be easily manipulated by well-moneyed political professionals. The people do not even know what the hero stands for, other than winning. For many, that's enough. Since this is a democracy, support from the people becomes support from their political representatives. The Senate plans to change the form of government to give the rising tyrant more power and authority. Yet here the Senate is remarkably silent: this supposed majority is never heard from in Shakespeare's play. The senators we hear are displeased with the centralization of power in one man but unwilling or unable to engage in public debate. The only open resistance comes from a small set of senators willing to play dirty, and they suffer two setbacks. First, they are just as arrogant and manipulative toward the working class as their opponents, and, second, their resistance is reeled in by the forces of law and order under the tyrant's control. The small number of independent-minded senators who refuse to go along with the conspiracy to depose the tyrant—the Ciceros of the world—are ineffective in their feeble opposition to him.

Here is the situation in modern terms. A celebrity whose only value is personal ambition (Julius Caesar) seeks to increase his power and prestige. Officials on the Left (Flavius and Murellus) offer principled but weak opposition. There is an impoverished working class (the crowds) whose desperation is easily manipulated by politicians on the Left and the Right. On the Right, cynical career politicians resentful of the celebrity's success and opposed to his entire project (Cassius) are engaged in debate with sincere lovers of liberty worried about the damage a tyrant can do to the public good (Brutus). A political operative on the far Right (Mark Antony) is willing to exploit the celebrity and change the form of government from democracy to monarchy for no other reason, it seems, than to consolidate the wealth and power of their circle of friends.

Antony's primary quality is loyalty. He values not freedom, honor, or even money, but simply the tyrant himself. He stands against the conspirators, but, because the government system has changed, that is not the same as standing for peaceful politics; it means standing up for monarchy. Antony romanticizes the tyrant, turns him into a martyr, and seeks out a successor in his image. He becomes duplicitous, manipulating the freedom fighters, doing to Cassius what Cassius did to others. He claims to enter into good-faith politics with opponents, while actually whipping up mutiny from the mob. His rhetoric incites vengeance, not virtue. He creates violent rebellion against the violent rebels, becoming a prophet of chaos, anarchy, and havoc. The joylessness of the second half of the play, where the conspirators turn against each other, then fall to the tyrant's heir, who promises order and stability but offers only anger, represents the shift in quality of life that occurs in the transition from democracy to empire. That's why, amid the Public Theater controversy, Shakespeare scholar Andrew Hartley told CNN, "To me, the Trump figure is Antony, not Caesar."[52]

The energy of the first half of *Julius Caesar* comes from the interplay between three forces—a mounting tyrant, a feeble political opposition, and a desperate populace. My argument, in sum, is that all three descend from civil war: discord engulfs a state's citizens, its political leaders, politicians in general, its system of government, and the society itself, which becomes a shadow of what it was. To the extent that a bitter and divisive election is a civil war of sorts—a culture war rather than a military one—Shakespeare's vision of postwar politics was startlingly relevant in 2017.

Who will be responsible for removing Trump from office? Not the Left, whose opposition—like Flavius and Murellus's—is already out in the open yet feeble. Effective opposition will come only from the Right, the heirs of Barry Goldwater. That is why the July 2018 cartoon in the *New Yorker* was such a good reading of *Julius Caesar*: Trump, on his knees, is saying, "Et tu, Cohen?" to his former attorney, who had turned on him by releasing damaging audio recordings.[53] And what will happen to the Republicans after they rid themselves of Trump? The same thing that happens to Shakespeare's conspirators, if we follow the analogy from physical to political war. They will be democratically unseated, one by one. The Republican Party (not the entire nation) will then fall into the hands of far-right radicals.

And seeing civil war as the origin of tragedy in *Julius Caesar* helps us answer our next question.

X. What Did Shakespeare Believe about Tyranny?

This is the question Stephen Greenblatt asks in his book *Tyrant*.[54] Emphasizing the *Henry VI* trilogy, *Richard III, Macbeth, King Lear,* and *Coriolanus,* he shows how tyrants come to power in Shakespearean tragedy through a combustible mixture of economic inequality, political partisanship, self-serving enablers, and incompetent demagogues. Greenblatt has less to say about what happens once Shakespeare's tyrants are in power, in part because his account of *Julius Caesar* is thin. I think he misreads the mixture of egotism and stupidity in the conspiracy as "a systematic, principled attempt to stop tyranny before it starts" (147). The most forceful of the brisk seven pages he devotes to *Julius Caesar* points out, chillingly, "Caesar is dead, but by the end of the play Caesarism is triumphant" (154). The devastating permanence of that fact, and Shakespeare's unflinching insistence upon it, render Greenblatt's effort to end his book on a note of optimism odd: "He was not without hope," he says, sentimentalizing some Shakespearean investment in the glorious mystery of the human spirit, "the sheer unpredictability of collective life, its refusal to march in lockstep to any one person's orders"—which (we are asked to believe) insulates us from tyrants (187–188). I sympathize with the effort to find a modicum of hope in Shakespearean tragedy, but the assertion that a tyrant cannot remain in power for long is hardly grounds for optimism, considering the lasting damage a tyrant can do in the short time he reigns. Thus, Greenblatt's final words in the book, a misty-eyed celebration of individual acts of courage by ordinary citizens, are unfulfilling:

> The best chance for the recovery of collective decency lay, [Shakespeare] thought, in the political action of ordinary citizens. He never lost sight of the people who steadfastly remained

silent when they were exhorted to shout their support for the tyrant, or the servant who tried to stop his vicious master from torturing a prisoner, or the hungry citizen who demanded economic justice. (189)

These allusions are delusions: the "people" in *Richard III* are bulldozed into subjugation by a plot to make Richard king; the "servant" in *King Lear* is immediately killed for his resistance; and the "citizen" in *Coriolanus* is berated into silence by a strongman politician. It is telling that this paragraph contains no allusion to *Julius Caesar,* Shakespeare's most pessimistic play (more pessimistic even than *King Lear*). A full account of Shakespeare's vision of tyranny would need to return in the end to unflinching tragedy: *But it is also possible that the greatest democracy in the history of the world up to that point can be changed, permanently, to limit the freedom and happiness of its subjects. Civil society usually finds a way to survive, but history offers examples of absolute tragedies that extinguish joy for centuries.*

XI. Why Was the Public Theater's *Julius Caesar* Controversial?

Our heading for this section could have been "Do Madonna, Snoop Dogg, Kathy Griffin, and Joe Piscopo appear in this story?" Yes they do.

The day after Trump's inauguration, Madonna told the Women's March on Washington that she had "thought an awful lot about blowing up the White House."[55] Former Speaker of the House Newt Gingrich said on *Fox and Friends* that she should be arrested. Two months later, Snoop Dogg released a music video in which he fires a toy pistol at the head of a clown costumed like Trump. Senator Marco Rubio is apparently a Snoop Dogg fan but chided, "We've got to be careful about that kind of thing because the wrong person sees that and gets the wrong idea and you could have a real problem."[56] Two months later—one week into previews of *Julius Caesar* at the Delacorte—comedian Kathy Griffin did a photoshoot holding a mockup of Trump's bloody, decapitated head. She quickly apologized but was fired as co-host of CNN's New Year's Eve program and disinvited from other events. Asked by the *New York Times* if the controversy made him queasy, Eustis said: "We noticed, and we went, 'Whoops!' But, of course, we knew we weren't doing anything like that. We were doing Shakespeare in the Park, for God's sake."[57]

The day after the Kathy Griffin controversy broke, May 31, CNN anchor Fareed Zakaria tweeted: "If you're in NYC, go see Julius Caesar, free in Central Park, brilliantly interpreted for Trump era. A masterpiece."[58] Four days later, a conservative media executive named Laura Sheaffer saw the play. On June 6, she voiced her displeasure in a radio interview with former actor turned talk-show host Joe Piscopo (who was weirdly fixated on the notion that, as a midwesterner, Sheaffer must have been shaken to her core by the onstage nudity). In a later interview with the conservative website *Mediaite*, Sheaffer said: "I don't love President Trump, but he's the president. You can't assassinate him on a stage."[59] The interview was picked up by conservative media, including *Breitbart*, *The Blaze*, and *Newsbusters*, their coverage written by political pundits who never saw the performance and were not very knowledgeable about the play (according to *Breitbart*, Caesar is stabbed in Act V).[60] A more informed but still disapproving review came on June 9 from Kyle Smith at *National Review*, including one of the best lines about the production: "Hey, it's . . . Orange Julius!"[61]

By that time, the Public was receiving threats. Security was increased. The cast was shaken, on edge. The Eustis family was being threatened at home. Eustis's wife filed a police report on June 9. Someone called their home eight or nine times in half an hour, then again several times the next day. "Your husband wants Trump to die. I want *him* to die," he told Eustis's wife. "It's sexual attacks on my mother," Eustis's daughter recalled. "'Grab her by the p—y,' raping her—threats on me, and physical threats on my father's life." [62] I asked Eustis what it was like to have that danger come into his home:

> It was awful, but I will say that my wife and daughter are really strong, courageous people, and they never suggested that I should do something different. I can promise you neither of them enjoyed the experience. And they both heartily wish the experience doesn't happen again. But neither of them have said to me, "You shouldn't have done that. Don't do that again." And I don't think they even thought it. I think—I hope—on some level they're proud to have been part of this.

How did it come to this? How did we get from people playing pretend in costumes to "I want him to die"?

In an essay published at the height of the controversy, Eustis's mentee, Rob Melrose—director of the 2012 Obama *Caesar*—put his finger on the origin of the controversy: "Most people who wrote about and talked about our production . . . actually *saw* the show, where it is clear that most of those outraged by The Public Theater's Trumpian emperor either didn't see the play or didn't stay to the end."[63] A year later, Eustis echoed those thoughts to me:

> I assumed—and this is where my naivety came in—I assumed that it would be controversial, not really with our audience, but that there would be some kind of debate about the production. What I completely didn't understand was that the debate was not going to be about my production. The debate was going to be about images from my production upon which a false narrative was created. And that's what *Breitbart* and then *Fox* did: they got access to a little illegal video of the show, and then the story they told was really simple. The story they told was: "Manhattan elites are cheering when President Trump is stabbed to death in Central Park." And there's no truth to that. They weren't cheering. They were sitting in horror watching it happen. There was no understanding. One of the early counterprotesters had a big sign that said, "Read the Fucking Play," which I admired.

XII. Why Did Corporate Sponsors Pull Out of Free Shakespeare in the Park?

On June 11, a Fox News story reported that "a New York City play appears to depict President Trump being brutally stabbed to death by women and minorities." The report buried the fact that the play was Shakespeare's *Julius Caesar,* taught every year in thousands of high schools in the United States.[64] Roping in the Kathy Griffin story, *Fox and Friends* ran multiple segments on the production. After seeing the story, Donald Trump Jr. tweeted, "I wonder how much of this 'art' is funded by taxpayers? Serious question, when does 'art' become political speech & does that change things?"[65] Delta Airlines discontinued its sponsorship of Shakespeare in the Park later that day, issuing the following statement: "The graphic staging of 'Julius Caesar' at this summer's Free Shakespeare in the Park does not reflect Delta Air Lines' values. Their artistic and creative direction crossed the line."[66] That night, Bank of America pulled support of this particular production, though it continued supporting the organization: "The Public Theater chose to present *Julius Caesar* in a way that was intended to provoke and offend. Had this intention been made known to us, we would have decided not to sponsor it."[67] The next day, American Express issued a statement saying that it had not supported the production, "nor do we condone the interpretation of the *Julius Caesar* play."[68] The Public battened down the hatches, declining to comment on stories and asking trustees to do the same.

Why did corporate sponsors drop out, especially when they did not run from earlier politicized productions of *Julius Caesar*? For one thing, the Public's *Caesar* was a higher-profile production. That matters because sponsors dropped out for financial, rather than ethical, reasons: they were less concerned about the offensiveness of an onstage pantomime of killing a sitting president of the United States, and more concerned about losing business from bad publicity. Sponsors did not drop out early in previews when they saw what the Public was doing; they dropped out when they saw what people were saying about it. That publicity came about because, as argued earlier, there are actual parallels between Caesar and Trump that were not present in earlier politicized Caesars. Those parallels matter because there were actual feelings of violent hostility toward Trump, and there was a real danger that someone might act on those feelings. For a corporation to be affiliated with a provocative theatrical production cited in an attempt on the president's life—however unintentional and distorted this connection might be—would be very bad for business.

XIII. How Much of This "Art" Was Funded by Taxpayers?

Here's a sentence I never thought I would write: conceptually, Shakespeareans never quite caught up to Donald Trump Jr. His questions were big ones, and smart ones, and ones I did not know the answers to until I looked them up. When does art become political speech? Legally, what makes something "political speech"? Are there limits on it when government funding is involved?

The First Amendment states, "Congress shall make no law . . . abridging the freedom of speech." U.S. citizens are free to create and enjoy—or not—any art they like. But the creation of art is also subsidized by the government because, like the military, art is a public good. It benefits the whole culture: even the street vendor who does not want to go to the Public Theater will gladly sell tacos to someone who does, and will benefit from taxes collected from theatergoers. Declaring that "the arts and the humanities belong to all the people of the United States," Congress passed the Arts and Humanities Act of 1965, declaring it "necessary and appropriate for the Federal Government to complement, assist, and add to programs for the advancement of the humanities and the arts."[69] The act established the National Endowment for the Arts (NEA) to provide stipends to deserving artists and museums, noting that "public funding of the arts and humanities is subject to the conditions that traditionally govern the use of public money."

NEA policies did not apply to the Public's *Caesar* for the simple reason that no NEA funds supported it. NEA policy is administered on a case-by-case basis; an organization accepting NEA funding for projects A, B, and C does not need to conform to NEA standards for unsupported projects X, Y, and Z. Organizations receiving federal money retain First Amendment rights, though that money cannot be used for political purposes; for that they must use nonfederal money. That would be a lawyer's defense of the Public's *Caesar*, but we can pursue the matter beyond the law into the concepts in play. Should an artistic organization that frequently receives government funding be prohibited from producing politically provocative art? Should the government be in the business of supporting distasteful or dangerous art? Or, more to the point, should the NEA deny funds to the Public Theater in the future?

Subsidized speech raises two First Amendment questions. First, are subsidized speakers agents of the government? Second, does the government have its own freedom of speech? The late 1980s saw a series of controversies about the regulation of publicly funded art that some found offensive, followed by a flurry of legislative proposals for content restrictions. Most were defeated, but in 1989 Congress passed a law stating that "none of the funds authorized to be appropriated for the National Endowment for the Arts . . . may be used to promote, disseminate, or produce materials which in the judgment of the National Endowment for the Arts . . . may be considered obscene."[70] In 1991, the NEA requirement that grant recipients certify that they would not produce "obscene" art was ruled unconstitutional (too vague and overbroad to pass muster under the Fifth Amendment's due-process clause, with a chilling effect on artists that violated the First Amendment's guarantee of freedom of speech). The NEA amended its language to say that "artistic excellence and artistic merit are the criteria by which applications are judged, taking into consideration general standards of decency and respect for the diverse beliefs and values of the American public."[71] In 1992, this policy was challenged by the NEA Four, a group of artists whose applications were vetoed because of the "decency and respect" provision. The Supreme Court upheld the constitutionality of the "decency and respect" clause but blunted its teeth, saying that "decency and respect" only need to be considered; they are not determining factors. More recently, however, arguments have suggested that the real First Amendment issues here are the rights of the NEA itself, an agency designed to promote the free exchange of ideas and to be insulated from partisan politics.

To be clear, the Supreme Court has repeatedly ruled that the government has no obligation to subsidize art or free speech. As lawyer Kathleen Sullivan explained in her 1991 testimony before Congress, however, "The First Amendment bars government from establishing a National Endowment for the Arts and saying that only the orthodox and the conformist need apply."[72]

XIV. When Does Art Become Political Speech, and Does That Change Things?

Trump Jr.'s tweet was an amateur attempt to enforce the Hatch Act. Passed in 1939 to fight political corruption by prohibiting federal employees from engaging in partisan political activity, the Hatch Act was extended in 1940 to state and local employees funded by the federal government. It does not apply to the Trump-themed *Caesar* on the obvious grounds that the Public is not a government entity. It receives federal funding, but it is a private nonprofit organization. Its employees are not government employees, so they are not barred from partisan political speech. That is the legal reason the Hatch Act does not apply; again, we can venture into conceptual terrain, for the Hatch Act can help Trump Jr., and others, determine when something becomes "political speech."

The Hatch Act says that government employees may "express opinions about candidates and issues" and "participate in campaigns where none of the candidates represent a political party," but may not "campaign for or against a candidate or slate of candidates in partisan elections," "make campaign speeches," or "organize or manage political rallies or meetings."[73] The Public's production did not throw support behind or against a candidate for office. When does a creative representation telling a story to entertain and provoke an audience become a statement advocating action? According to the Hatch Act, when it is "activity directed at the success or failure of a political party, candidate for partisan political office, or partisan political group."[74]

We now have answers to Trump Jr.'s three questions. "How much of this 'art' is funded by taxpayers?" None—if it had been, it would have raised concerns about the "decency and respect" provision of the NEA guidelines, but that provision also raises concerns about the institutional First Amendment rights of the NEA as an organization. "When does 'art' become political speech?" When it advocates for or against a candidate or party on partisan grounds, but not when it expresses ideas about politics, even if they are critical. "Does that change things?" No, the Public's First Amendment rights are not limited because it is not a government entity covered by the Hatch Act, and *Julius Caesar* was not supported by NEA funds.

XV. How Did People Respond to the Controversy at the Public Theater?

On the night of June 11, conservative critics like Fox News contributor Mike Huckabee sounded off in support of the corporate sponsors who had dropped the Public Theater: "Kudos to @Delta for pulling $$ from 'play' portraying assassination of @POTUS. No one should sponsor crap like that!"[75] The partisan back-and-forth was on. Counter-tweets came in from the likes of *House of Cards* writer Beau Willimon ("Disappointed in @Delta for turning its back on free expression. I've flown many thousands of miles with you. No more")[76] and author Joyce Carol Oates ("Have plans to see 'Julius Caesar' (Shakespeare-in-the-Park) in thrilled defiance of ignorant would-be censors").[77] Audiences inside the Delacorte may have been giddy about trolling Trump, but many interviewed outside the theater thought the play was disrespectful. Theater critic Frank Scheck echoed that attitude in a June 11 review for the *Hollywood Reporter:* "How about laying off mock representations of the murder of the president?"[78] Other early reviews were similarly unimpressed. A hostile first wave of responses was followed by a defensive second wave, aware of the gathering storm and intent on refocusing attention away from the spectacle of Caesar's assassination and back on the logic of the whole play and its critique of political violence. A clear trend emerged suggesting that the Public had done something very wrong.

Conservative critics noted that the Public's sponsors included the *New York Times* and *New York* magazine and saw signs of a conspiracy by liberal media to promote violence against Trump. On the night of June 11, in a statement to the Associated Press, Eustis stood his ground and sought to bring some nuance to the controversy:

> Anyone seeing our production of "Julius Caesar" will realize it in no way advocates violence towards anyone. . . . We recognize that our interpretation of the play has provoked heated discussion; audiences, sponsors and supporters have expressed varying viewpoints and opinions. Such discussion is exactly the goal of our civically engaged theater; this discourse is the basis of a healthy democracy.[79]

The Public issued a similar statement the next day, and a chorus of voices repeated those points. Fascinatingly, responses to the production—first it was seen as a call to action against tyranny, later as a reflection on the dangers of political violence—mirror an audience's usual response to the two halves of the play, as well as the development in Eustis's conceptualization of his production, and even the attitude on the Left during the first year of the Trump administration.

And then—after all this—opening night arrived on June 12. Before the show, a slightly defiant Eustis addressed the audience from the stage:

> Hamlet said, "The purpose of playing, from the first til today, was and is, to hold up as 'twere, a mirror to nature, to show the age his form and pressure." (Excuse the male pronoun: that's what he used.) That's what we do here in the theater: We try to hold a mirror up to nature. It's what Shakespeare was doing; it's what we're doing. When we hold the mirror up to nature, often what we reveal are disturbing, upsetting, provoking things. Thank God. That's our job. Anybody who watches this play tonight—and I'm sorry, there's going to be a couple of spoiler alerts here—but will know that neither Shakespeare nor the Public Theater could possibly advocate violence as a solution to

political problems, and certainly not assassination. This play, on the contrary, warns about what happens when you try to preserve democracy by nondemocratic means, and again, spoiler alert: It doesn't end up too good. But at the same time, one of the dangers that is unleashed by that is the danger of a large crowd of people, manipulated by their emotions, taken over by leaders who urge them to do things that not only are against their interest, but destroy the very institutions that are there to serve and protect them. This warning is a warning that's in this show, and we're really happy to be playing that story for you tonight. What I also want to say, and in this I speak, I am proud to say, for the Public Theater past, present, and, I hope, future; for the staff of the Public Theater; for the crews of the Public Theater; for the board of directors at the Public Theater; and for Patrick Willingham and myself when I say that we are here to uphold the Public's mission. And the Public's mission is to say that the culture belongs to everybody, needs to belong to everybody. To say that art has something to say about the great civic issues of our time, and to say that like drama, democracy depends on the conflict of different points of view. Nobody owns the truth—we all own the culture. Welcome to the Public, welcome to *Julius Caesar*.[80]

In an interview with the *New York Times* that night, Eustis played it cool. He declined opportunities to criticize corporate sponsors, assured everyone that the lost sponsorship would not affect operations at the Public, and affirmed his satisfaction with the show.[81] A year later, speaking with me, he was more reflective:

I think my response was inadequate. In terrifically classy PBS fashion, I got out on opening night and told everybody to take out their phones and film me, and I made a beautifully reasoned Brutus-like statement about how noble our intentions were. And, man, I think my base just thought I was the coolest thing. And I think, outside of that base, nobody even knew I talked. It was a non-event. And what I should have done, I realize now, is that the second it appeared on Fox, I should have started screaming that Hannity had to put me on and let me talk. I don't know if he would have or wouldn't have but, whatever would have happened, even if he had humiliated me, that would have been a more effective response because I would have been talking to the people who were actually protesting. And again, I think the people—and there were tens, maybe hundreds of thousands of people who took action, at one point calling Delta, American Express, and Bank of America and telling them to withdraw their sponsorship, to the other extreme of sending death threats to my family and slipping death threats under my front door, calling my daughter's cell phone and threatening violence against her, really bad shit—but all of those people didn't hear a word I said, or didn't know I responded. We didn't respond to them. We responded to our base, who love us, and isn't that nice that they love us. But it does nothing to try and actually make a dialogue between the bitterly divided poles in this country.

In a remarkable approximation of the progression of interpretation that *Julius Caesar* evokes from audiences, Eustis came to see his initial instinct to defend his production with passion and dignity as a politically ineffective response—one that appealed to a certain constituency yet left unresolved the larger cultural tensions driving the conflict.

XVI. Why Did People Protest the Public Theater's *Julius Caesar*?

Two days after opening night, on June 14, Congressman Steve Scalise was shot by an anti-Republican activist while practicing, with his Republican team, for the annual congressional charity baseball game. A congressional aide, a lobbyist, and a police officer were also shot. Within hours, Trump Jr. retweeted a comment from a Trump ally: "Events like today are EXACTLY why we took issue with NY elites glorifying the assassination of our President."[82] Publicly blamed, by the president's son, for a mass shooting, the cast of *Julius Caesar* grew fearful about going on stage.

The next day, June 15, conservative social media activist Mike Cernovich announced a reward for disrupting the play: "I need you to get up with either a 'CNN is ISIS' . . . or 'Bill Clinton's a rapist' or 'the media is terrorism,' and if you're able to get up and be escorted out by security then I will give you $1,000."[83] That night, a protestor standing in the park outside the theater shouted insults at the cast for the first hour of the show. At the end of the performance, Stoll recalled, "a man

FIGURE 5.4. Laura Loomer on Fox News on June 19, 2017, with inset of Loomer protesting *Julius Caesar* at the Delacorte Theater in New York on June 16, 2017.

wearing an American-flag jacket who had politely sat through the play stood and unfurled a Trump 2020 flag."[84] Stoll said they caught each other's eye, and exchanged respectful smiles.

The next night, June 16, just after the assassination, at Cinna's line, "Liberty! Freedom! Tyranny is dead!" (3.1.79), a young woman with bleached blond hair—she later identified herself on social media as Laura Loomer—walked up on stage rather nonchalantly and began berating the audience: "Stop the normalization of political violence against the right! . . . This is violence against Donald Trump" (Figure 5.4).[85] Initially, the cast and audience were stunned, unsure what to make of it; then, from the audience, someone yelled, not angrily, but annoyed that his Shakespeare was being interrupted, "Get off the stage!" The stage manager calmly announced, "Ladies and gentlemen, we're going to pause. Security. Security, please." The audience jeered and booed, drowning out Loomer as she shouted and wagged her finger at them.

On a video that Loomer was live-streaming online, you could hear her shouting through the boos, "You guys are ISIS! CNN is ISIS!"[86] She was surrounded and led away by security guards as the audience applauded. Outside the theater, she continued to scream: "This is an active attempt to get Donald Trump assassinated! . . . They are actually enacting their thought-out plan to kill Donald Trump!" As police ushered her out of the park, still streaming, one person approached her to say, "I just want to voice my support for what you did. Thank you." Seconds later, someone in the background can be heard saying, "Who's this crazy bitch?"

Later in the video, after calming down, Loomer fought back tears to explain to a few people drawn in by the spectacle, with a shake in her voice, "They would never ever depict an assassination of President Obama or any Democratic leader." She was arrested and charged with criminal trespassing and disorderly conduct. Soon the hashtag #Free-Laura was trending on Twitter as she used the website to make a fundraising appeal. It was later discovered that FreeLaura.com, a site that raised funds to cover her legal fees, was purchased on the day of the protest, six hours before the play began, by Ezra Levant, the far-right Canadian founder of the pro-Trump website *The Rebel Media*.[87] Loomer had just started at *Rebel,* having previously worked for political stunt artist James O'Keefe's Project Veritas, famous for largely incompetent exposé sting operations against liberal groups. Later that night, somebody made a $1,000 donation to Loomer's defense fund.[88]

During Loomer's protest, the actors, shaken out of their roles, milled about onstage. "We're not promoting it," one calmly told her. "This is *Julius Caesar.*" A man in the audience, who later identified himself as Jack Posobiec, had been recording Loomer's protest. He stood up, turned his camera on himself, and began shouting, "You are all Goebbels. You are all Nazis like Joseph Goebbels. This is Goebbels. You are all Joseph Goebbels. You are inciting terrorists. The blood of Steve Scalise is on your hands. The blood of Steve Scalise is on your hands. Goebbels would be proud. Goebbels would be proud. Goebbels would be proud." Loomer and Posobiec had seen each other in the audience before the show. They texted instead of talking, to avoiding drawing attention to themselves. "Are you here for the Cernovich contest?" he asked. "Just stay tuned," she replied.[89] Posobiec himself worked at Levant's *Rebel Media* until the end of May 2017. He was most widely known as a leading peddler of the Pizzagate story, which alleged that Hillary Clinton was running a child sex ring out of a Washington, DC, pizzeria. Posobiec had also recently claimed that Clinton was involved in the murder of Seth Rich, a Democratic National Committee staffer; the story got him fired from *Rebel*. The Delacorte audience did not know any of this; to them, he was just a guy shouting about gerbils. Once he was escorted out, the stage manager announced, "Actors, let's pick it up from 'liberty and freedom.'" The line got a life-affirming standing ovation.

Loomer and Posobiec met up later that night in a restaurant near the police station.[90] They giddily scrolled through their Twitter feeds. They could not wait to post, as Posobiec did the next day: "One of the NYPD: 'Look, we're just doing our jobs, but we are behind you guys 100%.'"[91] They proudly read Fox News commentator Laura Ingram's tweet: "The Left doesn't like it when their tactics are used against their 'expression.' How many wd storm stage if 'Obama' was stabbed?"[92] The answer, as we know, is zero. They reveled in Loomer's 20,000 new Twitter followers and clumsily game-planned their social media response to conservative commentators already denouncing the stunt as "obnoxious stupid snowflake crap."[93] They were hoping to raise $25,000.[94] Posobiec beamed: "This is gonna go down as the greatest production of *Julius Caesar* in history." Loomer agreed: "I redefined Shakespeare tonight."

Security was increased at the Delacorte. Tensions ran high for the final two shows. On June 17, protestors stood outside the theater holding signs saying, "Far Left Hates America," "Boo the Cast," and "Shut It Down."[95] Inside the theater, someone opening an umbrella was rushed by security, but it was a false alarm. There were no disruptions to the performance that night.

There were two on June 18.[96] In the first five minutes of the play, a protester ran on stage yelling, "Liberal hate kills! Goebbels would be proud! Goebbels would be proud!" Within seconds, five security guards and two police officers rushed him. "Ladies and gentlemen, we'll pause here," the stage manager announced, her voice a little shakier than last time. Surrounded, the protestor resisted and continued chanting, marching back and forth on stage. "Wow," an audience member deadpanned in disbelief; the audience booed the protester as he was led away, his hands restrained by security guards clearly trained for such moments. "Actors, let's pick up please with, 'It is no matter,'" the stage manager announced, pointing to Flavius's next line (1.1.67), to cheers of joy. During the assassination scene, another protester rushed through the audience yelling, "We're sick of your bullshit! Goebbels would be proud!" He took the stage at a full sprint, barreling past an actor who tried to stop him. It was nerve-wracking. There was panic in the stage manager's voice—"Hold. Hold. Hold." He was quickly tackled, restrained, and removed.

XVII. What Is It Like to Be Threatened Because of Your Art?

On June 19, a *Vanity Fair* story reported that Shakespeare acting companies across the United States were getting death threats in response to the media coverage of the controversy: "Apparently, vitriolic people are lazily Googling 'Shakespeare in the Park,' then messaging threats to the first result they see."[97] I asked Eustis what it was like for him and his team to find themselves in physical danger because of their art:

> What I honestly felt was that there was a real distinction between me and much of the staff. I felt great about it. I felt invigorated and excited: we were doing something real. And it was very shocking to me to realize how scared my staff was. We had a meeting about a month after *Caesar* closed where the staff let us know how upset they were. There was a lot of tears, a lot of anger. People felt really, really upset. So some of that, I think, is my insensitivity, but some of it is also, I think, a generational thing. My generation of radicals was brought up with the idea that *of course* we were going to be in danger if we protested. I've been thrown in jail; I've had ribs broken by billy clubs. That's what you do when you protest: you run into danger. And I feel like we've got a generation of young people now—and this is not true of all of them—who simultaneously are able to say to me, "No, no, no, don't withdraw one bit from how provocative and radical the art is. No, no, we're not saying that. We're just saying you have to create a completely safe space for us within that." And to me that's very characteristic of this generation—again, not of everybody—and me having to say, 'Guys, there's no such thing. I can't create a space of no danger for you. We're doing theater. We're doing theater for free in the park. If people want to do us harm, there's no amount of metal detectors or cavity searches in the world that will prevent them from doing that.' For my staff, the fact that there were people on the internet offering cash rewards to anybody who would physically interrupt the show was really frightening to them. And I get that it was frightening, but I also think that there's this completely illusory idea of safety that, frankly, some of us on the Left have promulgated—the universities, for example—the idea that there can be

safe spaces where nobody will be hurt. What world is that? And the argument we have a lot—and, because I run the place, I've kind of won—is to say, no, we are not going to search people coming into Free Shakespeare in the Park. I'll let you look in their bags. But we're not going to have metal detectors. We're not going to have body searches. We're not going to have police presence. We know that there is a real percentage of our audience that is undocumented. If you put police standing at those gates, they won't come to the theater. And we are not going to turn ourselves into a gated community. Because that's exactly what these guys want. None of them actually wanted to kill me, I don't believe. I felt it, but that was never the real threat. What they really wanted to do was to intimidate us into speaking less loudly, and withdrawing our ideas from the general circulation, making our ideas less accessible to the public. That's what they want. And we just have to work really hard not to give them what they want.

XVIII. Was the Public Theater Inciting Violence?

"The Left has systematically and programmatically used free speech and artistic expression as a pretext to incite violence against the Right and promote the assassination of Donald Trump," Laura Loomer told Sean Hannity on Fox News on June 19 (Figure 5.4). "I'm protecting the president's life. I'm protecting our Constitution. I'm using my constitutional right of free speech and protest to protest against the bastardization of Shakespeare."[98] It does not mention Shakespearean performance, but Title 18 of the United States Code makes it illegal to create and send "any letter, paper, writing, print, missive, or document containing any threat to take the life of, to kidnap, or to inflict bodily harm upon the President of the United States."[99] Freedom of speech is not absolute. It can be limited in certain situations, as in the Hatch Act, and as the Supreme Court has repeatedly affirmed: "These include the lewd and obscene, the profane, the libelous, and the insulting or 'fighting' words—those which, by their very utterance, inflict injury or tend to incite an immediate breach of the peace."[100] Was the Public's *Caesar* a threat against President Trump? Was it an incitement of violence, rendering the First Amendment void?

Similar questions arose in 1969 when eighteen-year-old Robert Watts became eligible for the draft and told a rally in Washington, DC, "If they ever make me carry a rifle the first man I want to get in my sights is L.B.J."[101] The Supreme Court deemed Watts's words "political hyperbole," not a sincere threat, noting that "the language of the political arena . . . is often vituperative, abusive, and inexact." *Watts v. United States* created the basis for the "true threat" doctrine: "'True threats' encompass those statements where the speaker means to communicate a serious expression of an intent to commit an act of unlawful violence to a particular individual or group of individuals."[102] Clearly the Public's *Caesar* made no effort to call audiences to enact the assassination it represented—quite the opposite. Even Eustis's harshest critic would have to echo the Supreme Court's conclusion about Robert Watts: "His only offense here was 'a kind of very crude offensive method of stating a political opposition to the President.'"[103] By these standards, however, the people sending death threats to Eustis and his family are criminally responsible.

It was not a threat, therefore, but was the Public's *Caesar* inciting violence? In 1969, the Supreme Court held that speech incites violence only "where such advocacy is directed to inciting or producing imminent lawless action and is likely to incite or produce such action."[104] *Intended* to produce crime *at that moment,* not days or even hours later, and *likely* to do so: those are the criteria for incitement, and the Public's *Caesar* did not meet them. Even "advocacy of illegal action at some indefinite future time" is not incitement.[105] Note that these criteria also govern ongoing disputes involving Trump's possible incitements during campaign rallies: "Get 'em out of here." "I'd like to punch him in the face." "Knock the crap out of him, would you? I promise you, I will pay your legal fees." They are applicable as well to hostile rhetoric toward the press, such as "enemy of the people."[106]

Could the Public Theater be liable if someone committed violence against Trump because of its production of *Julius Caesar,* even if it did not mean to incite violence? No—in 1969 the Supreme Court held that "words could not be punished by the State on the ground that they had a 'tendency to lead to violence.'"[107] In 1988 a California court found art not intended to cause people to commit a crime cannot be held liable for crimes carried out in its name: "musical lyrics and poetry cannot be construed to contain the requisite 'call to action' for the elementary reason that they simply are not intended to be and should not be read literally on their face, nor judged by a standard of prose oratory."[108] Even negligence in communicating a threat—as in a 2015 case where a man posted death threats against his wife on Facebook under the pretense that they were rap lyrics—is not sufficient for criminal intent; even the fact that statements are perceived as threatening by reasonable people is not enough to convict. Consciousness of an intent to threaten must be present. These legal conclusions are not just mine, as Eustis related:

> About two days after this all blew up, I got a call from my daughter, who said, "The Secret Service just called for you on my cell phone." And I said, "What!?" She said, "Yeah, they're going to call you." I said, "How did you know it was the Secret Service? You didn't give them my phone number, did you?" She said, "Sure I did." So then they called, and then I said, "I'm hanging up, and I'm going to call the field office of the Secret Service in New York, and you better be there." So I called, and it was indeed the Secret Service, and they said, "We are coming to interview you at 1:00 this afternoon." They didn't ask me; they told me they were coming, and said, "You better be in your office." So two guys who looked straight out of *Men in Black* came into my office, sat down, and introduced themselves very solemnly and asked me this long series of questions—about a half-hour interview—about my intentions toward the president, whether I meant to kill the president, whether I'd ever bought weapons, whether I was trying to incite people to kill the president. And, it was—I mean, I was not shaken up, but it was serious: the Secret Service was in my office investigating whether I was a threat to President Trump. And at the end of the interview, the agent—I hope I don't get him in trouble—but the agent closed the book and said, "Mr. Eustis, thank you for your cooperation. We were legally required to do this because of the number of complaints we received. And I want to assure you that this investigation is now closed. And, by the way, I love Shakespeare in the Park!"

XIX. Why Did the Right and Left Interpret *Julius Caesar* Differently?

The controversy surrounding the Public's *Caesar* invokes some big debates in literary theory. Plato banned literature from his ideal nation state because he worried that people will thoughtlessly imitate what they see or hear. Aristotle saw audiences as more intelligent and litera- ture as a good prompt for thought and conversation about society. Clearly Eustis was pursuing an Aristotelian model, but many feared the Platonic response.

Plato developed his theory of *mimesis,* "imitation," in dialogue with the pre-Socratic Sophists' notion that rhetoric—persuasive speech—has an almost magical ability to overwhelm the thinking capabilities of its audience and control their actions. That is why, according to the Soph- ist Gorgias, you cannot blame Helen of Troy for abandoning her hus- band (debating the issue was a frequent topic on cable news in the clas- sical world). To Gorgias, Helen went "unwillingly under the influence of speech as if she were seized by the violence of violators."[109] The speaker, Paris, is the one to blame, not the listener, Helen, because lan- guage can "benumb and bewitch the soul with evil persuasion" (14).

Adopting this view, Plato's Socrates detests rhetoricians "who, by the power of their language, make small things appear great and great things small."[110] How can we resist their deceptions when, like Helen, we are helpless against the force of language? In the right hands, language can be a force for good, leading to truth and beauty, but as a society we have no reliable mechanism to ensure that only the virtuous and just have access to eloquence. The same holds true for art, Socrates says. It is a discourse of deception because it exacerbates the divide between our mistaken perceptions of the world and what is actually real. His theory of art as thrice-removed from truth appears in Plato's *Republic* in the famous example of the three kinds of beds. The painter's bed is a de- graded imitation of the carpenter's bed, which is already a degraded imitation of the perfect bed made by god. One copy (art) imitating an- other (appearance) imitating what is true and good (reality): the situation is fraught with delusion and the potential for socially destructive behav- ior based on those misunderstandings. It is not so bad when it is about furniture, but what about history or politics? The utmost danger is that art will generate one more layer of imitation: audiences, thoughtlessly believing what they see in art to be good and true, will do what they see. A delusion thrice-removed from truth can become a very real tragedy if someone acts on it. Art therefore ruins the minds of people who lack the capacity to understand it, and those people, in turn, ruin society.

In the face of this chilling prospect, the state must do what is neces- sary, however harsh. In Plato's *Laws,* a grittier text dealing with the concrete realities of society, artists find themselves censored in a totalitarian state. Given the susceptibility of the public and the danger of art, some dictatorial arm of the state must monitor speech, allowing only words that will, in the state's view, lead the people to virtuous thoughts and actions.[111] In the *Republic,* a more ambitious work envisioning an ideal society, Socrates comes to an even harsher conclusion about literature: "Banish it from the city."[112]

But Socrates hedges: "If the poetry that aims at pleasure and imitation has any argument to bring forward that proves it ought to have a place in a well-governed city, we at least would be glad to admit it" (607c). Aristotle takes up this challenge in his *Poetics.* The entire Platonic account of artistic experience is misguided, he concludes, so the role of the artist in society must be rethought. When we look at art, Aristotle writes, it is obvious that artists do not try to imitate things exactly as they are. Their imitations are not thrice-removed from reality because artists are not aiming for reality (this is the origin of Philip Sidney's notion that literature "nothing affirms"). Artists imagine something that could be, might have been, or we wish would be. Artists create imaginary worlds; audiences easily recognize those worlds as imaginary. Even when Sophocles represents Oedipus, that is not really Oedipus, and everyone knows it. Instead, it is an opportunity to think about what happens in the story, why the people in it did what they did, and how it applies to our own lives. That is why, Aristotle says, art is a more ethical endeavor than history. We—as artists and audiences—use the imaginary world to think about the real world. This is how Aristotle recuperates the interpretive faculties of the audience, working up from that position to create a valuable role for art in society as a mechanism through which we as individuals reflect upon our thoughts, experiences, and desires.

Aristotle's respect for audiences and his affirmative view of the role of art in society appear in his famous definition of tragedy as "accomplishing by means of pity and fear the catharsis of such emotions."[113] Not only do audiences have the ability to interpret tragedy, even violent and challenging plays, but doing so actually makes the world a better, safer place because the emotions that exert control over people's actions—pity, fear, and, we could add, rage—are expunged when witnessed and experienced within the controlled environment of an artistic event. That theory of tragedy will help us answer our final question in the next section, but first I want to ask why the Right versus Left responses to the Public's *Caesar* matched so closely the Platonic versus Aristotelian theories of mimesis.

I think it is because, on the one hand, Plato is fundamentally conservative and Aristotle fundamentally progressive; and, on the other hand, conservatives are fundamentally Platonic and progressives fundamentally Aristotelian. Citing belief in an invisible realm of truth, both Plato and many on the American Right are centrally concerned with the preservation of social stability and traditional power structures. That concern leads both to be leery of art that challenges power, and to fear that people will imitate such art. Adopting a more scientific and humanistic approach, Aristotle and many on the American Left are centrally concerned with building a more just system based on a more realistic account of individual experience. That account affirms the capacity of free-thinking individuals to interpret controversial art, rejects the image of audiences as imitative monkeys, and resists state censorship conducted in the name of social order. That provides a basis for our final question, the big one raised by this production—a genuine and difficult ethical dilemma.

XX. Is It Wrong to Stage a Coded Version of an Assassination of a Sitting President?

We know it is not illegal. But is it virtuous, ethically permissible, considering the possibility of a Platonic response? What if someone imitates the radical political violence seen on stage, even if that was not the author's intent—was in fact the opposite of the author's intent?

It comes down to a risk-benefit calculation. What were the risks? Offending people, alienating audiences, losing sponsors, creating a partisan cloud over future work done at the theater, driving a deeper wedge between America's bitterly divided factions, exposing the theater to bad press were someone to cite it in an act of radical political violence, and—most seriously—potentially being a causal factor, however unintentionally, in that possible act. What about the benefits? Beyond the usual joys of a night at the theater, there was only one: prompting your audience to think long and hard about Donald Trump's presidency, their feelings toward it, their ways of talking about it, and their future actions in light of the larger Western tradition and its discourse about tyranny, as represented by the most insightful observer of human behavior in the English language. The gritty reality of the risks in light of the airy abstraction of the reward makes this a gut-wrenching wager.

Oskar Eustis and the Public Theater decided to take the risk. In doing so, they acted upon Aristotle's theories of tragedy, audience intelligence, and the social value of art. Their gamble paid off. Chatter about violence against Trump cooled as summer faded to fall. As the main point of reference, the Public Theater's *Julius Caesar*—with its insistence on reflection, nuance, and complexity in thought—played a leading role in the fizzling out of that conversation. Shakespeare gave to America the logic for rejecting radical political violence. This situation could have ended very badly: those risks were real, and there is probably some moral luck behind an ultimately affirmative judgment of the virtue of the Public's *Caesar*. But Eustis and the Public deserve credit for their faith. They had faith in their audience, even when that audience shifted into a national partisan conversation involving people who never set foot inside the Delacorte Theater, and they had faith in the productive social energy created by tragic drama, even by a play as unflinchingly pessimistic as Shakespeare's *Julius Caesar*. That was the point of the essay penned on June 23 by Corey Stoll, the actor playing Brutus, which recounted "What It Was Like to Star in the Trump-Themed *Julius Caesar*":

> In this new world where art is willfully misinterpreted to score points and to distract, simply doing the work of an artist has become a political act. . . . A play is not a tweet. It can't be compressed and embedded and it definitely can't be delivered apologetically. The very act of saying anything more nuanced than "us good, them bad" is under attack, and I'm proud to stand with artists who do. May we continue to stand behind our work, and, when interrupted, pick it right back up from "liberty and freedom."[114]

Conclusion

O THE PUBLIC, Trump is either the epitome of immorality—corrupt, lying, racist, misogynistic—or a return to the glory days of American exceptionalism. To political commentators, he is a post-truth demagogue spouting retrograde nationalistic gibberish on social media. To political theorists, he is the predictable outcome of the encounter between globalization and economic inequality in a capitalist society: the personification of the scapegoating of cultural differences in response to financial frustration. To lawyers, he is in jeopardy for alleged crimes. To politicians, he is a target for impeachment. These readings parse the particulars of the Trump phenomenon, but to a Shakespearean he is something much bigger that connects our moment with the patterns of past politics: Trump is a sign of tragedy ahead.

He was elected, in part, because of a failure of imagination—no one thought it could happen. A Shakespearean intervention activates a deeper understanding than we get from the nightly news, behind-the-scenes books, or even political science. Shakespeare moves us from the facts of the Trump story to their meaning, showing the social forces that created Trump, how our moment echoes the rhythms of history, and what comes next. The echo of Shakespearean tragedy in Trump forces us to take seriously the possibility that this is the beginning of the end of America. That is not a happy idea. Political commentators do not like to go there;

viewers tune out. As someone who feels that, on balance, America has been good for humankind, I don't like to think about it either. But Shakespeare was unflinching in his willingness to confront tragedy directly and in depth. We need to be too. We ignore Shakespeare at our own peril.

I. Shakespeare and Trump in the Classroom

Curious about how Shakespeareans were negotiating Trump, I asked around.[1] It became clear that our profession powerfully impacts our politics. First, as Louise Geddes at Adelphi University said to me, all academic training, regardless of discipline, gives one skills "to think more critically and step back to look at a larger picture, and also to approach a variety of news sources." Then there are the instrumental skills specific to the humanities. Humanists "tend to see the 'long-run effects' as opposed to short-term squabbles," one colleague noted; they tend to "avoid 'knee-jerk' responses to outrageous politics," said another. Those studying history and philosophy are equipped to recognize, as Andrew Moran at the University of Dallas put it, "the historical origins of contemporary ideological positions and the transience of those positions." Randall Martin at the University of New Brunswick similarly emphasized that "present-day politics has a historical and ideological past, and that past clarifies the motives, means, and rhetoric of contemporary politicians." Above all, English professors agreed with Marcia Eppich-Harris of Marian University: "It is a perfect moment to reengage with the basic skill of our profession: close reading. In an era in which the truth is slippery and fake news proliferates, it is *crucial* to build, reinforce, and practice close reading skills." Thus, in a talk at Harvey Mudd College, Ambereen Dadabhoy asked "What Can a Liberal Arts Education Offer in the Age of Trump?" and answered: "We need to think in the way that literary scholars and humanists think because those methodologies will make us better navigators of our social and political culture."[2]

Beyond the instrumental skills of literary studies, there are some transferable skills specific to Shakespeare studies. Shakespeareans receive "training in how to read complex political situations," Dan K. Nestor said, pointing to the layers of meaning in Shakespeare's plays and suggesting that Shakespeareans bring "a habit of seeking double meanings to [their] engagement with contemporary politics." Daniel

Spector of New York University added, "Politics, argument, and debate can all be examined through a dramaturgical lens." What are politicians if not actors reading lines to an audience, then exiting to backstage meetings with directors to plan their next performance? Pointing to Shakespeare's ability to inhabit the lives and minds of his characters, Sean Keilen of University of California, Santa Cruz, thought a career spent interpreting Shakespeare's plays helps one "understand why other people hold their beliefs" in the political realm as well. Another colleague ventured further to say that interpreting the political figures outside one's own political party is much like reading a Shakespearean play: "The way he approaches characters and understands them from the inside out would be a trait we should adopt in increasingly insane partisan times." It was noted that both Shakespeare and Trump elude simple understandings: "The totality of Trump, words and deeds, is complex and at times contradictory. I would relate that to the complexity of some of Shakespeare's characters. I understand that those who are high on the dogmatic scale won't see the complexity." Venturing beyond instrumental skills, Peter C. Herman of San Diego State University suggested a substantive relationship between Shakespeare and Trump: "If you are going to talk about, say, the Ancient Constitution (the unwritten rules limiting monarchic power), it's impossible not to segue into contemporary politics, especially since the English Revolution begat the American Revolution which begat our present system."

Shakespeareans may have the skills to read Trump, but doing so in class can be dicey. Many do not, for many reasons. "Simply not relevant," said one colleague. The syllabus says "Shakespeare"; a twenty-first-century politician is no more germane to the discussion than he would be in a class on molecular biology. Others ignore Trump for pedagogical reasons. To Andrew Cutrofello of Loyola University, Chicago, "It seems to me more productive to let the students themselves draw connections between the texts we discuss in class and the contemporary political scene." To Sean Keilen, "Literary studies in our period is excessively politicized, both from within and without the Academy, and I prefer to leave politics out of my classroom." Andrew Moran went further when asked if he brings Trump into Shakespeare classes:

No, because to do so would inevitably call forth ugly and vacuous partisan passions which would engender ill will and distract us from the literature. To ask "What does Shakespeare teach us about Trump?" inevitably leads to trite answers and a tedious middle-aged professor indoctrinating the students, who for the most part are still too young to be critical of the professor.

Even highly political left-wing Shakespeareans like Christian Smith can feel that politically efficacious teaching need not be explicitly political:

> The work of the radical teacher is to keep the student awake and aware to all the thoughts and feelings inside her. Help her stay dialectical—keeping all the contradictions present in her thought. Good Shakespeare close reading does not have to force the politics onto the student. The politics are already in the poetry. This is why Karl Marx loved Shakespeare so much and used his lines hundreds of times in his writings.

Clearly, Shakespeareans of different stripes see pitfalls in bringing Trump into the classroom.

Yet others see opportunities. At St. John's University, Steve Mentz designed an entire course entitled "Shakespeare and Political Rhetoric" in the fall of 2016: "We were talking about political rhetoric every day, both in the twenty-first-century and Shakespearean contexts. Class on Nov. 9 was devastating for everyone." Peter C. Herman assumed this mantle less eagerly, relating his own story about the blurred line between teaching and being human that many experienced on November 9, 2016: "After Trump's election, I spent the first ten minutes or so in the class engaging in a kind of therapy with my students. To my initial discomfort, at least some looked to me as an authority figure who could provide some answers. So, I tried to step up to the plate and do what I could." Marcia Eppich-Harris recalled her November 9: "I was teaching Machiavelli's *Prince* the day before the election. When Clinton lost, I was devastated. But I took the opportunity to say that if we are living in an era in which we elect a man who says 'grab em by the pussy,' then learning about Machiavelli's work is more important now than ever."

Louise Geddes signaled another benefit of bringing Trump into the Shakespearean classroom: "Students process affectively," she noted. Here the point is not to use Shakespeare to comment on the president but, instead, to more powerfully communicate the tensions of Shakespeare's texts by having students interpolate their emotionally charged experiences with modern politics. For his part, Daniel Spector "couldn't stop talking about [Trump] when working on Iago while teaching and directing *Othello*," noting that "most discussions of Trump *vis a vis* Shakespeare have to do with linguistic matters." But things can go awry when Trump is brought into the classroom, as one colleague recalled: "A student took offense and went to my chair. The student complained that I dismissed Trump voters as stupid (which is obviously not what I said). As a result, I talk about politics in a broader sense right now, and do not directly mention the president by name." Sometimes it doesn't work, said Hillary Nunn of the University of Akron: "I fished and fished for someone to make the comparison between Caesar and Trump. No one bit. They didn't particularly want to talk about it, or about Shakespeare's business in contemporary politics." Peter C. Herman had a different take on student interest:

> Shakespeare is already "politicized" in that he writes in several plays about the rights and duties of monarchs, why they should or should not be obeyed, even deposed. In one play, *The Winter's Tale,* he explores what you do when the monarch seems to go insane. So it's impossible, even unnatural, to restrict the conversation to sixteenth or seventeenth century contexts. Nor do students want that. In my experience, at least, they *want* literature to be both meaningful and active in the world. So connecting Shakespeare with contemporary politics is something they enjoy because it demonstrates how earlier literature can serve as a guide to contemporary issues.

Andrew Moran was leery, however, about echo-chamber conversations: "To whom does this way of reading literature appeal except to the students who already have strong left-wing commitments or who are terribly naive about the kind of indoctrination that they will be getting?"

Given the arguments for and against bringing Trump and Shakespeare together, many employ indirection. "I do not address him by name but sometimes address the policies as appropriate issues for moral debate," said one colleague. The biggest issue is a teacher's responsibility to create a space for learning that is respectful of the various political opinions students from diverse backgrounds bring to the room, as

Herman acknowledged: "You cannot come across as an ideologue and make students who might be sympathetic to Trump feel unwelcome." The takeaway from my conversations with colleagues is that many Shakespeareans do not know what to do with Trump, and for every Shakespearean who does, there is another who thinks we should do the opposite. The Shakespeare-and-Trump move is a delicate one. It's difficult to strike a posture that avoids therapeutic preaching to the choir, stating the obvious, alienating audiences, and coming across as hokey. Shakespeareans feel the same tension as other literary scholars and academics: we do not want to politicize our work, yet our work has been politicized by others. Responding by pretending that politics does not exist is the fastest way to ensure that we have no say in defining how our areas of expertise are understood by the general public. That strategy would show a lack of responsibility and a failure of leadership—and therefore many Shakespeareans think we need to be less embarrassed about addressing ethics and politics directly.

II. Shakespeare and Trump: A Typology

Outside the classroom, the three main venues for Shakespeare-and-Trump discourse are *performance, media,* and *writing*. Sometimes they intersect—as in writing about performance, writing on social media, performance on social media—and each venue has subtypes, as outlined below.

Performance

Orange-Face Shakespeare: Modern dress productions, usually serious and tragic, costuming Shakespearean characters as Trump to lodge a political critique.

Shakes-Trump Travesties: Shakespearean theatrical adaptations, usually irreverent satires, often low-budget one-person shows, that send up the chaos and absurdity of Trump's reign by impressionistically patterning it onto one of Shakespeare's texts (Figure C.1).

Shaxtivism: Disruptive political demonstrations, including guerrilla performances, leveraging Shakespeare and his cultural cachet to spur audiences to resistance.

FIGURE C.1. David Carl in *Trump Lear*, directed and co-created by
Michole Biancosino, written and co-created by David Carl
(New York: Under St. Marks Theater, 2018).
(Photograph by Anthony Velez/No Future Photography.)

Media

Shakes-Toons: Shakespeare-inflected political cartoons depicting storylines from the Trump saga in terms of the plays' well-known plots, characters, and dialogue (Figure C.2).

Shakes-Memes: Brief video clips, images, quotations, or witticisms spread on the internet, with variations, using Shakespeare to comment on modern cultural phenomena, or vice versa (Figure C.3).

Bard Blogs: Online lists and blog posts, usually witty and lighthearted, that map some aspect of the news onto quotations or characters from the plays.

Bardcasts: Audio interviews, discussions, and podcasts for a general audience bringing Shakespearean performers and scholars into conversation with current events—most notably Isaac Butler's *Lend Me Your Ears* on *Slate*.

Politicitation: Political commentators, usually well-educated but not specialists in literature, alluding to Shakespeare off-the-cuff to boost the power and prestige of their arguments.

FIGURE C.2. Steve Bell, "I am the noblest Roman of them all," commissioned for the Royal Shakespeare Company, *Draw New Mischief* (2017).

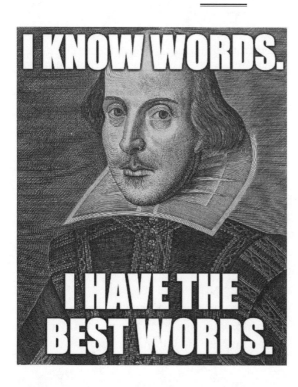

FIGURE C.3. Shakespeare "I have the best words" meme, quoting Donald Trump at a campaign rally in Hilton Head Island, South Carolina, on December 30, 2015. (Created by the author.)

Writing

The Really Bad Quartos: Similar to the *Shakes-Trump Travesties* (see above), satirical creative writing that tells Shakespearean stories in Trumpian language or vice versa.

Scholarly Conference Papers and Journal Articles at the Intersection of Shakespeare and Trump: Which Always Have Colons in Their Titles: Talks by academics for academics, usually leveraging a specialist's historical knowledge to disclose a new wrinkle in the Shakespeare-Trump discourse.

Public Shakespeare: Essays by Shakespeare scholars for public venues bringing the plays into discussion with current events.

III. Shakespeare and Trump: Some Best Practices

1. Shakespeare fans, including political commentators, can quote from the plays to enhance opinions on current events, elevate the conversation, and open up discourse—what I have called the *politicitation* of Shakespeare.

2. To avoid a liberal echo chamber, Shakespeare enthusiasts can meet retrograde right-wing trolls on their own turf by developing and distributing Shakes-memes, filling the world with Shakespearean humor and satire to counterbalance the hate-memes on the other side.

3. Literature lovers, especially in the U.S. heartland, can mount grassroots Shakespeare productions. Don't politicize them; that's alienating. The plays will take care of themselves, as they always have. Just get people in the same room, let them see Shakespeare, and get them talking.

4. Major Shakespearean companies can mount explicitly politicized adaptations (Richard III as Trump, Macbeth as Trump, Lear as Trump) to spark national conversations that put our current moment in dialogue with our cultural heritage.

5. In college classrooms, teachers do not need to preach to the choir. Instead, show students the stoicism in the tragedies (how to find solace in times of trouble), the skepticism in the late plays (how to doubt everything), and the sources of joy

in the comedies (how to laugh), as well as how live theater builds community.

6. Even if the historicized meaning of Shakespeare's texts is the end-all and be-all for Shakespeare scholars, they should vigorously support and speak to the public's clear desires to use literature to think ethically about life today, a practice I refer to as *Public Shakespeare.*

With that last point in mind, I conclude with the story of Trump as seen through Shakespeare.

IV. How We Got Here, a Tragedy in Five Acts

Act I

It starts with the people. They are fun-loving, but they worship money and ambition. The nation has bested its foreign rivals but neglected the homeland: there's disorder in the streets. Economic inequality is stark, the people hungry. There is plenty of food stored up, but the well-off hoard it for themselves. Working people blame immigrants. There are hate crimes against outsiders. Elites decry the ignorance of the masses—blocks, stones, worse than senseless things—yet not the politicians who deny money for public education. It starts with the people, but they are products of government policy.

The state is oblivious to those outside the aristocracy—a total disconnect. The people do not exist to the politicians in their palaces, except as gunpowder for partisan wars. The big fish eat the small. People are strangely fantasied, not knowing what they fear, but full of fear. Wealth makes the abhorrent adored, the rich celebrated for what the poor are despised for. The masses are changeable: some call it fickleness, but it is really diversity. Church clashes with state. Factions of feuding nobles vie for power and prominence. War against a foreign threat holds us together for a time. Once it is over, that energy turns to civil war, which then fractures future foreign campaigns. Soldiers die carrying out nobles' crusades. Postwar periods of demilitarization are ripe for tyranny. Knowing the nation's greatness gives greater feeling to its failings. The clearer the sky, the darker the clouds when they come. This country could never be conquered without wounding itself first.

The gap between people and government creates media: go-betweens, meant to connect the two, that drum up conflict where there is none. Sifting through consensus to find discord, they amplify it, creating rather than reporting public sentiment. It's a spectacle, Montagues and Capulets biting their thumbs at each other, audiences watching with delight. Quarrels between political masters become quarrels between everyday men and women. Thoughts that people take to be their own have been goaded on. The media is biased—not against a political party but against unity. Its existence depends on discord. It profits on division.

Laws prune noisome weeds; lenity makes robbers bold. Women have a diminished role in government, though they repeatedly prove to have precisely the skills lacking in the men whose machismo ran the nation into a rut. Hungry people grow desperate. They want an end to strife. The world is turned upside-down. Normal rules do not apply. Fair is foul, and foul is fair. A fragile populace becomes enamored of a celebrity exuding success and luxury. Our entertainments make instruments to punish us.

Act II

He seems anomalous but actually represents his culture's core values, the embodiment of a society that fosters men-children. The corrupt culture spawns the tyrant who conquers it, then is consumed by it. He is always the son of an aristocrat, never a politician. He is a child of privilege, with the best education money can buy, yet woefully unequipped with the technical skills needed to manage competing voices in government. He is oblivious to his privilege, believing that he deserves the life he was born into, and has no idea what life is like outside the aristocracy. He is contemptuous of the people but does not realize it.

His childhood was not infused with love. For most of his life, he was a decent enough guy but lacks social bonds. A father dies, sometimes a brother. He constantly feels wronged, claiming to be a victim. Anger fills him; hatred consumes. He does not experience love and resents those with happy lives, envious of others' talents and accomplishments. He is alone. He replaces the pleasure most take from intimacy, friendship, and family with pleasure from holding power over others. He throws himself into his work. His drive is impressive. He wants glory and fame, and to be liked, but will settle for respected. He brushes aside any dregs of conscience, but they drift back from time to time.

The essence of his personality is toxic masculinity. He is condescending toward women, with a performative sexual bravado. He emphasizes physical appearance to the extreme. When agitated, his anger surfaces in racism and sexism. He loves military culture. To some, his machismo has a sexual charm, but he is hideous by most standards, and oddly asexual, passionless with his wife. Sex for him is about power.

He can be charismatic, with a weird mix of etiquette and immorality: a very amiable monster. He is ruthless in pursuit of desire and power, bellicose, his words filled with violent imagery, but he avoids conflict. He immediately calms disagreement instead of moderating competing viewpoints. He is cowardly when confronted, weak-willed and childlike, though awkward around children. He is not traditionally noble, instead irreverent, jokey, riotous, dismissive of morality and decency. He constantly makes dick jokes. Audiences find it hilarious. No one takes him seriously. He is proud to a fault, a boaster, seeing himself as a lion, others as leopards. He was born to command, not to sue, a god to be worshiped by the people, not one of them. He is his own trumpet and chronicle, praising his own deeds, devouring the deeds in the praise: a strong will and a weak mind.

He definitely has talent; for one thing, he is good at being bad. He is opportunistic without scruples. Prudence is an obstacle. There is not a sincere bone in his body. But all he does is win, which makes him rich and celebrated. He would not be a wolf were the people not sheep. He feels destined for greatness. Sometimes he's the best, most accomplished of the nobles, sometimes a warrior, sometimes a culture warrior. But he cannot enjoy the pleasures of peace and prosperity. There is an emptiness that cannot be filled, his ambition insatiable. He wants the highest office in the land, but the pathway is blocked: many people, vestiges of honor. His conscience won't let him catch the nearest way. He experiences this as a challenge to his masculinity: is he man enough to do what needs to be done to win?

Act III

The future tyrant asserts himself only when the ruling powers have proven woefully inadequate, and the people are rioting. A plague on both their houses, they say. We are not the first who with good meaning incurred the worst.

Sometimes the tyrant illegally usurps power from the rightful ruler. More often, there is an election, with campaigns, candidates, and rallies. Sometimes the common voice chooses someone else, but that person declines. Those who could run the country won't; those who want to can't. Sometimes the people defer to political elites. Their candidate serves only them. Sometimes the would-be tyrant is a stupid demagogue propped up in a shadow campaign by Machiavellian aristocrats to secure their own interests, but, in his self-conceit, he thinks that sovereignty is his birthright.

He is desperate to be elected—the ultimate affirmation. He does not love the people; he loves himself, positive that his prowess will carry over to government. His misplaced confidence is infectious, inspiring people tired of losing. He is wise enough to play the fool, deafening ears with his superfluous breath, speaking an infinite deal of nothing. There's method in his madness. He can insult people to their faces, and they smile along with him. He makes absurd populist promises with no intention of delivering on them. He would govern with perfection. He defies other nations, especially France. He opposes education, intelligence, and expertise as elitist. Sexuality and aggression infuse his politics. He asks the people to fight for him, seeing them as materials to be manipulated to serve his will. He rises by sin; others fall by virtue.

He wants the same as everyone else—wealth and power—but his total commitment silences the pangs holding the rest of us back. To him, "conscience" is a word cowards use, honor a scutcheon. He lies without compunction, claiming that political opponents are illegitimate by birth, counterfeiting religious piety. He equivocates, and cites scripture for his purpose. Insisting that he cannot scheme and lie is one of his schemes and lies. Supporters believe him, though they know he is lying. He becomes an actor, a role-player, a deceiver, a dealmaker. He has the time of his life pulling off his schemes: it is fun beating idiots. He mocks the simplicity of his victims, and his willingness to say the unsayable astonishes. His wicked energy draws people into transparently evil plots. Supporters embrace him with unusual fury.

He attracts a team of clowns—conscienceless henchmen, adoring family members, Machiavellian puppeteers, advisors out of their depth—lesser demons that he lords over. Many who hate his manners say nothing because they see profit in him. His orders and desires come in half-statements and vague commands, pocketing deniability. Delusion vies with malice in his mind; he bends facts to fit pre-formed opinions. He will not acknowledge truths that everyone else sees. His lies are transparent: he does not expect you to believe them, but he wants you to display your loyalty by affirming them. He produces political theater, performing planned routines as if spontaneous, manipulating the public sentiment he claims to represent. He brags of massive support that he does not have, planting loyalists in public to simulate it.

He pledges a desire to be friends with rivals while working against them and explains his schemes directly to those who stand in his way, making them accomplices. Everyone knows what he is doing. People love watching him win and want to be on the winning team. Their goals shift: from achieving the greatest good for the greatest number to beating an opponent. People who are usually ethical become strategic instead, violating their previous codes of conduct. Victory rather than virtue becomes the measuring rod.

People are no longer fighting for a cause but for a person. Military leaders throw their authority behind him. Politicians love him, but the people hate him, would devour him like the wolf the lamb. Really, his opponents just want him to be decent. He thinks he deserves support based on his accomplishments—it is his right—but they want him to show the kindness and humility we all bring to our daily lives. They want him to show his wounds—his humanity and vulnerability. Many are amazed that a man of such feeble temper could enjoy such success. The furor of the opposition causes its warnings to be dismissed as ranting. Those seeking to create unity from fractious discord are seen as hokey and out-of-touch. Traditional nobility is shown to be feeble. His supporters ignore all warnings, indifferent to history, thinking it will be different this time. We bid this be done when evils have a permissive pass and not the punishment. The people get the sovereign they deserve.

He is the paragon of justice, and virtue exudes from his being, he insists, becoming known as a law-and-order candidate who will reform corrupt government. But he doesn't care about law. All he cares about is his family because they are an extension of himself. Desire for sovereignty outweighs obligation to act legally. Sight of the means to do ill deeds makes them done instantly. He sees his willingness to do wickedness as a mark of his manhood. He sanctions crimes in service of his ambition, sometimes a treasonous arrangement with a foreign competitor, trading money for power. And an imperfect election process results in leaders that are not fit and capable. A nation used to conquering others conquers itself. Future ages will look at this and groan. Falstaff becomes king.

Act IV

Suspicion surrounds the man because of his shadowy path to sovereignty. To be thus is nothing; he must be thus safely. Power grabbed by an unruly hand is maintained as gained.

He rules for himself and his family, not the people, forsaking responsible government for personal pleasure. He is negligent, appointing others to run the country while he enjoys his opulent lifestyle, surrounding himself with flatterers, inviting parasites into his circle of advisors, building policy around them. He loves pomp and ceremony. He makes decisions of enormous political consequence based on emotion and personal interest rather than reason and the public good. He purchases alliance abroad to secure power at home. Servants perform his ill-conceived bidding. He vaguely suggests that his people attack his enemies, then denies his orders, and rejects responsibility for miscarriages. When decisions turn out to be disastrous, underlings take the fall. He hates to hear the sins he loves to act. Excuses make his faults worse by the excusing. He is demeaning to servants, makes them dress in ways that please him, and dotes on his children but domineers their will, responding with shock when asked to be ethical. He demands loyalty but shows none, wants total obedience and devotion, must be loved, or else. Supporters must see the world as he does. He relishes the power he has over them. Commonwealth is a bizarre concept to him; he wants dictatorship. Things begun badly strengthen themselves by more ill. People look around and notice that the comical fools that earlier followed the tyrant have mysteriously disappeared from the story.

He encourages loyalists to break the law, not punishing crimes when committed, promising rewards for support and servitude. He floats trial balloons of illegality to see who will support him. He can do what he likes. His will is law, his power disjoined from remorse. His decree will stand unchecked and unrevoked. His false overweighs your true. He oversteps custom, believing he is singular—an exception to the way government is usually done.

Poor personnel decisions start to eat the government from the inside.

He seeks foreign aid from nations with their own best interests at heart. He is filled with aggression, hatred, and ruthlessness—great when trained against foreign enemies, but not when directed against those who oppose him at home. He is creative—even artistic—in punishments devised for enemies. He relishes abuses against them, acting with more savagery than the "animals" he complains of.

His fire blazes hot but soon burns out. Thrills grown common lose their delight. Opposition works in the dark of night, with back-room scheming rather than public debate. The people lack power or desire to resist. He overwhelms enemies with the full force of the state. Some are destroyed, so others refuse to resist, though they want to. Many curse his name. Women see and speak the tyrant's evil, but they have not traditionally held positions of power in this culture. The tyrant's sharpest critics are children, who innocently describe things as they see them, and whose ethics are basic and simple—*be kind, tell the truth, don't be violent*—unrefined with adult sophistry. The people would love to have the tyrant's talents used in government for the good of the nation, but they cannot accept his attitude that he is above them and the rules do not apply to him. They lament the nation's lost dignity. Victims of his crimes and policies publicly call for justice. People protest his abuse of the country's interests, loudly but not effectively. Opposition on moral grounds goes nowhere.

But prosperity mellows. The resistance gains traction only when the tyrant takes the wealth of the upper class and fails as a steward of the people's resources, wasting their money on projects that enhance his personality. He is removed from the realities of war in his comfortable palace, yet bellicose and boastful when dealing with other countries and eager to wage war. The thunder of his cannon will be heard. He seizes resources of enemies and friends for political campaigns. Gross mismanagement of state funds makes resistance real.

Now there's anger. Sometimes it goes too far. It can be alienating for work-a-day citizens but activates a political establishment whose disposition is complacency. An emboldened resistance fights openly, accusing the tyrant of obtaining power illegally. People who support the logic of the resistance but not its militancy ultimately join the cause, seeing the tyrant's crimes as the greater evil. Griefs, not manners, reason now. The resistance merely wants to check his behavior, not depose him; it wants him to follow the law. He can only conceive of resistance to his policies as resistance to him. He feels insecurity for the first time, blustering that he is the legitimate sovereign, accusing the resistance of treason. He cannot understand the demand that he act in accord with law rather than whim and will.

A dog's obeyed in office. Some loyalists are complacent. Some are obsequious, eager to please the tyrant. Some stifle their conscience when he offers wealth and status. Some justify his villainies as necessary, given the grossness of the age. Some see loyalty as the greatest virtue, regardless of its recipient. Some serve the nation honorably, blind to its hollow leadership. Some are talented and noble but are absorbed in the tyrant's schemes. Some try coupling power with wisdom. Some try saving the tyrant from himself. Others use that dissent to lobby for their removal.

Policy battles and foreign campaigns are lost. A populace that tolerated corrupt leadership in exchange for national prosperity grows restless. Young and old rebel. Riots break out. Neighbors turn against neighbors, daughters against fathers, mothers against sons. The tyrant's weakness awakens the ambition of his advisors. They grow resentful of his demands, exasperated with his antics. Some have a crisis of conscience. Some resign in protest. Some work behind closed doors with his enemies. His wife exercises her political muscle. Honorable loyalists are swallowed up by the sea of corruption surrounding the tyrant. The resistance picks off his forces one by one. He is shown to be less talented than people thought. He is implicated in the death of children—beautiful, playful, and innocent—shocking a dazed nation back to its senses.

Act V

An entity emerges with the power to make the tyrant feel the force of justice. The totality of his villainy creates the conditions for tragedy, but it is some silly little mistake that sets his downfall in motion.

Realizing that he does not have absolute authority devastates him. He cannot fathom being subject to the rules and customs governing prior politicians and other citizens. He cannot change his ways but undergoes a change of personality, growing anxious, stubborn, spiteful, vengeful, cruel, and erratic. He insists upon validation, changes his mind constantly, agrees with whomever he spoke to last, trusts no one, is suspicious of everyone. Unavoided is danger now. He is wrathful when reminded of promises to supporters. Demanding that family and servants please him, he fumes when disobeyed. He must eliminate any threat to

204 | Shakespeare and Trump

his authority. He is no longer fun and funny. His creepy sexuality becomes grotesque. He rants and rages alone, unhinged, increasingly misogynistic, increasingly explicit about the misdeeds he orders from his henchmen. Crime will have crime; sin plucks on sin. He is so far in he cannot turn back. He wrongly accuses family members of betrayal, creates elaborate loyalty tests for friends, turns against his closest advisors and bars them from his presence. He becomes verbally abusive, often sexually aggressive and perverse, railing against enemies and advisors alike. The toxic masculinity that made him mars him: the thing that made him "great" brings his world crashing down. He is cordoned off, removed from supporters, isolated. People worry about his mind. He longs for release from the emptiness of government.

He starts negotiating with the resistance to maintain his power, enraging loyalists. He loses public support when he cannot deliver on his populist promises. He cannot deliver for loyalists either, who know that his promises of status and wealth are hollow. He threatens their families if they defect. With each passing second the rebellion gains momentum. He vows desolation, death, and decay if his authority is not preserved. His family seeks sanctuary.

He is severed from any greatness he once had. He orders heinous crimes to shore up his power. Minions hesitate, shrink from him, defect to the resistance. Some confront him directly and are banished. He hunkers down in his castle. Those who worshiped him when he had power forsake him when it is gone. Even his bad advisors turn against him. Some are dragged down with him; some never see their families again; some of the fools end up hanged. He mourns the loss of his favorites. His family flatters him in public but despises him in private. His spark and verve are gone.

Women's anger fills the air. The virtue of the resistance weighs more than the fear of his wrath. The wonder is that he endured so long. He releases his followers. Chaos swirls, and the tyrant is powerless to stop it. He can only watch. He's doomed, though his struggle against the inevitable is admirable.

V. Act V, Scene 3; Or, How This All Ends

The details do not match up. Trump will not visit the Weird Sisters in the woods. We will not see Mike Pence exit, pursued by a bear. I doubt that an Empress Melania will eat her children baked in a pie. But Shakespeare's visions of tyranny suggest several possible endings, arranged here from the most tragic to the most likely.

It could end like *Julius Caesar,* the tyrant made a martyr as the nation moves toward the death of democracy. Or like *Coriolanus,* the proud man consumed by the multiple armies of enemies he has made throughout his life. Or like *King Lear,* a once-great family decimated because the inseparability of the personal and the political means that the family's fate is tied to the fortunes of the tyrant's government. Or like *Measure for Measure,* the tyrant getting a slap on the wrist, and the government's leniency inviting more tyranny. Or *King John,* the tyrant's party retaining power, but in a greatly diminished nation. Or *Henry VI,* where the tyrant falls to an equally corrupt faction, and nothing changes because both parties stand for the exact same thing: the success of their family, their friends, and their party. The counterpoints are *Richard II* and *Macbeth,* where the plume-plucked tyrant yields to a resistance that is then left to negotiate its contradictory status: it is a better government, but the unsavory means its partisans employed to win power lead to questions of legitimacy.

Let's not close off the possibility suggested by *The Winter's Tale:* redemption and restoration. The tyrant, forced to reckon with the truth he has denied, has a moment of clarity and, guilt-stricken and griefridden, accepts responsibility for his villainies. Time passes (sixteen years in *The Winter's Tale*) as people not involved in the affair grow up far from court. They find joy in the simple things in life—family, feasting, singing, dancing, joking, storytelling, holidays, art, nature, romance, love. They order their lives according to the personal, not the political. The tyrant learns to do the same. He feels shame and regret and asks for forgiveness. Even those he wronged come to pity him. A fairy-tale atmosphere emerges: the honorable poor folk are really princes and princesses, and good deeds are rewarded with worldly success. All that was lost is magically restored; order returns.

That is the world as we wish it were, but not as it actually is. A more realistic version comes in *The Tempest,* where the restoration of order is a veneer. The deposed tyrant comes back into power, promising to reform his ways. He doesn't. The traitor who deposed him is apprehended but not punished. The old order of government is restored. It is hard to shake the feeling that it is going to happen again. That is what we may be left with: political elites who remain in power despite demonstrable failings.

Or it could end like *Richard III,* with the dawning of a new day. The tyrant fights until the bitter end, somewhat admirably, but the tide turns in favor of the resistance. Its leader is not particularly fun or inspiring, is in fact pious and boring but represents a return to decency and order. It will turn out to be an age of peace, prosperity, and progress. We can all go back to our lives—backyard barbeques, family vacations, piano recitals, book clubs, high-school reunions, sports radio, date nights, Thanksgiving dinner, swimming pools, Shakespeare in the park—without constant conversation about the evil plaguing national politics.

Notes

INTRODUCTION

1. Stanley Fish, *Save the World on Your Own Time* (Oxford: Oxford University Press, 2008).

2. Historians Against Trump, "An Open Letter to the American People," July 11, 2016, historiansagainsttrump.org.

3. Stanley Fish, "Professors, Stop Opining about Trump," *New York Times,* July 15, 2017.

4. "Oxford Dictionaries Word of the Year 2016 is . . . Post-truth," *Oxford Dictionaries,* November 16, 2016, languages.oup.com.

5. David Remnick, "An American Tragedy," *New Yorker*, November 9, 2016, newyorker.com.

6. David Moye, "Trevor Noah: Clinton Email Scandal Straight out of Shakespeare," *Huffington Post*, November 2, 2016, huffpost.com.

7. Elizabeth Drew, "How It Happened," *New York Review of Books,* November 12, 2016, nybooks.com.

8. Stephen Greenblatt, *Tyrant: Shakespeare on Politics* (New York: W. W. Norton, 2018), 14.

9. Folger Shakespeare Library, "Stephen Greenblatt on 'Tyrant: Shakespeare on Politics,'" *Shakespeare and Beyond,* May 11, 2018, shakespeareandbeyond. folger.edu.

10. Stephen Greenblatt, *Renaissance Self-Fashioning: From More to Shakespeare* (Chicago: University of Chicago Press, 1980), 193.

11. Speech after *A Winter's Tale*, dir. Blanche McIntyre, July 13, 2018, available at https://twitter.com/katymfallon/status/1018072174828097537.

12. Daniel Spector, "Shakespeare Studies and Performance: Free Speech and Identity Politics," paper presented at the annual convention of the British Shakespeare Association, Queens University, Belfast, Northern Ireland, June 2018, available at https://tisch.nyu.edu/content/dam/tisch/CreativeResearch/deans-grants/daniel-spector.pdf.

CHAPTER 1

1. Julia Jones and Stephen K. Bannon, *Andronicus* (manuscript), 51–52; Rex Weiner, "Titus in Space," *Paris Review,* November 29, 2016, theparisreview.org. Quotations are verbatim.

2. Gary Anthony Williams, quoted in "Behind the Scenes: Steve Bannon's Rap Musical Table Read," *NowThis Politics,* web video, April 30, 2017, facebook.com/NowThisPolitics.

3. Julia Jones and Stephen K. Bannon, *Coriolanus: The Thing I Am* (manuscript), 30. Quotations are verbatim.

4. I am indebted to conversations with Abigail Simon about the scripts, and to her essay, "Understanding Steve Bannon through His Shakespeare Adaptations: A Closer Look at Populism and Violent Conflict," written for my *Why Shakespeare?* class, Harvard University, 2017.

5. Unless otherwise attributed, quotations from Jones are from my interviews with her on May 23 and September 29, 2018.

6. Quoted in Joshua Green, *Devil's Bargain: Steve Bannon, Donald Trump, and the Nationalist Uprising*, paperback ed. with a new preface (New York: Hudson, 2018), 51.

7. Green, *Devil's Bargain,* 52.

8. Quoted in Green, *Devil's Bargain,* 204.

9. René Guénon, *The Crisis of the Modern World*, trans. Marco Pallis, Arthur Osborne, and Richard C. Nicholson (Hillsdale, NJ: Sophia Perennis, 2001), 7.

10. Quoted in Green, *Devil's Bargain,* 71.

11. Green, *Devil's Bargain,* 74.

12. Quoted in Green, *Devil's Bargain,* 81.

13. Green, *Devil's Bargain,* 58, 148.

14. Green, *Devil's Bargain,* 85.

15. PBS, "Bannon's War," *Frontline,* May 23, 2017.

16. Quoted in Green, *Devil's Bargain,* 207.

17. J. Lester Feder, "This Is How Steve Bannon Sees the Entire World," *BuzzFeed News,* November 16, 2016, buzzfeednews.com.

18. Quoted in Green, *Devil's Bargain,* xvi, xiii.

19. Quoted in Green, *Devil's Bargain,* xxiii.

20. William Strauss and Neil Howe, *The Fourth Turning: An American Prophecy* (New York: Broadway, 1997), 2–3.

21. See David Von Drehle, "Is Steve Bannon the Second Most Powerful Man in the World?" *Time,* February 2, 2017, 28; Neil Howe, "Where Did Steve Bannon

Get His Worldview? From My Book," *Washington Post,* February 24, 2017; David Kaiser, "What's Next for Steve Bannon and the Crisis in American Life," *Time,* February 3, 2017, time.com.

22. Asawin Suebsaeng, "Steve Bannon, Donald Trump's Campaign CEO, Once Wrote a Rap Musical," *Daily Beast,* August 23, 2016, thedailybeast.com; Todd Van Luling, "Steve Bannon's Failed 'Star Wars'-Meets-Shakespeare Movie Script," *Huff Post,* May 10, 2017, huffpost.com.

23. Quoted in Van Luling, "Bannon's Failed 'Star Wars.'"

24. Quoted in Weiner, "Titus in Space."

25. Quoted in Suebsaeng, "Rap Musical."

26. Quoted in Weiner, "Titus in Space."

27. Stephen K. Bannon and Julia Jones, pitch for "Those Who Knew: A Twenty-Six Part Series for Television" (manuscript), 1.

28. Quoted in Simon, "Bannon through His Shakespeare," 7.

29. Ian Mason, "Steve Bannon: Same Causes of Roman Empire's Decline Can Be Seen in America Today," *Breitbart,* November 13, 2017, breitbart.com.

30. Quoted in Mason, "Roman Empire's Decline."

31. Quoted in Mason, "Roman Empire's Decline."

32. Edward Gibbon, *The History of the Decline and Fall of the Roman Empire* (London: Strahan and Cadell, 1776–1789), 6.363–364.

33. Quoted in Mason, "Roman Empire's Decline."

34. Thomas North, "Amiot to the Readers," in Plutarch, *The Lives of the Noble Grecians and Romanes Compared Together* (London: Thomas Vautroullier and John Wight, 1579), iii.

35. Quoted in Weiner, "Titus in Space."

36. Quoted in Van Luling, "Steve Bannon's Failed 'Star Wars.'"

37. Quoted in Van Luling, "Steve Bannon's Failed 'Star Wars.'"

38. Adam White, "Shakespeare in Space, with 'Ectoplasmic Sex': The Bizarre Story of Donald Trump Strategist Steve Bannon's Titus Andronicus Script," *Telegraph,* December 5, 2016, telegraph.co.uk.

39. Quoted in Weiner, "Titus in Space."

40. Quoted in Suebsaeng, "Rap Musical."

41. Quoted in Suebsaeng, "Rap Musical."

42. Suebsaeng, "Rap Musical."

43. Quoted in Suebsaeng, "Rap Musical."

44. "The Uninvited," panel discussion, March 16, 2013, https://www.youtube.com/watch?v=jQt38F9Mqlo.

45. Quoted in Green, *Devil's Bargain,* 146.

46. Quoted in Robert Kuttner, "Steve Bannon, Unrepentant," *American Prospect,* August 16, 2017, prospect.org.

47. Quoted in Scott Shane, "Combative, Populist Steve Bannon Found His Man in Donald Trump," *New York Times,* November 27, 2016.

48. Green, *Devil's Bargain,* 124.

49. Quoted in Green, *Devil's Bargain,* 213–214.

50. Quoted in Green, *Devil's Bargain*, 214.

51. Donie O'Sullivan and Drew Griffin, "Cambridge Analytica Ran Voter Suppression Campaigns, Whistleblower Claims," *CNN,* May 17, 2018, cnn.com.

52. Quoted in Kuttner, "Steve Bannon, Unrepentant."

53. Adam Nossiter, "'Let Them Call You Racists': Bannon's Pep Talk to National Front," *New York Times,* March 10, 2018.

54. Quoted in Suebsaeng, "Rap Musical."

55. Asawin Suebsaeng, "Breitbart Boss Stephen Bannon Bragged in 2015: 'I'm Trump's Campaign Manager,'" *Daily Beast,* October 11, 2016.

56. Suebsaeng, "Rap Musical."

57. Quoted in Green, *Devil's Bargain*, 89.

58. Quoted in Green, *Devil's Bargain*, 212.

59. Green, *Devil's Bargain*, 146.

60. Donald J. Trump, Inaugural Address, January 20, 2017, whitehouse.gov; Bannon quoted in Michael Wolff, "Ringside with Steve Bannon at Trump Tower as the President-Elect's Strategist Plots 'an Entirely New Political Movement,'" *Hollywood Reporter,* November 18, 2016, hollywoodreporter.com.

61. Quoted in Green, *Devil's Bargain*, 145.

62. Green, *Devil's Bargain*, 146.

63. Green, *Devil's Bargain*, 147.

64. Green, *Devil's Bargain*, 208.

65. Green, *Devil's Bargain*, 5, 140.

66. Green, *Devil's Bargain*, 148.

67. Green, *Devil's Bargain*, 219.

68. Ronald Radosh, "Steve Bannon, Trump's Top Guy, Told Me He Was 'a Leninist,'" *Daily Beast,* August 22, 2016.

69. Quoted in Conor Friedersdorf, "The Radical Anti-Conservatism of Stephen Bannon," *The Atlantic,* August 25, 2016, theatlantic.com.

70. Quoted in Wolff, "Ringside with Steve Bannon."

71. Philip Rucker and Robert Costa, "Bannon Vows a Daily Fight for 'Deconstruction of the Administrative State,'" *Washington Post,* February 23, 2017.

72. Errol Morris, dir., *American Dharma* (film, Fourth Floor Productions, 2018).

73. Green, *Devil's Bargain*, 140.

74. Errol Morris and Deborah Chasman, "Errol Morris on Steve Bannon's Dangerous 'Dharma,'" *Boston Review,* August 24, 2018, bostonreview.net.

75. John Dryden, *Of Dramatick Poesie, An Essay* (London: Henry Herringman, 1668), 51.

76. John Dryden, "The Grounds of Criticism in Tragedy," in *Troilus and Cressida* (London: Able Swall and Jacob Tonson, 1679).

77. *The Second Part of King Henry the Fourth*, in vol. 4 of *The Plays of William Shakespeare*, ed. Samuel Johnson (London: J. and R. Tonson, 1765), at 5.5.109.

78. John Dover Wilson, *The Fortunes of Falstaff* (Cambridge: Cambridge University Press, 1943), 20.

79. *The Interlude of Youth*, in *Two Tudor Interludes: The Interlude of Youth, Hick Scorner*, ed. Ian Lancashire (Baltimore: Johns Hopkins University Press, 1980), 210–214.

CHAPTER 2

1. Frank Bruni, "From 'Hamlet' to Hillary," *New York Times*, May 2, 2015.

2. Daniel Wattenberg, "The Lady Macbeth of Little Rock," *American Spectator* 25.8 (1992): 25.

3. Robert Anderson, *Macbush*, dir. Alan Woods, performed by the Ohio State University Theatre Company, Columbus, 1992; Michael Hettinger, *Macbush*, Alice Arts Theater, Oakland, CA, 2003.

4. Harold Bloom, "Macbush: The Tragicomical History of Dubya the Great, King of America and Subsequently Emperor of Oceania," *Vanity Fair*, April 2004, 286–289.

5. Mackubin Thomas Owens, "George W. Bush as Henry V," *National Review*, February 12, 2004, nationalreview.com.

6. Scott L. Newstok and Harry Berger Jr., "Harrying after VV," in *Shakespeare after 9/11: How a Social Trauma Reshapes Interpretation*, ed. Matthew Biberman and Julia Reinhard Lupton, *Shakespeare Yearbook* 18 (2011): 141–152.

7. Stephen Greenblatt, "Friends, Americans, Countrymen . . . ," *New York Times*, October 3, 2004.

8. "Stephen Greenblatt—Shakespearean Candidates," *Colbert Report*, October 2, 2008, http://www.cc.com/video-clips/nkfn9g/the-colbert-report-shakespearean -candidates---stephen-greenblatt.

9. "The Colbert Report: A Rare Behind-the-Scenes Look," https://www.you tube.com/watch?v=DfiL2hpnmZ0.

10. Emily Uecker, "'Hell Is Empty and All the Devils Are Here': A Shakespearean Guide to the 2016 Republican Primary," *McSweeneys*, August 6, 2015, mcsweeneys.net.

11. Emily Uecker, "'The Crown Will Find an Heir': A Shakespearean Guide to the 2016 Democratic Primary," *McSweeneys*, October 13, 2016.

12. Katy Weniger, "The 2016 GOP Presidential Candidates: As Told by Shakespeare," *Odyssey*, January 25, 2016, theodysseyonline.com.

13. "About Odyssey," *Odyssey*, https://www.theodysseyonline.com/about (accessed August 1, 2016).

14. Tom Blunt, "The Bard's Ballot: 2016 Candidates as Shakespeare Characters," *Signature*, April 18, 2016, signature-reads.com (accessed August 1, 2016).

15. Michael Judge, "Shakespeare on Our 'Scurvy Politicians,'" *Wall Street Journal*, September 20, 2016.

16. Common Core State Standards, "English Language Arts Standards » Reading: Literature » Grade 11–12," http://www.corestandards.org/ELA-Literacy/ RL/11-12/7 (accessed October 5, 2019).

17. Chris Anderson, Emily Bell, and Clay Shirky, "Post-Industrial Journalism:

212 | Notes to Chapter 2

Adapting to the Present" (New York: Columbia Journalism School, Tow Center for Digital Journalism, 2012).

18. See "The 155 Craziest Things Trump Said This Election," *Politico Magazine,* November 5, 2016, politico.com. Quotations from Trump in this section come from this page.

19. See Asawin Suebsaeng, "Marvel Artist Who Made a Trump Supervillain Thinks Donald Is a 'Goddamn Idiot,'" *Daily Beast,* July 6, 2016, thedailybeast.com.

20. Gary Schmidgall, "What Would Shakespeare Make of Trump?" *Chronicle Review,* February 7, 2016, chronicle.com.

21. Aryeh Cohen-Wade, "Donald Trump Performs Shakespeare's Soliloquies," *New Yorker,* April 6, 2016, newyorker.com.

22. Jaime Fuller, "Shakespeare's Latest Tragedy: The 2016 Election," *MTV News,* April 25, 2016, mtv.com.

23. Andrew Cutrofello, "Shakespeare and Trump: What's in a Name?" *Public Seminar,* December 15, 2015, publicseminar.org.

24. Brian Leiter, "Shakespeare on Trump: Money Made the Man," *Huffington Post,* February 29, 2016, huffpost.com.

25. Donald Hendrick and Bryan Reynolds, "Shakespace and Transversal Power," in *Shakespeare Without Class: Misappropriations of Cultural Power,* ed. Donald Hendrick and Bryan Reynolds (New York: Palgrave Macmillan, 2000), 3.

26. Julia Lupton, "The Minority of Caliban: Thinking with Shakespeare and Locke," *REAL: Yearbook of Research in English and American Literature* 22 (2006): 4.

27. Terence Hawkes, *Shakespeare in the Present* (London: Routledge, 2002), 21–22.

28. Charles McNulty, "The Theater of Trump: What Shakespeare Can Teach Us about the Donald," *Los Angeles Times,* May 26, 2016.

29. A. D. Nuttall, *Shakespeare the Thinker* (New Haven, CT: Yale University Press, 2007), 173.

30. John Morgan, "Shakespeare Scholar, Detained," *Inside Higher Ed,* January 29, 2016, insidehighered.com.

31. Paul Hamilton, "Trumping Shakespeare: Donald Trump, Boris Johnson, and the Rise of the Clown Politician," *Kingston Shakespeare Seminar,* July 11, 2016, kingstonshakespeareseminar.wordpress.com.

32. See Peter C. Herman, "Shakespeare's 'Macbeth,' Donald Trump, and the Republican Party," *Times of San Diego,* August 7, 2016.

33. Stephen Greenblatt, "Shakespeare Explains the 2016 Election," *New York Times Sunday Review,* October 8, 2016.

34. Scott Rappaport, "Anger in Politics: From Shakespeare to Donald Trump," *UC Santa Cruz News Center,* September 22, 2016, news.ucsc.edu.

35. Quoted in Rappaport, "Anger in Politics."

36. Neema Parvini, "Interview with Stephen Greenblatt," *Shakespeare and Contemporary Theory,* no. 32, podcast, November 11, 2016.

37. Neema Parvini, "Shakespeare and Cultural Materialist Theory with

Christopher Marlow," *Shakespeare and Contemporary Theory,* no. 31, podcast, November 4, 2016.

38. Amanda Gordon, "Shakespeare Has Words for Trump, Dr. Who Actor Tennant Says," *Bloomberg,* April 4, 2016, bloomberg.com.

39. See Gordon, "Shakespeare Has Words for Trump."

40. Ben Brantley, "Review: Petruchio Is a Woman, and Courtship Is a Beauty Pageant, in This 'Taming of the Shrew,'" *New York Times,* June 13, 2016.

41. Melena Ryzik, "Meryl Streep Does a Number on Donald Trump at Public Theater's Gala," *New York Times,* June 7, 2016.

42. Chris Jones, "'Civil Strife' Concludes Barbara Gaines' Epic Comment on Conflict," *Chicago Tribune,* September 27, 2016.

43. Noah Millman, "The Age of Trump, as Explained by Shakespeare," *The Week,* November 2, 2016, theweek.com.

44. George Bernard Shaw, Preface to *Three Plays for Puritans* (New York: Brentano's, 1901), xxxi.

45. See Scott L. Newstok, "How to Think Like Shakespeare," *Chronicle Review,* August 29, 2016, chronicle.com.

CHAPTER 3

1. Comment quoted in Olivia Sylvester, "Students Remove Shakespeare Portrait in English Dept., Aiming for Inclusivity," *Daily Pennsylvanian,* December 12, 2016, thedp.com.

2. See Kim F. Hall, *Things of Darkness: Economies of Race and Gender in Early Modern England* (Ithaca, NY: Cornell University Press, 1995); Hannah Ehrenberg, Kim F. Hall, and Peter Erickson, "Early Modern Race/Ethnic/Indigenous Studies: A (Crowdsourced) Annotated Bibliography," available at http://bit.ly/ShakeRaceBib.

3. For the character count, see Heather Froehlich, "How Many Female Characters Are There in Shakespeare?" blog post, February 8, 2013, hfroehli.ch (accessed October 5, 2019).

4. "The Mystery of the Borrowed Bard; Or, All's Well That Ends Well," *Pennsylvania Gazette,* September/October 1998, upenn.edu/gazette.

5. National Association of Scholars, "Top Authors, 1964–65," in *Losing the Big Picture: The Fragmentation of the English Major since 1964* (Princeton, NJ: National Association of Scholars, 2000), 76.

6. See Richard Bernstein, "In Dispute on Bias, Stanford Is Likely to Alter Western Culture Program," *New York Times,* January 19, 1988.

7. Rachel Donadio, "Revisiting the Canon Wars," *New York Times Book Review,* September 16, 2007, nytimes.com.

8. Selwyn Duke, "Cultural Affirmative Action," *American Thinker,* March 25, 2008, americanthinker.com.

9. See "Borrowed Bard."

10. See Sylvester, "Students Remove Shakespeare."

11. Quoted in Tim Dickinson, "How the GOP Became the Party of the Rich," *Rolling Stone,* November 9, 2011, rollingstone.com.

12. Audre Lorde, *Zami: A New Spelling of My Name* (Berkeley: Crossing Press, 1982), 226.

13. Audre Lorde, "Power" and "The Black Unicorn," in *The Black Unicorn* (New York: W. W. Norton, 1978), 108, 3.

14. Cheryl Clarke, Introduction, in Audre Lorde, *Sister Outsider: Essays and Speeches* (Berkeley: Crossing Press, 2007), 8.

15. Audre Lorde, "The Master's Tools Will Never Dismantle the Master's House" (1979), in *Sister Outsider*, 112.

16. Lorde, "The Uses of Anger: Women Responding to Racism" (1981), in *Sister Outsider*, 127.

17. Lorde, "The Transformation of Silence into Language and Action," in *Sister Outsider*, 43.

18. Lorde, "Age, Race, Class and Sex: Women Redefining Difference" (1980), in *Sister Outsider*, 115. On the misquotation, see Lavelle Porter, "Dear Sister Outsider," *Poetry Foundation,* May 18, 2016, poetryfoundation.org.

19. Laura Sydell, "On Both the Left and Right, Trump Is Driving New Political Engagement," *NPR*, March 3, 2017, npr.org.

20. Tim Dickinson, "How a New Generation of Progressive Activists Is Leading the Trump Resistance," *Rolling Stone,* August 24, 2017.

21. Dickinson, "New Generation."

22. Dickinson, "New Generation."

23. Zachary Lesser, Twitter post, December 12, 2016, quoted in "Penn: Shakespeare Portrait Is Moving, Not Disappearing," *Inquirer/Daily News,* December 14, 2016.

24. *OED Online,* www.oed.com, s.v. "Affirmative Action."

25. Franklin Roosevelt, Transcript of Executive Order 8802: Prohibition of Discrimination in the Defense Industry, June 25, 1941.

26. Lyndon B. Johnson, Commencement Address at Howard University, June 4, 1965.

27. James P. Gannon, "Factory-Bias Right," *Wall Street Journal,* January 5, 1967, quoted in Dennis Deslippe, *Protesting Affirmative Action: The Struggle over Equality after the Civil Rights Revolution* (Baltimore: Johns Hopkins University Press, 2012), 1.

28. Anthony Rachal, speech to Middle Tennessee Federal Executive Council Seminar, November 11, 1968, quoted in Deslippe, *Protesting Affirmative Action*, 23.

29. Quoted in Sylvester, "Students Remove Shakespeare." Quotations in the next three paragraphs all come from the online comments section of this article.

30. James Baldwin, "Why I Stopped Hating Shakespeare," *The Observer,* April 19, 1964, 21.

31. Quotations in this paragraph are from Maya Angelou, "The Role of Art in Life," *Connections Quarterly,* September 1985, 14, 28, excerpted from a keynote address to the National Assembly of Local Arts Agencies Convention, Cedar Rapids, Iowa, June 12, 1985.

32. Keith Hamilton Cobb, *American Moor* (2013).

33. The fifty-book master list is available at http://www.english.upenn.edu/graduate/requirements-rules-procedures/first-year-oral-exam/50-book-list.

34. Lorde, "The Uses of Anger," 132.

35. Yascha Mounk, *The People vs. Democracy: Why Our Freedom Is in Danger and How to Save It* (Cambridge, MA: Harvard University Press, 2018), 208.

36. Nikole Hannah-Jones, "The New York Times Presents the #1619Project," August 13, 2019, https://www.youtube.com/watch?v=XrfV7w3EyGI.

37. See Chris Bodenner, "The Surprising Revolt at the Most Liberal College in the Country," *The Atlantic*, November 2, 2017, theatlantic.com.

CHAPTER 4

1. Stephen Greenblatt, "Shakespeare Explains the 2016 Election," *New York Times Sunday Review*, October 8, 2016; and see the discussion in Chapter 2.

2. Thomas Blount, *Glossographia* (London: Tho. Newcombe for George Sawbridge, 1656), K7.

3. Thomas More, *The History of King Richard the Third*, in William Shakespeare, *Richard III*, ed. Thomas Cartelli (New York: Norton, 2009), 136.

4. This chapter was written in the summer of 2017, shortly before Kevin Spacey was accused of sexual harassment and assault by more than a dozen people, including crew members on *House of Cards* who described a toxic work environment. Spacey was fired from Netflix, which halted production on the show, and he was written out of the final season. I do not attempt here to reckon fully with the impact of the scandal on the show. I will note, however, that a post-scandal audience is likely to respond to Frank Underwood's charismatic machismo more with disgust than with delight.

5. Beau Willimon, writer, *House of Cards* (Netflix, 2013–2018). References to *House of Cards* appear in the text according to season and episode.

6. Vince Gilligan, quoted in David Segal, "The Dark Art of 'Breaking Bad,'" *New York Times Magazine*, July 6, 2011, nytimes.com.

7. "Complicit," *Saturday Night Live*, Season 42, Episode 15, March 11, 2017.

8. "Ivanka Trump: 'I'll Weigh In with My Father on the Issues I Feel Strongly About,'" *CBS News*, April 5, 2017, cbsnews.com.

9. "Sean Spicer: Lying to Media Not Acceptable," *Reliable Sources* on *CNN Politics*, January 22, 2017, cnn.com.

10. Glenn Kessler, "Spicer Earns Four Pinocchios for False Claims on Inauguration Crowd Size," *Washington Post*, January 22, 2017.

11. Quoted in Brian Stelter, "White House Press Secretary Attacks Media for Accurately Reporting Inauguration Crowds," *CNN*, January 21, 2017.

12. Quoted in Meridith McGraw, "Trump Adviser Doubles Down on Claims of Voter Fraud and of 'Thousands' of Voters Bused into New Hampshire," *ABC News*, February 12, 2017, abcnews.go.com.

13. Halim Shebaya, "Trump 'Tells It Like It Is,'" *Huffington Post*, May 5, 2016; rev. May 6, 2017, huffpost.com.

14. John G. Bullock, Alan S. Gerber, Seth J. Hill, and Gregory A. Huber, "Partisan Bias in Factual Beliefs about Politics," *Quarterly Journal of Political Science* 10 (2015): 519–578.

15. "U.S. Voters Send Trump Approval to Near Record Low; Quinnipiac University National Poll Finds; No Winner in Media War, but Voters Trust Media More," *Quinnipiac University Poll*, May 10, 2017, poll.qu.edu.

16. See "Trump Approval to Near Record Low."

CHAPTER 5

1. Plutarch, "The Life of Iulius Caesar," in *The Lives of the Noble Grecians and Romanes Compared Together*, trans. Thomas North (London: Thomas Vautroullier and John Wight, 1579), 789, 764, 765, 770, 774, 790, 791.

2. William Hazlitt, *Characters of Shakespeare's Plays* (London: C. H. Reynell, 1817), 34.

3. Henry N. Hudson, Introduction to *The Tragedy of Julius Caesar*, in William Shakespeare, *Works* (Boston: Nichols and Noyes, 1867), vol. 8, 322.

4. George Bernard Shaw, "Tappertit on Caesar," *Saturday Review* 85.2205 (January 20, 1898): 139.

5. Donald J. Trump and Tony Schwartz, *Trump: The Art of the Deal* (New York: Ballantine, 1987), 58.

6. Quoted in Char Adams, "Why Donald Trump Has Been Sending *Vanity Fair* Editor Pictures of His Hands for 25 Years," *People*, October 26, 2015, people.com.

7. Quoted in Maureen Dowd, "Living La Vida Trumpa," *New York Times*, November 17, 1999.

8. Donald J. Trump (@realDonaldTrump), Twitter post, May 8, 2013.

9. Donald Trump, interview on *Meet the Press*, NBC, August 9, 2015, nbcnews.com.

10. "Clown Runs for Prez" (cover), and Erin Durkin and Adam Edelman, "Donald Trump Enters 2016 Presidential Race with Bizarre Speech Insulting Mexican Immigrants, Lambasting Obama," *New York Daily News*, June 17, 2015.

11. Quoted in Steve Guest, "Trump: 'I Know Words, I Have the Best Words'— Obama Is 'Stupid,'" *Daily Caller*, December 30, 2015, dailycaller.com.

12. Chris Cillizza, "The Dangerous Anger of Donald Trump," *Washington Post*, November 13, 2015.

13. Jeremy Diamond, "Trump on Looking Presidential: 'How Handsome Am I?'" *CNN*, April 25, 2016, cnn.com.

14. Emily Heil, "Donald Trump says D.C.'s Dress Shops Are Sold Out of Inauguration Gowns. Wrong!" *Washington Post*, January 9, 2017.

15. Daniella Diaz, "Trump: I'm a 'Very Stable Genius,'" *CNN*, January 6, 2018.

16. Charles Ventura, "J. K. Rowling, Merriam-Webster Mock Trump over Misspelled 'Pour' Tweet," *USA Today*, July 4, 2018, usatoday.com.

17. Quoted in Michael Cooper, "Why 'Julius Caesar' Speaks to Politics Today. With or Without Trump," *New York Times,* June 13, 2017.

18. John Ripley, *Julius Caesar on Stage in England and America, 1599–1973* (Cambridge: Cambridge University Press, 1980), 100.

19. Quoted in Carl J. Richard, *The Founders and the Classics: Greece, Rome, and the American Enlightenment* (Cambridge: Cambridge University Press, 1994), 65.

20. Quoted in Richard, *The Founders and the Classics*, 65.

21. Michael Kauffman, *American Brutus: John Wilkes Booth and the Lincoln Conspiracies* (New York: Random House, 2004), 200.

22. Quoted in Kauffman, *American Brutus*, 400.

23. Rob Melrose, "Obama/Trump/Caesar," *Medium*, June 14, 2017, medium.com.

24. Quoted in Rebecca Mead, "Stage Left: Oskar Eustis, the Public Theatre's Latest Radical," *New Yorker*, March 22, 2010, newyorker.com.

25. Kevin Kelly, "Trinity's 'Caesar': Bold, Yes, but Does It Have to Be So Loud?" *Boston Globe*, February 16, 1990.

26. Tony Kushner, "The Importance of the Taper's 'Caesar,'" *Los Angeles Times*, May 20, 1991.

27. Eustis confirmed to me that Kushner's characterization of the production was true.

28. Oskar Eustis, "A Note from Oskar Eustis," in the playbill for *Julius Caesar*, dir. Eustis (New York: Delacorte Theater in Central Park, 2017).

29. Public Theater, "Julius Caesar," https://www.publictheater.org/Tickets/Calendar/PlayDetailsCollection/SITP/Julius-Caesar/ (accessed June 1, 2018).

30. Quoted in Michael Paulson, "Oskar Eustis on Trump, 'Julius Caesar' and the Politics of Theater," *New York Times*, June 14, 2017.

31. Corey Stoll, "What It Was Like to Star in the Trump-Themed Julius Caesar," *Vulture*, June 23, 2017, vulture.com.

32. Quoted in Paulson, "Oskar Eustis on Trump."

33. Emily Palmer and Maya Salam, "Protesters Outside 'Julius Caesar' in Central Park, and Laughs Inside," *New York Times*, June 18, 2017.

34. Marcus Gilmer, "Trump's Cabinet Meeting Was a Lot Like the Opening of 'King Lear,'" *Mashable*, June 12, 2017, mashable.com.

35. Timothy Snyder, *On Tyranny: Twenty Lessons from the Twentieth Century* (New York: Tim Duggan Books, 2017).

36. *OED Online*, www.oed.com, s.v. "Tyrant," etymology.

37. Euripides, *Suppliants*, in *Early Greek Political Thought from Homer to the Sophists*, trans. and ed. Michael Gagarin and Paul Woodruff (Cambridge: Cambridge University Press, 1995), 65.

38. Xenophon, *Memorabilia*, trans. E. C. Marchant (Cambridge, MA: Harvard University Press, 1923), 4.6.12.

39. Solon, "The Danger of Tyranny, a Warning against Peisistratus," in *Early Greek Political Thought*, 28.

40. Aristotle, *Politics*, trans. B. Jowett, in *The Complete Works of Aristotle*, ed. Jonathan Barnes (Princeton, NJ: Princeton University Press, 1984), 1279b.

41. Roger Boesche, *Theories of Tyranny: From Plato to Arendt* (University Park: Pennsylvania State University Press, 1996), 459–460.

42. John Ponet, *A Short Treatise of Politic Power* (Strasbourg: Heirs of W. Köpfel, 1556), Gvi.

43. John Milton, *The Tenure of Kings and Magistrates* (London: Matthew Simmons, 1649), 17–18.

44. Thomas Hobbes, *Leviathan* (London: Andrew Crooke, 1651), 95.

45. John Locke, *Two Treatises of Government* (London: Awnsham Churchill, 1690), 420.

46. James Madison, *The Federalist*, No. 47, ed. Terence Ball (Cambridge: Cambridge University Press, 2003), 234.

47. Tina Fey, writer, *Mean Girls*, dir. Mark Waters (Paramount, 2004).

48. Carlos Morton, *Trumpus Caesar*, dir. Irwin Appel (University of California, Santa Barbara, Studio Theater, 2017), theaterdance.ucsb.edu/news/event/592.

49. Stoll, "What It Was Like."

50. Philip Sidney, *An Apology for Poetry (or the Defence of Poesy)* (ca. 1579–1581), ed. Geoffrey Shepherd, rev. R. W. Maslen (Manchester: Manchester University Press, 2002), 103.

51. John Keats, "To George and Tom Keats" (December 21/27[?], 1817), in *The Letters of John Keats*, ed. Hyder Edward Rollins, vol. 1 (Cambridge: Cambridge University Press, 1958), 193.

52. Frank Pallotta, "Trump-like 'Julius Caesar' Isn't the First Time the Play Has Killed a Contemporary Politician," *CNN*, June 12, 2017.

53. Jason Adam Katzenstein, "Et tu, Cohen?" *New Yorker*, July 23, 2018.

54. Stephen Greenblatt, *Tyrant: Shakespeare on Politics* (New York: W. W. Norton, 2018).

55. Quoted in Eric Levenson, "In R-Rated Anti-Trump Rant, Madonna Muses about 'Blowing Up White House,'" *CNN*, January 21, 2017.

56. Lisa Respers France, "Snoop Dogg 'Shoots' Trump Clown 'Ron Klump' in New Video," *CNN*, March 15, 2017.

57. Paulson, "Oskar Eustis on Trump."

58. Fareed Zakaria (@FareedZakaria), Twitter post, May 31, 2017.

59. Aidan McLaughlin, "Senators Stab Trump to Death in Central Park Performance of Shakespeare's Julius Caesar," *Mediaite*, June 6, 2017, mediaite.com.

60. Daniel Nussbaum, "'Trump' Stabbed to Death in Central Park Performance of 'Julius Caesar,'" *Breitbart*, June 6, 2017, breitbart.com.

61. Kyle Smith, "A Trump-ified *Julius Caesar*," *National Review*, June 9, 2017, nationalreview.com.

62. Quoted in Tina Moore and Max Jaeger, "'Julius Caesar' Director Gets Death Threats at Home," *New York Post*, June 21, 2017.

63. Melrose, "Obama/Trump/Caesar."

64. See Fox News, "NYC Play Appears to Depict Assassination of Trump," June 11, 2017, foxnews.com. The story now includes an "Editor's Note": "This article has been amended to more prominently state that the mock assassination occurred in a production of 'Julius Caesar.'"

65. Donald Trump Jr. (@DonaldJTrumpJr), Twitter post, June 11, 2017.

66. Liam Stack, "Et tu, Delta? Shakespeare in the Park Sponsors Withdraw from Trump-like 'Julius Caesar,'" *New York Times*, June 11, 2017.

67. Stack, "Et tu, Delta?"

68. American Express (@AmericanExpress), Twitter post, June 12, 2017.

69. National Foundation on the Arts and the Humanities Act of 1965 (P.L. 89–209), https://www.neh.gov/about/history/national-foundation-arts-and-humanities-act-1965-pl-89–209.

70. Quoted in Bella Lewitsky Dance Foundation v. Frohnmayer, 754 F. Supp. 774 (C.D. California 1991).

71. Quoted in National Endowment for the Arts v. Finley, 118 S. Ct. 2168, 2178 (1998).

72. Kathleen M. Sullivan, "Are Content Restrictions Constitutional?" *Journal of Arts Management and Law* 21.4 (1992): 323–325.

73. Cynthia Brown and Jack Maskell, "Hatch Act Restrictions on Federal Employees' Political Activities in the Digital Age," *Congressional Research Service*, April 13, 2016, 11–14.

74. Brown and Maskell, "Hatch Act Restrictions," 11.

75. Mike Huckabee (@GovMikeHuckabee), Twitter post, June 11, 2017.

76. Beau Willimon (@BeauWillimon), Twitter post, June 11, 2017.

77. Joyce Carol Oates (@JoyceCarolOates), Twitter post, June 12, 2017.

78. Frank Scheck, "'Julius Caesar': Theater Review," *Hollywood Reporter*, June 11, 2017, hollywoodreporter.com.

79. Travis M. Andrews, "Trump-like 'Julius Caesar' Assassinated in New York Play. Delta, Bank of America Pull Funding," *Washington Post*, June 12, 2017.

80. A video of this address is available with "A Note About Julius Caesar," at https://www.youtube.com/watch?v=1eZQr72JJto.

81. Paulson, "Oskar Eustis on Trump."

82. Harlan Z. Hill (@Harlan), Twitter post, June 14, 2017.

83. Quoted in Andrew Wyrich, "Alt-right Figure Offers to Pay Protesters to Disrupt Controversial 'Julius Caesar' Play," *Daily Dot,* June 21, 2017, dailydot.com.

84. Stoll, "What It Was Like."

85. A video recording of the protest was posted on YouTube by a group called Now The End Begins, under the headline "Fed Up Patriots Shut Down Performance Of Anti-Trump 'Julius Caesar' in New York City," June 16, 2017, https://www.youtube.com/watch?v=Xyu8AhvQ8hk.

86. Laura Loomer (@LauraLoomer), "Julia Caesar Meets Laura Loomer," formerly available at https://www.pscp.tv/LauraLoomer/1gqxvbVXbrexB (accessed June 1, 2017).

87. Ben Collins and Gideon Resnick, "The Domain Troll Behind Pro-Trump Stunts," *Daily Beast*, June 20, 2017, thedailybeast.com.

88. Andrew Marantz, "Behind the Scenes with the Right-Wing Activist Who Crashed 'Julius Caesar,'" *New Yorker,* June 20, 2017.

89. Marantz, "Behind the Scenes."

90. Unless otherwise attributed, quotations and information in this paragraph

come from Marantz, "Behind the Scenes," which includes much more colorful detail than I have space for here.

91. Jack Posobiec (@JackPosobiec), Twitter post, June 16, 2017.

92. Laura Ingram (@IngrahamAngle), Twitter post, June 16, 2017.

93. Ben Shapiro (@benshapiro), Twitter post, June 16, 2017.

94. Charlie May, "'Julius Caesar' Stage Crasher Nets Financial Windfall," *Salon,* June 21, 2017, salon.com.

95. Palmer and Salam, "Protesters outside 'Julius Caesar.'"

96. These protests were posted by Mark F to YouTube under the heading "ANOTHER Protester Storms the Stage Trump 'Julius Caesar' Tonight!" June 18, 2017, https://www.youtube.com/watch?v=eFG7ALWLC68.

97. Yohana Desta, "Multiple Shakespearean Theaters Are Getting Death Threats after New York's Trump-Inspired Julius Caesar," *Vanity Fair,* June 19, 2017, vanityfair.com.

98. Fox News, "Protester Who Stormed 'Julius Caesar' Stage Speaks Out," June 19, 2017, https://www.youtube.com/watch?v=x0fnyC72SVs.

99. 18 USC section 871(a), http://uscode.house.gov/view.xhtml?req=granuleid: USC-prelim-title18-section871&num=0&edition=prelim.

100. Chaplinsky v. New Hampshire, 315 U.S. 568 (1942).

101. Watts v. United States, 394 U.S. 705 (1969).

102. Virginia v. Black, 538 U.S. 343 (2003), citing Watts v. United States.

103. Watts v. United States.

104. Brandenburg v. Ohio, 395 U.S. 444 (1969).

105. Hess v. Indiana, 414 U.S. 105 (1973).

106. All quotations in "Did Donald Trump Encourage Violence at His Rallies?" *Snopes,* February 21, 2018, snopes.com.

107. Brandenburg v. Ohio, 444.

108. McCollum v. CBS, Inc., 202 Cal. App. 3d 989, 249 Cal. Rptr. 187 (1988).

109. Gorgias, "Encomium of Helen," in *Early Greek Political Thought,* 13.

110. Plato, *Phaedrus,* trans. Alexander Nehamas and Paul Woodruff, in *Plato: Complete Works,* ed. John M. Cooper (Indianapolis: Hackett, 1997), 267a.

111. Plato, *Laws,* trans. Trevor J. Sanders, in *Complete Works,* 802c, 817b.

112. Plato, *Republic,* trans. G.M.A. Grube, rev. C.D.C. Reeve, in *Complete Works,* 607b.

113. Aristotle, *Poetics,* trans. Richard Janko (Indianapolis: Hackett, 1987), 1449b.

114. Stoll, "What It Was Like."

CONCLUSION

1. Unless otherwise attributed, the quotations in this section come from a survey of Shakespeare scholars that I conducted in July 2018.

2. Ambereen Dadabhoy, "Why We Need a Trump Shakespeare," paper presented at a panel discussion entitled "What Can a Liberal Arts Education Offer in the Age of Trump?" September 26, 2017, Harvey Mudd College, Claremont, CA.

Index

Page numbers followed by the letter *f* refer to figures.

Jeffrey R. Wilson is a faculty member in the Writing Program at Harvard University.